ELLA HEPWORTH DIXON

Ella Hepworth Dixon

The Story of a Modern Woman

VALERIE FEHLBAUM
University of Geneva, Switzerland

ASHGATE

Published by
Ashgate Publishing Limited
Gower House
Croft Road
Aldershot
Hampshire GU11 3HR
England

Ashgate Publishing Company
Suite 420
101 Cherry Street
Burlington, VT 05401-4405
USA

Ashgate website: http://www.ashgate.com

British Library Cataloguing in Publication Data
Fehlbaum. Valerie
Ella Hepworth Dixon : the story of a modern woamn. – (The nineteenth century series)
1. Dixon, Ella Hepworth 2. Dixon, Ella Hepworth – Criticism and interpretation 3. Women authors, English – 19th century – Biography 4. Authors, English – 19th century – Biography
I. Title
823.8

Library of Congress Cataloging-in-Publication Data
Fehlbaum, Valerie.
Ella Hepworth Dixon : the story of a modern woman / Valerie Fehlbaum.
p. cm. — (The nineteenth century series)
Includes bibliographical references (p.) and index.
ISBN 0-7546-3877-4 (alk. paper)
1. Dixon, Ella Hepworth. 2. Authors, English—20th century—Biography. 3. Authors, English—19th century—Biography. 4. Journalists—Great Britain—Biography. 5. Editors—Great Britain—Biography. I. Title. II.
Series: Nineteenth century (Aldershot, England)

PR6007.I84Z66 2006
818'.5209—dc22

2005010838

ISBN 0 7546 3877 4

Printed and bound in Great Britain by MPG Books Ltd, Bodmin, Cornwall

Contents

List of Figures

The Nineteenth Century Series
General Editors' Preface

The aim of the series is to reflect, develop and extend the great burgeoning of interest in the nineteenth century that has been an inevitable feature of recent years, as that former epoch has come more sharply into focus as a locus for our understanding not only of the past but of the contours of our modernity. It centres primarily upon major authors and subjects within Romantic and Victorian literature. It also includes studies of other British writers and issues, where these are matters of current debate: for example, biography and autobiography, journalism, periodical literature, travel writing, book production, gender and non-canonical writing. We are dedicated principally to publishing original monographs and symposia; our policy is to embrace a broad scope in chronology, approach and range of concern, and both to recognize and cut innovatively across such parameters as those suggested by the designations 'Romantic' and 'Victorian'. We welcome new ideas and theories, while valuing traditional scholarship. It is hoped that the world which predates yet so forcibly predicts and engages our own will emerge in parts, in the wider sweep, and in the lively streams of disputation and change that are so manifest an aspect of its intellectual, artistic and social landscape.

Vincent Newey
Joanne Shattock
University of Leicester

Acknowledgements

Thanks are due to more people than I can name individually. So many friends and scholars have helped with this work in countless ways that such cursory acknowledgements as I can offer will, I fear, always be woefully inadequate.

This work has in fact grown out of my doctoral thesis, so I should begin by thanking Ella Hepworth Dixon herself for being such a fine subject. I would then like to express my gratitude to my supervisor, Lyn Pykett, for her indispensable advice and long-standing encouragement, and to Patricia Duncker and Barbara Onslow for their enthusiastic response. I am also grateful for earlier guidance from Michele le Doeuff and Paul B. Taylor, and to Jennifer Gascoigne, Mark Samuels Lasner, Denise Noel, Arnold A. Rogow, Margaret Stetz and Angela Thirlwell for their expertise and kindness.

I am naturally indebted to the staff in several libraries, in particular to everyone at Colindale without whose unstinting assistance much of this research would have been simply impossible. My thanks also go to the British Library for permission to quote from the typescript copies of the plays by Ella Hepworth Dixon and Lena Ashwell, and to reproduce the photograph of Ella Hepworth Dixon taken by Mrs Fred. Wilkinson which appeared in the *Lady's Pictorial* of February 10, 1894. I would like to thank the Controller of Her Majesty's Stationery Office for permission to reproduce Ella Hepworth Dixon's birth and death certificates, and The Royal Literary Fund for kindly allowing me to quote from correspondence from Mary Ann Dixon. I also owe thanks to the University of Reading, Archives and Manuscripts Department, for providing copies of correspondence from Chatto and Windus, and to University of Illinois Library at Urbana-Champaign for permission to use material from the Grant Richards Collection. I am grateful to A. P. Watt Limited on behalf of Jacques Eldin for permission to quote from the correspondence of Arnold Bennett. Here in Geneva I am indebted to Victoria Espinosa, Lise Magnollay and Viviane Siffert for their invaluable help. I must also thank the secretaries in Aberystwyth and Geneva: Joan Crawford, Sylvie Forel, Ancilla Stefani, and Clare Tierque, and my editors at Ashgate: Ann Donahue, Anne Keirby, Emma McBriarty and Emma Williams. If I have inadvertently omitted to mention individuals or collections, I hope they will forgive me.

Special thoughts must go to those who have not been able to witness the completion of this project: Jim Curtis, Mair G. Davies, and Avice Masters, and extra-special thanks must go to Ryme and her parents who unfailingly lifted the spirits of her little Bajaja whenever they were flagging. As for the many others whose support and friendship contributed significantly to this work, whenever I begin to give thanks, I am regularly told they already know; I sincerely hope this is so. To you all, much gratitude.

Whilst every effort has been made to trace copyright holders, any further information would be welcomed from any other parties who may feel they hold rights in any material that has been included.

Foreword

> With a feeling of relief the busy journalist will learn that the columns of 'stuff' which he scribbles while the printer's devil dances impatiently in the hall will never be handed down to a coldly critical posterity. A *Daily Chronicle* young man has been interviewing the Superintendent of the British Museum reading-room, who is strongly of the opinion that all the newspapers in that sanctuary of learning will be as dust and ashes in the year 1996. … And this is as it should be. I have a misgiving, for instance, that these 'Pensées de Femme' would be justly held to be the drivellings of a fogey, the maunderings of a benighted intelligence, were they to survive to the enlightened scrutiny of the women of a century hence.[1]

This short extract from one of Ella Hepworth Dixon's weekly magazine columns neatly encapsulates the essence of both her life and her style, and I hope to show in the course of my work that present-day readers may be relieved that the esteemed 'Superintendent of the British Museum reading-room' was mistaken. With the added *frisson* of hindsight, far from reading like 'the drivellings of a fogey', Ella Hepworth Dixon's writing is highly revelatory of the early days of mass media when journalists in general were learning to write for immediate consumption and almost as immediate *oubli*. Moreover, perhaps even more interesting for my present purposes is the fact that her elegant prose is laced with typical self-deprecation, not to be confused with self-abnegation, apparently 'so devoutly to be sought' by Victorian Women, and contains a willfully elusive quality which makes any attempt to submit the writer to scrutiny problematic.

Having benefited from an unusually liberal education at home and abroad, Ella Hepworth Dixon initially intended to pursue an artistic career. To this end, in the late 1870s she contributed to exhibitions of the Society of British Artists at the Suffolk Street Gallery as well as those of the Society of Lady Artists in Great Marlborough Street, and with her sister Marion studied art in Paris at the famous Julian Academy at the same time as Marie Bashkirtseff. Then, for a variety of reasons, she exchanged her paint brush for a pen, and, although for women of her class marriage was often considered the ultimate career and few were adequately prepared for earning a living, by her own account she enjoyed 'a singularly happy working life', and even merited an obituary in *The Times*.

In a career which spanned more than four decades, Ella Hepworth Dixon met and worked with most of the luminaries of her day including Oscar Wilde, George Bernard Shaw, Aubrey Beardsley, H.G. Wells, George Meredith, Sarah Bernhardt, Cecily Hamilton, Elizabeth Robins, as well as public figures in other domains such as politicians including Lloyd George and media magnates such as William

---

[1] 'Pensées de Femme', *Lady's Pictorial* (February 8, 1896), p. 173.

Heinemann and Alfred Harmsworth, later Lord Northcliffe. During that time she was alternately journalist, critic, essayist, short story writer, novelist, editor of a woman's magazine, dramatist, autobiographer. For this reason, I have taken a generic rather than a thematic approach. Such multiplicity of output was not uncommon for the New Woman writer, nor was it by any means limited to New Woman writers; many eminent men and women of letters, better known today for one aspect of their writing, engaged in a wide variety of literary enterprises. What is significant is that women were entering spheres previously considered beyond their bounds, and enjoying a certain success.

For many of her contemporaries, therefore, she typified the 'Modern Woman', leading a rather more fruitful existence than she allowed some of her fictional representations. Her own definition of this term may be understood not only from her celebrated 1894 novel, *The Story of a Modern Woman*, but also from her description of Eleanora Duse as '"The Modern Woman": a creature all intelligence, dignity, and charm, and with a brain highly developed, though not at the expense of her affections'.[2]

Both then and now, however, Ella Hepworth Dixon has also been closely associated with the New Woman, who came to the fore at a time of intense interrogation of the term 'woman' on every imaginable level. Throughout the nineteenth century and particularly in the last decades there was much heated debate about woman's nature. The primary questions 'What was a woman?' and 'What does a woman want?' were accompanied by subsidiary controversies about what precise role she was to play in society and the best means to prepare her for her ascribed part. As Ella Hepworth Dixon recognized, 'Woman, in a word, has always been hedged round with a prickly wall of prejudice, and the pioneer who attempted to tear it assunder and let in daylight always ran the risk of lacerating her own fingers.'[3] Such was indeed the case for many a New Woman writer. Perhaps to reassure both men and women, Ella Hepworth Dixon also claimed, 'The centuries go by, and human nature - especially feminine human nature - has a trick of remaining unchanged in the essentials of life. ... By giving woman the franchise, or even by educating her to the same level as her brothers, you will not alter one jot of her nature and disposition.'[4] Clearly, what precisely that 'nature and disposition' meant was perennially contentious.

As more and more attention is focused on the New Woman of the late nineteenth century, she becomes ever more elusive. Just as she defied the comprehension of her contemporaries, so she continues to escape neat categorization by more recent literary critics and cultural historians who have subjected her to scrutiny. Through a close study of the life and work of Ella Hepworth Dixon, I propose to provide more insight into the multi-faceted character of the New Woman writer and her epoch.

In some ways, Ella Hepworth Dixon appears to have been consciously writing against stereotypes of various sorts, including that of the New Woman. When, for

---

[2] *Ibid.* (June 22, 1895), p. 955.
[3] *Ibid.* (December 12, 1896), p. 867.
[4] *Ibid.* (August 1, 1896), p. 193.

example, she began her weekly column in the *Lady's Pictorial* on June 22, 1895, she explained her choice of title, '*Pensées de Femme*', thus:

> How odd it is that to express the purely feminine one should turn instinctively to that agreeable tongue which is spoken on the hither side of the Straits of Dover. ... Here, ... one dreads to put down in black and white the letters which form the word 'woman', so bedraggled has it become with the cheap sneers of the pert journalist *(who generally associates it, for pecuniary purposes, with the much-battered word 'new'),* the shrill vindictiveness of the elderly literary lady who sees her public forsaking her, and the infuriated malice of that army of Anglo-Saxon Philistines who resent any discussion about their female goods and chattels (my italics).

Nevertheless, later in the same periodical she declared, 'It is significant, indeed, of the resiliency of woman that she survives all ... indiscriminate abuse and smilingly progresses on her way.'[5] Such optimism, accompanied as it often was with a note of humour, was by no means rare in her writing and is arguably one of its most distinguishing features. This might explain why, unlike many of her peers, although in her own way she was no less innovatory, she appears to have avoided attracting the corrosive criticism which was so copiously meted out to more prolific or more overtly polemical writers such as Mona Caird, George Egerton or Sarah Grand.

After an initial popularity, like the majority of her contemporaries, Ella Hepworth Dixon's work remained largely unread for decades. It is my contention that much of her writing remains as lively and as pertinent today as it was when it was first published. In succeeding chapters I hope to show how a re-evaluation of Ella Hepworth Dixon's life and varied literary output might serve to enhance our understanding of a period which, to employ her own words, witnessed 'a change such as the world ha(d) not yet seen'.[6]

---

[5] *Ibid*. (November 27, 1897), p. 765.

[6] *As I Knew Them* (London, 1930), p. 281.

Chapter 1

As I Knew Them: Ella Hepworth Dixon's Own Story of a Modern Woman

'Most people of parts (and some of no pretensions) have, at some time or other of their lives, an irresistible desire to publish their reminiscences,' declared Ella Hepworth Dixon in one of her weekly newspaper columns.[1] 'Usually, to be sure,' she continued, 'they leave this adventure into the world of books too late, essaying, when they have nearly reached four-score, to amuse their younger contemporaries with an account of bygone experiences … . We should not wait till we are senile before we begin to talk.' Why, then, at the age of seventy-five, did Ella Hepworth Dixon herself embark on what she had described elsewhere as 'that most tiresome of all forms of entertainment – a monologue about oneself'?[2]

Clearly she was not writing for her children, nor, apparently, was she settling old accounts. It may be that she was in a sense tidying up, for she died on January 12, 1932, a year after the publication of her memoirs, and only a month earlier, on December 11, 1931, she had made a will leaving everything except two legacies to her sister-in-law Sybil Maud Dixon, to whom she also dedicated *As I Knew Them*. Her estate was then valued at £1193-1-6 gross, £996-16-0 net, and on her death certificate[3] she is described as a 'spinster of independent means', so it seems unlikely that she was writing for fame or money. As she remarked, it is not uncommon to indulge in self-writing, and the 1930s did indeed see a flurry of memoirs by several of Ella Hepworth Dixon's notable contemporaries, for example Evelyn Sharp's *Unfinished Journey* was published in 1933, and Cecily Hamilton's *Life Errant* in 1935. Perhaps, as often in her career, Ella Hepworth Dixon was picking up on a trend, and making a success of it.

One further explanation may lie in her claim that 'the chief *danger* of memoir-writing is that the author is more apt to "give himself away" to his readers than to give away his contemporaries'[4] (my italics). Surely an autobiography is justly expected to reveal more about the writing-self. If, however, there are 'dangers' in writing about oneself, how much greater must be the menace of others undertaking

---

[1] 'Woman's Ways' – 'The Dangers of Memoirs', *The Sketch* (January 15, 1908), p. 31.

[2] 'My Faith and My Work', *Woman* (September 23, 1896), p. 8.

[3] See Appendix 1. The cause of death given on the Register of Deaths is I (a) Syncope, (b) Bronchial Asthma and II Aortic Disease.

[4] 'Woman's Ways' – 'The Dangers of Memoirs', *The Sketch* (January 15, 1908), p. 31.

the task. 'It is a dangerous thing to have your life written when you are dead and helpless and can do nothing to protest against the judgement,' [5] Mrs Oliphant had declared in her review of Harriet Martineau's *Autobiography*. Nevertheless, she had gone on to suggest that 'there is a still more fatal art … . This terrible instrument of self-murder is called autobiography'. Ella Hepworth Dixon, I would argue, managed to avoid both perils. Not only did she preclude a biography by anyone else; she also managed to construct a self-protective image of herself. To this end, she appears to have re-read all her writing, selected what she considered relevant and discarded the rest. I have found no trace of diaries, personal papers or letters except for those she uses to validate her anecdotes and a few others in the archives of publishers, in the collected letters of George Meredith, and in a few private collections.

Ella Hepworth Dixon's subtitle, 'Sketches of People I have Met on the Way' at once, however, reveals the fragmentary nature of her text. One could argue that this would be true of any memoirs. Evelyn Sharp likewise in her subtitle, '*Selected* Reminiscences from an Englishwoman's Life' (my italics), and in her introduction draws attention to the fact that her reminiscences 'will not profess to tell the whole story of my life, they will be sincere, I hope, as far as they go.' Nevertheless, her account is a good deal fuller than Ella Hepworth Dixon's. The term 'sketches' was in fact often used to designate cursory or incomplete studies. Helen C. Black employed it to describe her biographies of 'Notable Women Authors of the Day' which had originally appeared in the *Lady's Pictorial* before being collected together and published in book form in 1893. Similarly, W. Robertson Nicholl in the 'Introduction' to Eliza Lynn Linton's unfinished autobiography calls her 'reminiscences of Dickens, Thackeray and George Eliot' 'sketches'. These, too, had been commissioned for a periodical and only later collected together in book form. Mary Cholmondeley in her introduction to *Under One Roof: A Family Record* wrote of her intentions 'to make a pencil sketch' of her family and especially of her sister Hester whose diary inspired much of the work. Nearer to our own time, Virginia Woolf also used the term for some autobiographical material she wrote shortly before her death, published posthumously as 'A Sketch of the Past' in *Moments of Being*.

From the outset, then, the reader is cautioned not to expect an autobiography in the conventional sense of an exhaustive womb-to-tomb record of a first-person narrator. Some feminist critics would maintain that in the case of a woman writing about herself this is not unusual. Fragmentation is often seen as characteristic of a woman's life in general and consequently of her writing. Furthermore, considerable close study of autobiography *per se*[6] over the past twenty years has lead some

[5] *Blackwood's Magazine* 121 (April, 1877), p. 472.

[6] See for example Carolyn G. Heilbrun, *Writing a Woman's Life* (New York, 1988), Estelle C. Jelinek, *The Tradition of Women's Autobiography: From Antiquity to the Present* (Boston, 1986), Laura Marcus, *Auto/Biographical Discourses: Theory, Criticism, Practice* (Manchester, 1994), Linda H. Peterson, *Traditions of Victorian Women's Autobiography: The Poetics and Politics of Life Writing* (Virginia, 1999), Sidonie Smith, *A Poetics of*

critics to suggest that the genre is essentially androcentric. The very idea of putting oneself forward as the centre of attention is in itself diametrically opposed to the reticence long considered a feminine virtue and inculcated in women. Thus, it has been argued, male authors, in writing their own histories, contrary to their other works, primarily place the accent on their inner lives, often to show that even out of the public eye they are still Great Men. Women, on the other hand, who are stereotypically more often associated with personal matters, when writing autobiographies almost invariably concentrate, as to a certain extent Ella Hepworth Dixon does, either on their professional or public achievements, or on those around them, especially husbands and children. Nor should this simply be read as more evidence of women's customary subordination of their own lives to those of others; their intention may be specifically to keep their private selves hidden. In her evaluation of nineteenth century autobiographies by middle-class literary women Mary Jean Corbett remarks, 'Self-representation becomes its writer's last performance of a role she writes to protect herself against the deformations of publicity and celebrity, the final mask that will survive her, a mask that can shield the private individual from public view.'[7] Although she examines more famous self-representations such as those of Eliza Lynn Linton and Mrs Oliphant, her description of 'most secular woman autobiographers ... carefully shaping the personae they present and, more especially, by subordinating their histories of themselves to others' histories' could equally apply to Ella Hepworth Dixon. Indeed, Mary Jean Corbett almost appears to be quoting the latter when she writes, 'In this way, the middle-class woman writing autobiography both avoids self-exposure and attains a narrative stance closer to the fiction writer's; it is not her story she represents, but the story of others *as she sees them*' (my italics).

Nevertheless, even if self-writing might be motivated as much by a desire for self-protection as for self-promotion, this is surely not necessarily contingent on one's gender, and the final outcome of any attempt to recount one's life might be rather different from the writer's initial, or professed, intent. Moreover, some critics such as Liz Stanley and, more recently, Linda H. Peterson have accentuated the plurality amongst women writers. Finally, like Jane Marcus after her analysis of the 'autobiographical acts' of several public women, including Marie Bashkirtseff and Elizabeth Robins, one is led to ask 'whether there is indeed any common thread running through women's autobiographies'.[8]

A further difficulty in any appraisal of the self-writings of women such as Eliza Lynn Linton, Mrs Oliphant, and, perhaps even more significantly, Marie

---

Women's Autobiography: Marginality and the Fiction of Self-Representation (Bloomington, 1987), Sidonie Smith and Julia Watson (eds), *Women, Autobiography, Theory: A Reader* (Wisconsin, 1998), and Liz Stanley, *The Auto/biographical I: The Theory and Practice of Feminist Auto/biography* (Manchester, 1992).

[7] 'Literary Domesticity and Women Writers' Subjectivities', *Women, Autobiography, Theory: A Reader* (Wisconsin, 1998), pp. 255-263.

[8] 'The Private Selves of Public Women', in Shari Benstock (ed.), *The Private Self* (London, 1988), pp. 114-146.

Bashkirtseff is that they did not live to oversee the publication of their life-stories which, consequently, might have been rather different from the versions which appeared in print. Nor, of course, are such reservations valid only for the writing of women's lives. The polemic surrounding James Anthony Froude's revelations from papers entrusted to him by his friend Thomas Carlyle would testify that even one of the century's Great Men could not control the public image of his life after his death.

Marie Bashkirtseff's *Journal* caused a sensation when it was first published in 1887 and translated into English two years later, partly because it was considered an absolutely honest unexpurgated account of a woman's inner thoughts. A recent new edition,[9] however, suggests that, in spite of the fact that she wrote the preface herself, much in the actual diary had been specially arranged for sensational publication. Eliza Lynn Linton's memoirs, *My Literary Life,* were also published posthumously in 1899, the year after her death, with a 'Prefatory Note' by Miss Beatrice Harraden wherein she regrets that her 'dear friend' had not started earlier and was no longer there 'to tone it down' since 'her pen was harsher than her speech'.[10] Likewise, the *Autobiography and Letters of Mrs O.W. Oliphant,*[11] 'arranged and edited by Mrs Harry Coghill', only appeared in 1899, two years after her death, although Mrs Oliphant had clearly been working on her autobiography for many years. For the publication of her memoirs Ella Hepworth Dixon appears to have controlled the entire enterprise, contributing both a foreword and an afterword, as well as undertaking some promotion, as a letter[12] from Arnold Bennett testifies. This might explain also why, ultimately, she remains more hidden than Marie Bashkirtseff, Eliza Lynn Linton and Mrs Oliphant.

In the opening sentences of the 'Foreword' to *As I Knew Them* Ella Hepworth Dixon alerts the reader further to some of the intrinsic difficulties in writing about the self. An un-named literary expert's advice and her response to it are indicative of the whole work. 'You must write a page or two to say who you are and why you met so many interesting people,' she claims to have been told, although, again, one

---

[9] Edited by Lucile Le Roy and published by L'Age d'Homme, (Lausanne, 1999). The first of six proposed volumes, instead of the original two, is in fact volume 4 and covers the period September 28, 1887-December 21, 1879.

[10] Ella Hepworth Dixon once described Eliza Lynn Linton as 'a lady who has spent a long life and brilliant talent in assiduously belittling woman and belauding man ...'. 'Pensées de Femme', *Lady's Pictorial* (July 20, 1895), p. 87.

[11] In the *Ladies' Field* (May 20, 1899), p. 499, writing of great women such as George Sand, Ella Hepworth Dixon includes Mrs Oliphant, and declares that, despite being untouched by her novels, she found the autobiography very moving. Mrs Oliphant's accounts of her family tragedies and her strong religious beliefs are, however, far removed from Ella Hepworth Dixon's own style and experiences.

[12] See letter dated February 26, 1930 (to be found in the Harry Ransom Humanities Research Centre, University of Texas, Austin, Texas) in which Arnold Bennett thanks Ella Hepworth Dixon for her book, admits to having 'turned first to the reference to myself' and promises to 'see what can be done' about discussing it in *The Evening Standard.* I have so far found no evidence that he succeeded.

would imagine that the autobiography would do precisely that. 'My experience is that nobody knows anything', continues the expert, but most readers in 1930 would, on the surface at least, know who Ella Hepworth Dixon was. The reviewer in *The London Illustrated News*, for example, while regretting that she does not 'accept certain advice mentioned in her preface', at the same time acknowledges that 'the author's name is so well-known'.[13] The 'Foreword', therefore, raises doubts about the voice of authority in general and warns 'the public (which) likes a name'[14] that the book in hand will not furnish more in-depth details of a personal nature. Ella Hepworth Dixon's declared reluctance to speak of herself except in relation to others,[15] and significantly not through her family, as one might expect, but through her 'priceless friendships' and her 'singularly happy working life', again makes clear from the start that this will be neither a soul-searching confessional of the most intimate kind, nor a typical cradle-to-grave biography.

On the other hand, the 'little tale' which she does tell, besides characteristically attempting to minimize her own importance and emphasize the anecdotal nature of the text, exemplifies some of the complications inherent both in knowing and recounting oneself and others, and hence in writing and reading autobiographies. A sense of self is intrinsically dependent upon others, but their judgement may be as flawed and as unreliable as that of the first-person narrator. At the end of her 'Foreword', sounding rather like Gertrude Stein whose *Autobiography of Alice B. Toklas* first published three years later in 1933 would further stretch the limits of the genre, Ella Hepworth Dixon draws the reader's attention to such issues: 'This book may contain a portrait; on the other hand it may not. Is it possible that I may have met, dressed in white tulle, or stained with oil-paint and ink, myself, too, on the way?' Self-writing can, and often does, lead to self-revelation, but Ella Hepworth Dixon seems to suggest that the self is perforce so multi-faceted and has so many guises that any representation can only ever be partial and any interpretation problematic.

Significantly, but perhaps not surprisingly since she originally set out to pursue an artistic career, Ella Hepworth Dixon begins by positioning herself in relation to the world of Art, rather than the world of Letters. Strangely enough, in the memoirs the only other occasion on which she mentions her artistic practices is when she describes her initial encounter with Oscar Wilde: 'The first time Oscar Wilde loomed on my horizon I was painting, together with Charlotte McCarthy and my sister, a portrait of Justin McCarthy the younger, in their hospitable house in Bloomsbury.'[16] From 1878 to 1884 both Ella Hepworth Dixon and her sister

---

[13] Signed C.E.B., *The London Illustrated News* (March 29, 1930), p. 516.

[14] *The Story of a Modern Woman* (1894, repr. Peterborough, 2004), p. 109. This seems to be a leitmotiv in Ella Hepworth Dixon's work, re-echoing, for example, the literary editor's advice to the novice writer, Mary Erle, 'The name, of course, ... the name counts for something' p. 108.

[15] In 'A Sketch of the Past' (1939, repr. London, 1978) Virginia Woolf discusses at greater length 'this influence ... the consciousness of other groups impinging upon ourselves' p. 80.

[16] *As I Knew Them* (London, 1930), p. 34.

Marion exhibited works, especially oil paintings, in various exhibitions at the Society of Women Artists and the Royal Society of British Artists. The *Art Journal* review of the Society of Lady Artists Spring Exhibition 1879 even comments on Miss Hepworth Dixon's progress,[17] but so far I have been unable to unearth much evidence of their exact dates and places of study. The names of the Hepworth Dixon sisters do not figure, for instance, in the archives of the Académie Julian, but on several occasions in their periodical contributions both Ella and Marion mention having studied there at the same time as Marie Bashkirtseff. Marion Hepworth Dixon's 'Marie Bashkirtseff: A Personal Reminiscence' in the *Fortnightly Review*[18] is the most famous example, but in her 'Pensées de Femme' Ella Hepworth Dixon regularly makes references to when she 'studied painting in the studio of M. Charles Chaplin and afterwards in the more Bohemian *Atélie*r Julian in the passage des Panoramas'.[19] Moreover, she appears to have drawn on her experiences there not only for her novel, but also for several short stories such as 'Condemned'[20] and 'His Sweet Disaster'.[21]

In the 'Foreword', however, she presents herself from both sides of the canvas. She first describes the admiration aroused in an un-named captain of a well-known regiment by a portrait of herself[22] 'draped in white tulle' whom a 'French painter had grossly flattered', according to her sitter. The picture had hung in the Royal Academy and the young man had come to her house in an attempt to purchase it. He is unfortunately merely enamoured of an artistic representation, or *mis*representation, and immediately flees from the real-life model who, 'grubby with oil-paint ..., dressed in an unbecoming black jersey', bursts in on the discussion. Woman as the object of art is 'very earnestly' worthy of admiration; woman as the agent of art, on the other hand, is shied away from. It should also be noted that the flesh and blood woman is not engaged in the 'eminently ladylike occupation'[23] of painting water-colours.

Later, when she has traded her paint brush for a pen, Ella Hepworth Dixon offers a similarly complex image: 'journalistic activities were mixed up with a great deal of dancing and dining out; white tulle skirts and natty little laced up bodices took the place of an evening of inky fingers.'[24] Once more a young man, this time basing his opinion on the living presence again dressed in white tulle, equally

---

[17] 'Review of The Society of Lady Artists' Spring Exhibition', *Art Journal* (Spring 1879), p. 114 b. The 'Miss Hepworth Dixon' here referred to must obviously be Marion, the elder sister. In the catalogues paintings are ascribed to Miss Hepworth Dixon and Miss Ella Hepworth Dixon.

[18] *Fortnightly Review* (February, 1890), pp. 276-282.

[19] *Lady's Pictorial* (August 10, 1895), p. 197.

[20] *Woman* (April 9, 1891), pp. 15-16.

[21] *Lady's Pictorial* (November 26, 1898), pp. 4-9.

[22] I have as yet not been able to identify the artist or locate the portrait. The Royal Academy merely lists works exhibited, but in those days kept no visual copies.

[23] Vincent Hemming's comment on Mary Erle's announcement of her 'intention of adopting art as a profession'. *The Story of a Modern Woman* (1894, repr. Peterborough, 2004), p. 79.

[24] *As I Knew Them* (London, 1930), p. 31.

misjudges her, although by then she is not so entirely innocent of what was going on. He begins by mentioning one of *The World's* 'Town and Country Tales', which at that time were rarely signed, and then corrects himself, telling her it is 'not quite the kind of story you should read', whereas, unbeknown to him, it was she who had written it. Unlike her younger self, however, having now learnt to adapt to the expectations of others, Ella Hepworth Dixon manages to camouflage the evidence that she stains her hands, exerts more self-control and remains silent.

Her reaction might be interpreted as the typical silencing of the female voice, but her comment 'Why spoil my evening?' suggests that she knowingly compromises for her own ultimate ends. Since in *As I Knew Them* so much is left unsaid, one cannot help wondering if, whether wilfully or not, it is written with an analogous desire to meet the expectations of her readers. Unlike the short story, it is not anonymous and thus the author might be consciously more guarded about keeping up appearances. Furthermore, the self-mocking tone which 'the subject of this memoir'[25] adopts from the beginning could be interpreted as a mask, or as a deliberate distancing technique. In her chapter on 'Fictions and Lives',[26] Liz Stanley draws attention to the fact that women are often ironic about autobiography as a genre, and cites Gertrude Stein and Colette as prime examples. It is moreover typical of Ella Hepworth Dixon's writing in general, whether fiction or non-fiction, and reveals an equal reluctance to take herself too seriously. Nevertheless, that she relies on humour, often at her own expense, does not necessarily mean that there is no underlying seriousness. On the contrary, in speaking of one of her old friends, Judge W.H. Thorne, in a moment of rare gravity she expresses what might be her fundamental credo: 'He looks on life with the ironic smile we should all attain; otherwise it appears unsupportable.'[27]

As if to remind the reader of her more familiar public image Ella Hepworth Dixon provides two photographs (Figures 1.1 and 1.2) of herself, one facing the frontispiece as she appeared in 1930 and one when she 'commenced author', significantly placed in the chapter entitled 'People in the Gay 'Nineties'. She had, in fact, already enjoyed a considerable amount of success by then, but the last decade of the nineteenth century certainly witnessed the high-water mark of her celebrity, and perhaps she wished to be especially associated with the *fin de siècle*, 'the untidy, happy-go-lucky Bohemia of the 'nineties'.[28] The photograph of the débutante still reveals a rather demure figure, while the 1930s writer, although apparently still dressed for 'gay and brilliant evening parties',[29] looks out of the page with greater confidence and possibly the prescribed ironic detachment. The choice of images might therefore have been dictated by a desire to show herself as

---

[25] Virginia Woolf's term employed in 'A Sketch of the Past' (1939, repr. London, 1978), p. 80.

[26] Liz Stanley, *The Auto/biographical I: The Theory and Practice of Feminist Auto/biography* (Manchester, 1992), pp. 56-88.

[27] *As I Knew Them* (London, 1930), p. 40.

[28] *Ibid.* p. 272.

[29] *Ibid.* p. 137.

Figure 1.1 'Myself When I began to Write'

Photo *Hoppé, London*

Figure 1.2 Ella Hepworth Dixon (1930)

she was seen by others at the beginning and at the end of her long career.

It may, initially, appear somewhat contradictory for one who modestly claims to find it 'distasteful to write about myself' to include not one, but two portraits of herself. Nor was such self-deprecation new. Much earlier, precisely in the heyday of her fame, when interviewed by *Woman* in the series 'My Faith and My Work',[30] Ella Hepworth Dixon expresses similar reticence. Some might argue that 'such becoming modesty' is, or at least was, considered a quality, especially in a woman, and might simply have been another mask adopted for the circumstance. At this stage it is worth remembering that Ella Hepworth Dixon's long career ran parallel to many developments in media representation, and from her early experiences with the periodical press she had perhaps retained the habit of accompanying written texts with visual support. Moreover, the photographs remind readers that the emphasis throughout is on a public image, often a deliberate construct in itself. They also serve to illustrate further the protean nature of identity; one image can never encompass the entirety of a person. Both the title and subtitle of the work indicate as much. Ella Hepworth Dixon's avowal that she is describing those she 'met on the way' not as they were or as they are, but as *she* knew them, emphasizes the momentary nature of the observations and the subjectivity of her own vision. The admission that she is not providing a complete picture is picked up again on the last page of the book, as the reviewer in *The London Illustrated News* remarks:

> Seeing that a woman's postscript is supposed to contain the pith of her letter, it may be well to add that in her *envoi* she writes: 'I have not attempted to put any of the people into their proper niche - or even on a shelf - but only to set down, while they were fresh in my memory *certain traits* of famous men and women who will be remembered in the coming years.'[31] (my italics)

These 'pen-portraits', to use the term employed by the same critic, 'delightfully life-like' though they may be, are manifestly incomplete representations. Moreover, many 'excellent photographic reproductions'[32] of those 'she met on the way' also complement Ella Hepworth Dixon's verbal vignettes.

To a certain extent it could be said that in content and style *As I Knew Them* reflects the artistic movements of Ella Hepworth Dixon's youth and, even if no direct mention, somewhat surprisingly, is ever made of her studies at the Académie Julian in Paris or elsewhere, allusions from the register of the visual arts permeate the text to remind the reader throughout that the 'I' who speaks and the 'eye' that sees were trained in a 'serious French studio'.[33] The fragmented structure of the narrative recalls both 'the broken strokes of unmixed pigment'[34] that constitute

---

[30] 'My Faith and My Work', *Woman* (September 23, 1896), p. 8.

[31] Signed C.E.B., *The London Illustrated News* (March 29, 1930), p. 516.

[32] Peter Renny, *The Empire Review* LI (1930), p. 298.

[33] Alison Ives' unfavourable comparison between Mary Erle's studies at the London School of Art and the Parisian equivalent in *The Story of a Modern Woman* (1894, repr. Peterborough, 2004), p. 88.

[34] *The New Britannica-Webster Dictionary and Reference Guide* (1988).

Impressionist paintings and the dots of colour of Pointillist art, the overall image being held together by Ella Hepworth Dixon's consciousness or memory. Some feminist critics might argue that the result is similar to the quilting effect often associated especially with American women's writing, but even if one were to accept the underlying notion, quilting would seem too prosaic and too tangible for Ella Hepworth Dixon. The critic in *The Times Literary Supplement* rightly notes, 'there is not much substance to these sketches of well-known people'.[35] The overall impression is thus more in keeping with what Virginia Woolf calls the 'luminous halo'[36] of life, or the 'illuminations, matches struck unexpectedly in the dark'[37] evoked by her fictional woman artist, Lily Briscoe. As a result the two photographic images of Ella Hepworth Dixon can also be seen as providing a sort of frame for the sketches she draws of her milieu, with the occasional wayward brushstroke, as she refers very fleetingly to events beyond the borders of adulthood.

As I Knew Them covers the period 'from her childhood in late Victorian times to the present day',[38] and is 'full of memories of personalities who have left their mark on the world of time'.[39] 'She seems to have met nearly everybody', remarks the critic in the *Daily News*,[40] reminiscent of Miss Beatrice Harraden's comment in her 'Prefatory Note' to Eliza Lynn Linton's autobiography that Mrs Linton had 'known all the interesting people of her day'. H. Charles Woods in the *Sunday Times* is more explicit:

> Miss Hepworth Dixon, who has seen Society and written during three reigns, now manages to provide her readers with sidelights upon the countless people she has known. Combined and intermingled with these sidelights are powers of vivid description, of shrewd observation about the times in which she is living and of making witty remarks upon the things which she has seen and done.[41]

This sounds rather like a description of Ella Hepworth Dixon's lifelong contributions to the periodical press, and *As I Knew Them* often does read like more 'Pensées de Femme' or 'Woman's Ways', the titles of her weekly columns in, respectively, *Lady's Pictorial* and *The Sketch*. As the reviewer in *The Morning Post* points out, 'people are made to deport themselves in accordance with the old French song quoted on the title-page:

Ainsi font, font, font,
Les petites marionettes,

[35] (Unsigned) *The Times Literary Supplement* (March 13, 1930), p. 217.
[36] Virginia Woolf, 'Modern Fiction' (1925, repr. London, 1984), p. 150.
[37] Virginia Woolf, *To The Lighthouse* (1927, repr. London, 1963), p. 186.
[38] Signed C.E.B., *The London Illustrated News* (March 29, 1930), p. 516.
[39] Peter Renny, *The Empire Review* LI (1930), p. 298.
[40] Robert Lynd, 'Famous People', *Daily News* (March 12, 1930), p. 4.
[41] H. Charles Woods, *Sunday Times* (March 23, 1930), p. 11.

Trois petits tours, et puis s'en vont.[42]

This is seen as an advantage: 'The best of this happy book is that the author keeps her celebrities moving on; even the most notable are not allowed to stand long enough to bore her fellow-spectator.'[43] Ella Hepworth Dixon is thus doing exactly what she claims to set out to do; without lapsing into caricature, she provides 'sketches', a genre she had perfected over the years. The critic in *The Times Literary Supplement* notes, 'one meets them, has a word or two with them, and passes on', and pertinently adds, 'perhaps a journalist's life is like that.'

In this way, Ella Hepworth Dixon's style can be ascribed not so much to her gender as to her profession and to the life and times in which she learnt and exercised that profession. In her evaluation of the 'Private Selves of Private Women', Jane Marcus draws interesting parallels between 'the *form* of women's autobiographical writing and female identity'[44] (her italics). She suggests, for example, that Elizabeth Robins structures her life-story[45] as drama, whilst Ethel Smyth, the composer, recounts her life[46] 'on the huge scale of nineteenth-century opera'. Ella Hepworth Dixon's life and work certainly follow this pattern. She therein reflects not only the artistic trends of her day, but also the changes taking place in the literary world. It must be remembered that, as I shall discuss at greater length in chapter three, in the last decades of the nineteenth century the journalistic world was in a process of upheaval. The new vogue for titbits, causeries, or short pithy articles proved ideally suited to Ella Hepworth Dixon's 'prentice pen. It is surely significant that she only wrote one full-length novel and even that, in comparison with the voluminous writings of contemporaries such as Sarah Grand or Mona Caird, is more of an extended short story.

Nor was it only in the literary world that her skills in dealing with small details proved successful. At the outbreak of the First World War when her friend Sir Claude Phillips[47] declared, 'We must do something, and immediately. We must make shirts,' her reaction was, 'Well, I can't cut out, but I'm first-rate at buttonholes.' Looking back, she adds, 'My button-holes were workmanlike, and this accomplishment stood me in good stead to the end of the War. Even when employed by the Ministry of Information to write propaganda articles for neutral newspapers, I continued faithful to my buttonholes.'[48] Again rather than making

---

[42] Mary Cholmondeley likewise quotes from a French song on the title page of *Under One Roof: A Family Record* (London, 1918).

[43] Signed E.B.O., *The Morning Post* (March 7, 1930), p. 15.

[44] 'The Private Selves of Public Women', in *The Private Self* ed. Shari Benstock (London, 1988), pp. 114-146.

[45] Elizabeth Robins, *Way Stations* (London, 1913).

[46] Ethel Smyth, *Impressions That Remained* (London, 1920).

[47] Brother of Eugénie Phillips, to whom in 1904 Ella Hepworth Dixon dedicated her collection of short stories, Sir Claude Phillips (1846-1924) was art critic for the *Daily Telegraph* and first keeper of the Wallace Collection when it opened at Hertford House in 1900. He received a knighthood on his retirement in 1911.

[48] *As I Knew Them* (London, 1930), pp. 85-86.

this a gender issue, I would argue that it furnishes further evidence of Ella Hepworth Dixon's own recognition of her limitations; in life and literature her range was narrow, and she had no pretentions about either. Unlike Mrs Oliphant, for example, she never draws parallels between her own work and that of writers such as Jane Austen and George Eliot, and, in a different vein, unlike Eliza Lynn Linton, who rather titillates the reader about the secret lives of Dickens and Thackeray, Ella Hepworth Dixon never claims to know more than she tells. Naturally, it is rather incongruous to compare the sewing of buttonholes with the physically dangerous, traditionally unwomanly work undertaken by many of her sex during the war, and Ella Hepworth Dixon herself often expressed great admiration in her articles both during and after wartime for 'the variety of accomplishments which the war-woman or girl has achieved'.[49] No further mention is made of her own propaganda articles which are understandably difficult to identify.

Consequently, *As I Knew Them* also tells 'the story of a generation' and offers 'a slice of representative life in a specific period',[50] bearing witness to what, in the *envoi*, Ella Hepworth Dixon calls 'a change such as the world ha(d) not yet seen'.[51] As Mary Jean Corbett argues, such writing is typical of Victorian women's self-representation. In a footnote she defines: 'the term "memoir" to denote not an autobiographical text that tells a story about a centred self, but one in which the writing subject recounts stories of others and events or movements in which she and/or her other subjects have taken part.'[52] Superficially, *As I Knew Them* appears to fit such a description perfectly, signifying that Ella Hepworth Dixon was very much a product of her era. On another level, however, within the narrative, Ella Hepworth Dixon also reveals the extent to which she was a-typical of her class, gender and generation. In the 'Preface' to her autobiography, Netta Syrett expresses initial doubts about recounting her life, considering it 'too ordinary' to be of interest to others until she realized that some contemporaries had not had her advantages. She then consents to 'write a few reminiscences, chosen, so far as possible, for the light they may throw upon the past'. Incidentally, she and Ella Hepworth Dixon had several friends or acquaintances in common, such as Max Beerbohm, Arnold Bennett, and H.G. Wells, and yet neither ever mentions the other in her autobiography.

Ella Hepworth Dixon's memoirs then help to explain why she could allow herself to be less polemical than some of her contemporaries. As in more traditional autobiographies, childhood is presented, albeit briefly, as formative. From the outset Ella Hepworth Dixon recognizes her privileged position within the family

---

[49] 'Adaptable Woman', *Lady's Pictorial* (August 3, 1918), p. 108.

[50] Valerie Sanders, *The Private Lives of Victorian Women: Autobiography in Nineteenth-Century England* (New York, 1989), pp. 10-11.

[51] *As I Knew Them* (London, 1930), p. 281.

[52] Mary Jean Corbett, 'Literary Domesticity and Women Writers' Subjectivities' in *Women, Autobiography, Theory: A Reader* (Wisconsin, 1998), pp. 255-263.

and society in general: 'I was born[53] the seventh child, and the youngest of three sisters; therefore by all the laws of fairy-land, bound to be lucky.'[54] 'The little girl with hair hanging down her back' clearly benefited from 'being brought up in a literary and social milieu of the best class',[55] but 'the fat schoolgirl in pigtails' equally enjoyed the 'warlike' company of her siblings. She also inherited admirable traits from both parents: like her father, whom she describes as 'a Knight of the Inkstand', she, too, would take up her pen to defend others, especially friends such as Max Beerbohm,[56] and like her mother she would be a lifelong proponent of women's rights, as her *envoi* reveals, a subject to which I shall return. She recounts how her mother:

> Went to all Ibsen's plays (by herself) when they were first produced; and was, almost, the first woman in London to call in a woman doctor when my youngest brother, Sydney, was born.[57] It was she who presented me, on my return from school-days in Germany, with a petition to sign for women's suffrage.[58]

Her avant-garde parents gave her access to the same education as her brothers, including study abroad, so, unlike some women writers such as Virginia Woolf, who was also born into a literary family, she grew up with no sense of exclusion. Like Sarah Grand[59] from a very young age she was given a free reign in the library, but was never sent to a girls' school and 'never had a lesson from a woman in (her) life'.[60] Her account of her life at the Villa Felseck in Heidelberg, a school also frequented by the future George V and his eldest brother, the Duke of Clarence, makes a stark contrast to the un-named establishment which Sarah Grand attended

---

[53] For reasons I have yet to fathom, Ella Hepworth Dixon's birth-date is variably given as 1855 or 1857. I enclose her birth certificate (See Appendix 1) to dispel any remaining doubts. Her sister Marion was born a year earlier on March 17, 1856.

[54] *As I Knew Them* (London, 1930), p. 13.

[55] H. Charles Woods, *Sunday Times* (March 23, 1930), p. 11.

[56] See for example 'The Real Max Beerbohm: The Beau and the Caricaturist' in the *Westminster Gazette* (June 4, 1923, p. 6) written in response to what she considered unfair criticism. She draws attention to this in her chapter on Max Beerbohm and includes a copy of his letter of thanks.

[57] Sydney Hepworth Dixon was born on March 6, 1868.

[58] *As I Knew Them* (London, 1930), p. 14.

[59] At this point it is perhaps worth comparing her dates (1857-1932) with those of Eliza Lynn Linton (1822-1898), Mrs Oliphant (1828-1897), Ouida (Marie Louise de la Ramée) (1839-1908), Louise Jopling (1843-1933), Sarah Grand (1854-1943), Olive Schreiner (1855-1920), Iota (Kathleen Mannington Caffyn) (1855?-1926), Evelyn Everett-Green (1856-1932), Marie Bashkirtseff (1858-1884), Mona Caird (1858-1932), Mary Cholmondeley (1859-1925), George Egerton (Mary Chavelita Dunne Bright) (1859-1945), George Paston (Emily Morse Symonds) (1860-1936), Elizabeth Robins (1863-1952), Netta Syrett (1865-1943), Menie Muriel Dowie (1867-1945), Evelyn Sharp (1869-1955), Cicely Hamilton (1872-1952), and Virginia Woolf (1882-1941).

[60] *As I Knew Them* (London, 1930), p. 22.

between the ages of twelve and fourteen. Besides receiving 'special lessons, including German Philosophy', Ella Hepworth Dixon 'spent many happy days' skating in winter, swimming in summer, marching over the mountains, going to students' *Kneipes* and helping to entertain the Professor's class once a week at supper'.[61] Sarah Grand, in contrast, laments:

> We had none but the most babyish books; our recreation in the grounds was limited to monotonous walks up and down the gravelled paths; we had no games of any sort - nothing to develop our physique at all but the making of our little beds every morning and an hour's 'deportment' once a fortnight.[62]

Consequently, Ella Hepworth Dixon had none of Sarah Grand's inducements to marry at sixteen, 'the great inducement being that I should be able to study thoroughly any subject I liked, learn languages so that I could speak them, and music so that I could play it, have the command of good books, and escape from routine.'[63]

The fact that Ella Hepworth Dixon never married or had children does not automatically signify that she became a stereo-typical 'Odd Woman'. The autobiography ultimately defies the notion, hinted at in her own novel, *The Story of a Modern Woman*, that the lot of a single woman is 'a dreary battle'. She seems to have been at ease with herself and with others, and to have led a rich, fulfilling alternative life. Unlike some women writers, particularly those of an older generation, such as Charlotte Yonge, Mary Ward and Eliza Lynn Linton, Ella Hepworth Dixon makes a working woman's life attractive, as indeed it seems to have been for her. She is thus writing against several stereotypes including the embittered old maid, the middle-class lady writing for leisure, and the over-zealous New Woman journalist in pince-nez and mackintosh.

And yet, on many issues, *As I Knew Them* still leaves a great deal unsaid. Besides being absolutely discreet about suitors, Ella Hepworth Dixon remains silent about much of her personal life. This is perhaps partly a result of her class and upbringing, and partly because she is consciously not writing confessions of an intimate kind. In '"Fathers' Daughters": Three Victorian Anti-Feminist Women Autobiographers'[64] Valerie Sanders suggests this is not unusual in most autobiographies by Victorian women writers. Likewise, there is no sense of any soul-searching, practically no mention of religion, little politics,[65] few references to contemporary writers and no indication of her own struggles, disappointments or suffering. For example, her own bouts of serious ill-health are passed over with great rapidity, the deaths of her mother[66] and siblings are not even mentioned, and

---

[61] *Ibid*. pp. 23-24.
[62] 'Some Recollections of My Schooldays', *Lady's Magazine* (January, 1901), p. 42.
[63] *Ibid*.
[64] In Vincent Newey and Philip Shaw (eds), *Mortal Pages, Literary Lives* (Aldershot, 1996).
[65] 'There is not a scrap of political prejudice in the chronicler's mental make-up', comments the reviewer in *The Morning Post*.
[66] Mary Ann Dixon died on June 1, 1917.

that of her father, which left the family 'in most straightened circumstances',[67] is barely touched upon. An entry in William Michael Rossetti's diary for January 9, 1880, indicates that the financial difficulties of the Hepworth Dixons were no secret:

> Mrs Gilchrist and her younger daughter called: also Mrs Garnett who says that Mrs Hepworth Dixon and her family will certainly be unable to continue living in their present house (tho' it is their own property), and that the chief support of the family at present is a son, Harold, who has a Chemical Professorship at Oxford estimated (but Mrs G. fears overestimated) at £400 or £500 a year. An effort will be made to obtain a good literary pension for Mrs D.[68]

By this stage only three of Ella Hepworth Dixon's siblings were still alive – an older brother Harold aged 27, her sister Marion aged 23 and her younger brother Sydney. A few months after the death of her husband, Mary Ann Dixon in fact wrote to the Royal Literary Fund requesting financial assistance, as her 'present means of income being actually £100 p. a.' were 'quite inadequate' for 'two unmarried daughters and a boy, a child of eleven who will require educating for some years to come'. The recent deaths of his eldest children, William and Edith 'who assisted (her father) in his literary work', had apparently added to the strains on William Hepworth Dixon's failing health. Within ten days the Royal Literary Fund responded generously with a cheque for £150. In her letter of thanks Mary Ann Dixon indicated that the money would 'be of great service in educating my children; my daughters in their Art and my little boy in his general education'. *Galignani's Messenger*[69] indicates that a month later 'The Misses Dixons' were in Paris, staying at the Hotel Meurice, suggesting perhaps that this was a time when they were pursuing their artistic ambitions alongside Marie Bashkirtseff.

For Ella Hepworth Dixon such details might have been too personal or painful to place before the public, or even to recall to herself. In a similar vein, Netta Syrett openly admits, 'On the subject of sorrows, I will be brief',[70] and in her cursory recollections Sarah Grand declares, 'The tendency of human nature is to allow unpleasant things to lapse from the memory.'[71] Readers, therefore, who expect intimate revelations about the author in *As I Knew Them* will be rather disappointed. In many ways Ella Hepworth Dixon lives up to the nickname given to

---

[67] Letter dated March 2, 1880 from Mary Ann Dixon to the Royal Literary Fund, Archives of the Royal Literary Fund, M 1077/83, File 2087, to be found in the British Library.

[68] From William Michael Rossetti's unpublished MS Diary, University of British Columbia, Rare Books and Special Collections. William Michael Rossetti's diaries are also on microfilm at the Bodleain Library, Department of Western Manuscripts. I am indebted to Angela Thirlwell for drawing my attention to this.

[69] 'List of English and Americans registered yesterday', *Galignani's Messenger (*April 5, and May 3, 1880).

[70] *The Sheltering Tree* (London, 1939), p. 242.

[71] 'Some Recollections of My Schooldays', *Lady's Magazine* (January, 1901), p. 42.

her by Francis, Count Lützow: 'Lesniptak' or the 'Voice-of-the-bird-in-the-wood, an unseen but vocal character in "Siegfried"'.[72] Whilst her voice is heard, she herself remains camouflaged. In keeping with most of her writing, she deftly manages to conform to society's expectations of women by not becoming too public, but at the same time she challenges certain constraints by breaking silence and speaking out.

Her *envoi* should perhaps receive more careful attention. One is immediately tempted to quote again from her first weekly column in the *Lady's Pictorial* and ask why for her parting words she 'should turn instinctively to that agreeable tongue which is spoken on the hither side of the Straits of Dover'.[73] An extract from an old French song also appears on the title page and French expressions season her prose throughout. Recourse to French, it should be noted, was not at all unusual. Ella Hepworth Dixon reglarly employed French expressions in her writing. Likewise, Lady Violet Greville, for example, for many years wrote articles in *The Graphic* entitled '*Place aux Dames*', and *The Ladies' Field*, to which Ella Hepworth Dixon also contributed, had an unsigned column entitled '*Entre Femmes*' when it began in 1896 and a series in 1903 called '*Bavardages de Femmes*' signed '*L'Inconnue*'. Not everyone approved of such practices. John Strange Winter, for one, in her advice on 'How To Become A Lady Journalist', vituperated against 'French words (being) dragged in wholesale', and advocated 'the use of sound English'.[74] Curiously enough, Ella Hepworth Dixon almost never resorts to German although she writes at greater length about her time spent there and clearly mastered the language. It may simply be that for those of her class and culture a working knowledge of French was to be expected. For Ella Hepworth Dixon it may have been associated with happier times such as her youth in Paris and summers spent in pre-war France. Not that she ever expresses regret for the past. On the contrary, she claims to 'feel at home in the modern world, with its absence of hypocrisy, its broader outlook, its deeper sympathy, its collective conscience'. As in most of her work, Ella Hepworth Dixon's attention is primarily turned outwards, and French, long considered the language of diplomacy, may constitute yet another screen for the first person narrator.

As I Knew Them thus ends, as its title implies, with the emphasis firmly placed on others, and on women in particular. Like all of Ella Hepworth Dixon's books, it is dedicated to a woman, this time her sister-in-law, and her final words are about 'the revolution effected by the higher education of women, (and) their admittance to citizenship along with men'. With her concluding wish, 'May they prove worthy of their privileges', Ella Hepworth Dixon one last time directs the reader's gaze firmly away from herself. We may have caught a glimpse of her on the way, but it is my suspicion that we must look elsewhere to complete the picture.

References to her may be found, for instance, in a few letters to or from friends such as Max Beerbohm and Arnold Bennett, and in the memoirs of fellow artists

---

[72] *As I Knew Them* (London, 1930), p. 238.
[73] 'Pensées de Femme', *Lady's Pictorial* (June 22, 1895), p. 955.
[74] *Winter's Magazine* (December 2, 1898), p. 79.

and writers such as Louise Jopling,[75] Mrs C.S. Peel, or Francis Toye. For example, when recounting her meetings with celebrities in the 'naughty 'nineties' Mrs Peel describes Ella Hepworth Dixon as a 'the only woman star'[76] amongst the likes of Max Beerbohm and Somerset Maugham, an opinion shared by Francis Toye who writes of her as possessing 'something very like genius for social intercourse'.[77] Tantalisingly, however, again they provide mere sketches.

In 'Writing Fictions: Women's Autobiography in France'[78] Nancy K. Miller offers an alternative in suggesting that one must read the autobiography with the fiction: 'the historical truth of a woman writer's life lies in the reader's grasp of her intratext: the body of her writing and not the writing of her body.'[79] In that sense, therefore, one might find more of Ella Hepworth Dixon in Peggy Wynman, the first-person narrator of *My Flirtations,* Ella Hepworth Dixon's first book, which appeared under the pseudonym 'Margaret Wynman' in 1892, and in *The Story of a Modern Woman,* which lends itself even more easily to an autobiographical reading.[80] The initials of her two female protagonists, Mary Erle and Alison Ives, are surely significant: M.E. and A.I., and might indicate that there is perhaps as much of Ella Hepworth Dixon in one as in the other. The changes made between the serialized version and Heinemann's edition, such as deleting the whole of chapter three which deals with one heroine's experiences in a German school, might imply that the author wanted to create a greater sense of distance between herself and her fictional representation. Nevertheless, many similarities still remain between the novel and the memoirs, such as the account of the atmosphere surrounding the death of the father. Furthermore, Ella Hepworth Dixon's other non-fiction writing could also prove to be a rich source of information. For example, her account of her dislike of dolls in the *Lady's Pictorial* is notably resonant of Mary Erle's 'high scorn' for 'the whole race of dolls':[81] 'Personally, when I wore a pinafore and latchet shoes, I cared little for the smirking wax doll of Teutonic manufacture, and allowed my brothers to make an *auto da fé* of those dolls which were given to me ... .'[82]

In succeeding chapters, by examining both her milieu and her varied literary output, I shall attempt to supplement the self-evasive sketch of herself Ella Hepworth Dixon provides in her memoirs.

---

[75] Louise Jopling, *Twenty Years of My Life 1867-1887* (London, 1928).
[76] C.S. Peel, *Life's Enchanted Cup: An Autobiography, 1872-1933* (London, 1933), p. 104.
[77] Francis Toye, *For What We Have Received* (London, 1950), p. 77.
[78] In Brodzki and Schenck (eds) *Life/Lines* (Ithaca, 1988).
[79] In her autobiography, Netta Syrett recognizes only in retrospect that she put some of own past experience into her novels.
[80] In *The Longman Companion to Victorian Fiction* John Sutherland describes *The Story of a Modern Woman* as 'painfully autobiographical', p. 190.
[81] *The Story of a Modern Woman* (1894, repr. Peterborough, 2004), p. 51.
[82] 'Pleasing Things at Christmas', *Lady's Pictorial* (December 27, 1919), p. 862.

Chapter 2

Ella Hepworth Dixon and the New Woman

In her memoirs, Ella Hepworth Dixon only once mentions the term 'New Woman' with regard to herself:

> (At) a party given by Sir Gilbert Parker in his bachelor flat, when all the resources of the establishment were employed to house the guests, Edmund Gosse, in his old-fashioned way, offered me his arm to go and find a cup of tea. In much pomp we approached an open door which was quite obviously our host's bedroom. 'No, no,' exclaimed Edmund Gosse, coyly: 'I cannot take even "The New Woman" in there!'[1]

Whilst such sexual inuendoes were by no means rare whenever the New Woman was mentioned and whilst this anecdote may reveal a great deal about Edmund Gosse,[2] more interesting for my present purposes is Ella Hepworth Dixon's comment: 'Why I should have been so called I never knew, except that I had always been in favour of the Women's Franchise.' This not only emphasizes her own very different association of the New Woman with serious social and political concerns, but, as discussed in the preceding chapter, it also raises numerous questions about the reliability of a first person narrator, especially of autobiography.

For, in fact, particularly after the celebrity of *The Story of a Modern Woman* in 1894, often referred to as the '*annus mirabilis*' of New Woman fiction, Ella Hepworth Dixon was very closely associated with the avant-garde 'Emancipated Woman'. When, for example, in his July *Review of Reviews* W.T. Stead chose to review not one book of the month, as was his wont, but to publish a general overview of the literary phenomenon, he entitled his article 'The Novel of the Modern Woman',[3] echoing almost word-for-word the title of Ella Hepworth

---

[1] *As I Knew Them* (London, 1930), p. 41. Typically, no precise date is given.

[2] Ella Hepworth Dixon mentions that Edmund Gosse was caricatured by Max Beerbohm, Osbert Sitwell and 'other irreverent writers', but adds that he 'was always gracious and kindly disposed to young writers', and she 'always found him civil, and sometimes playful', as in the incident described here.

[3] *The Review of Reviews* 10 (July, 1894), pp. 64-74. In a footnote W.T. Stead lists them as follows:

Dixon's famous work, and, by way of introduction, began with a quotation from her novel. In her memoirs Ella Hepworth Dixon mentions that:

> W.T. Stead, whom I did not know personally, requested an interview, and 'did me' handsomely enough, in the *Review of Reviews*, which was then held in high esteem as a literary organ. It was the strangest interview. Stead was a shaggy, bearded, restless individual continually striding about, or sitting cross-wise on a chair. ... He was most outspoken in speech. .... I can remember almost every word which passed.[4]

The Review of Reviews had already published a review of Ella Hepworth Dixon's novel the previous month, and described it as 'one of the most powerful and, at the same time, least "platformy" of all the stories called forth by the constant discussions upon woman's present position and future.'[5] W.T. Stead had always shown an interest in promoting women, for example in his first *Review of Reviews*[6] a Scholarship of £100 *per annum* for three years had been offered to stimulate women readers and journalists, but he was not the only critic to attempt such an overview. In September and October 1894 the *Lady's Pictorial* also ran a three-part series on 'Emancipated Fiction'.[7] Although it was signed 'By One Who Has The Misfortune To Be A Man', it does attempt a fair, albeit less generous, appraisal of the 'New Fiction', beginning with Iota's *A Yellow Aster* and covering several of the works discussed by W.T. Stead, including *A Superfluous Woman*, *The Heavenly Twins*, and *The Story of a Modern Woman*. Also included were Mrs Lynn Linton's *The One Too Many*, which, not surprisingly, 'treats the emancipated sisterhood from the standpoint of an unsympathetic critic', and *A Daughter of To-day* by Sara Jeanette Duncan, described as 'a careful and clever picture of a peculiarly unpleasant type of girl, drawn, apparently, with the definite and deliberate purpose of disgusting us with a product of the new movement.'

'The Story of an African Farm,' by Olive Schreiner. (Hutchinson) 3s.6d.
'The Daughters of Danaus,' by Mona Caird.
'Dr. Janet of Harley Street,' by Arabella Kenealy. (Digby) 2s.
'The Heavenly Twins,' by Sarah Grand. (Heinemann.) 6s.
'The Superfluous Woman,'(Heinemann) 6s.
'Keynotes,' by George Egerton. (Mathews) 3s.6d.net.
'The Yellow Aster,' by Iota. (Hutchinson) 6s.
'The Story of a Modern Woman,' by Ella Hepworth Dixon. (Heinemann) 6s.
'Joanna Traill, Spinster,' by Annie E. Holdsworth. (Heinemann) 3s.net
'A Sunless Heart,' Two Volumes.Ward and Lock. 21s.
In the article he then discusses them in the same, apparently chronological, order supplying a photo-portrait of each writer and 'giving, wherever it is possible, their own statement in their own words of the message which in their novels they sought to deliver to the British public'.

[4] *As I Knew Them* (London, 1930), pp. 172-173.
[5] *The Review of Reviews* 9 (June, 1894), p. 634.
[6] *Ibid.* 1 (June, 1890), pp. 470-471.
[7] *Lady's Pictorial* (September 8), p. 339, (October 6), p. 504, and (October 13), p. 534.

In August of the same year when *The Idler* interviewed a number of celebrities, including Mrs Mannington Caffyn, John Oliver Hobbes, Lady Greville, Miss Pendered and Dr Arabella Kenealy on 'How to Court the "Advanced Woman"',[8] Ella Hepworth Dixon's opinion was sought along with that of other notorious New Women such as George Egerton and Sarah Grand, and subsequently commented upon in *The Illustrated London News.*[9] The 'Advanced Woman' is here described by Angus Evan Abbott, 'so courteously and humorously' according to Ella Hepworth Dixon with her usual irony, as 'she for whom Man will not risk his life, whom Man will not take as a gift, nor can Man be bribed to receive'. Perhaps not unusually, the journalist misrepresents Ella Hepworth Dixon in saying she 'declares that if the Average Man wants to marry the Advanced Woman, he won't find it difficult', and significantly omitting her proviso - 'provided he sets about it in a proper sense of enterprise'. In a later series on 'My Faith and My Work' published in *Woman* in 1896, after Roy Devereux, Mrs Andrew Dean, Alicia Ramsay and Mrs Meynell, Ella Hepworth Dixon admitted, 'I was called a number of names by several estimable elderly persons writing for Conservative newspapers ... . I was called a New Woman - or some such *quaint* appellation'[10] (my italics).

Ella Hepworth Dixon's disdain for such name-calling is evident in one of her numerous weekly columns when she writes:

> It has long been a cherished theory of our masculine critics - and particularly that of the second-rate journalist - that she who, in his sarcasm, he has blasted with the name of the New Woman, is invariably one who has been left withering on the parental tree, unplucked by a superior and discerning sex.[11]

She then goes on to declare, 'this theory never had even the spurious attraction of a half-truth', and, to prove her point, enumerates a long list of eminent women in politics, literature, religion and reform who were not only wives, but also mothers. The article begins with praise of Olive Schreiner, and then includes other New Woman writers such as Sarah Grand, George Egerton, and Mona Caird, besides women from other domains such as Mrs Fawcett, Josephine Butler, Mrs Booth, and Annie Besant.

What Ella Hepworth Dixon understood by the term can best be seen in her admiration for Shakespeare's women - Rosalind, the 'immortal prototype',[12] Portia and Beatrice: 'Be sure that all three, had they lived today, would have been branded with the epithet "New Woman"',[13] and in her references to writers such as

[8] *The Idler* 6 (August, 1894), pp. 192-211.
[9] (Unsigned), 'A Magazine Causerie', *The Illustrated London News* (September 15, 1894), p. 348.
[10] *Woman* (September 23, 1896), p. 8.
[11] *Lady's Pictorial* (January 18, 1896), p. 85.
[12] *The Idler* 6 (August, 1894), p. 209.
[13] *Lady's Pictorial* (October 5, 1895), p. 524.

Elizabeth Barrett Browning, 'one of the earliest of the "new women"',[14] and Charlotte Bronte. 'Was Charlotte Bronte a New Woman?' she asks in one of her 'Pensées de Femme':

> It needs no lantern to discover under the somewhat prim and priggish exterior of this little provincial governess, a soul which questioned all things, which rigidly demanded justice, which never failed to urge the dignity of feminine labour, the eternal right of the woman to equal chances of love, of work, of a fulfilled life, as the man.[15]

Her response thus makes it easy to see why in the above-mentioned *Woman* interview, in spite of its many derogatory connotations, Ella Hepworth Dixon could add:

> I have, I may as well state once for all, not the slightest objection to being called a New Woman, or an advanced female, or even one of the shrieking sisterhood. Most of the 'shrieking' nowadays, I find, is done by the exasperated champions of the old *régime.*[16]

A glance at almost any review or periodical of the time does indeed reveal heated arguments about the 'Novissima', 'Revolting Daughters', a 'Shrieking Sisterhood', 'Odd Women', 'Superfluous Women', 'Wild Women' as well as rather dubious visual representations which show that whoever or whatever was referred to aroused passions, often of a decidedly vitriolic nature.

The term 'New Woman' is generally ascribed to Sarah Grand after the publication of her essay 'The New Aspects of the Woman Question' in *The North American Review* in March 1894.[17] It should be mentioned that she also employs the term 'Bawling Brothers', obviously the male equivalent of 'Shrieking Sisters'. The phenomenon had, however, disturbed for some time. Already in 1865 in an article entitled 'Belles Lettres' published in the *Westminster Review* mention is made of:

> The New Woman, as we read of her in recent novels, (who) possesses not only the velvet, but the claws of the tiger. She is no longer the Angel, but the Devil in the House ... . Man proposes, woman disposes, is the new proverb. The Fathers, after all, were right when they said Adam was more tempted by Eve than by the Devil.[18]

---

[14] 'Why Women Are Ceasing To Marry', *The Humanitarian* 14 (June, 1899), p. 393.
[15] *Lady's Pictorial* (November 21, 1896), p. 748.
[16] *Woman* (September 23, 1896), p. 8.
[17] Sarah Grand, 'The New Aspects of the Woman Question', *The North American Review* 158 (March, 1894), p. 271.
[18] (Unsigned, but in fact John R. de C. Wise), *Westminster Review*. New series. LVI (October, 1865), p. 568.

These few lines, identifying woman as usual with original sin, reveal many of the underlying and ever-growing anxieties about what women, *and* men, hence the world in general, were coming to.

What became known as the 'Woman Question' had grown in prominence throughout the nineteenth century. As society adapted, albeit haltingly, to tremendous changes brought about largely by technology and science, more and more questions were raised about the changing roles of women. In fact, fundamental questions were being raised about society itself but it was, as ever, easier to find a scapegoat than to probe the possible deep-rooted sources of unrest. As Sander L. Gilman writes:

> When ... the sense of order and control undergoes stress, ... an anxiety appears ... . We project that anxiety onto the Other, externalising our loss of control. The Other is thus stereo-typed, labelled with a set of signs parallelling (or mirroring) our loss of control. The Other is invested with all the qualities of the 'bad' or the 'good'.[19]

The Other in this case who was made to bear the burden of society's anxieties was identified by most people as woman. The seemingly unending discussions about the 'female', the 'feminine', the 'womanly', the 'ineffable she' ultimately led to little short of a cultural crisis. This was consequently reflected in some of the literature of the period, and then, not surprisingly, such literature found itself relegated to the *oubliettes* of literary history for decades. The 'Sensation Novels' of the 1860s, such as Mrs Henry Wood's *East Lynne* (1861) and Mary Braddon's *Lady Audley's Secret* (1862), had already kindled controversy when they had revealed that the Victorian ideal, an angel in the house, could conceal a devil in disguise. In the last decade of the century the debate reached a new crescendo when the New Woman, a better educated, more articulate and ultimately more subversive figure than the Girl of the Period, appeared. Eliza Lynn Linton's concluding wish in her essay,[20] which had provided this name for the type of woman who particularly upset conventional expectations of femininity, that it was simply a question of waiting 'patiently until the national madness had passed, and our women have come back again to the old English ideal - once the most beautiful, the most modest, the most essentially womanly in the world' had clearly not been fulfilled.

'We of course called everything advanced "the New" at that time,' declares George Bernard Shaw in 1898 in his Preface to *Plays Pleasant and Unpleasant*, and goes on to refer to the New Theatre and the New drama. Likewise in her autobiography, Netta Syrett mentions 'the "new" everything. "The New Woman", "The New Morality", "The New Paganism"'.[21] In one of her short stories, 'Like to

---

[19] Sander L. Gilman, *Differences and Pathology: Stereotypes of Sexuality, Race and Madness* (New York, 1985), quoted by Kimberley Reynolds in *Girls Only?* (Hemel Hempstead, 1990), p. 66.

[20] Eliza Lynn Linton's anti-feminist essay 'The Girl of the Period' was first published, unsigned, in the *Saturday Review* (March 14, 1868), pp. 339-340.

[21] *The Sheltering Tree* (London, 1939), p. 80.

Like',[22] Ella Hepworth Dixon herself makes fun of such 'newness': the sister of the hero, an American newspaper tycoon, 'talks all the time of Browning, and George Meredith, and Ibsen, and of all the newest of new young men in Art, and Literature, and the Drama.' At one point in the story when she and the narrator have risen early to see the sun-rise in the Straits of Messina, she declares, 'Oh, Laura, isn't it perfectly divine? ... Why I have had a new emotion!'

After a century which has hailed the New Deal and even New Labour, it is at times a little difficult to appreciate fully the derogatory implications of the term as understood by most people then.[23] In Sydney Grundy's 1894 play, *The New Woman*, described by Clement Scott, the drama critic of *The Illustrated London News*,[24] as 'a fierce onslaught on "The New Woman", the latest of many *new* movements' (my italics), one of the characters, Lady Wargrave, who has been away from England for many years, taken aback by the outspokenness of another female character, asks, 'Can this be the New Woman I have read about?' The reply is a resounding chorus of 'Everything's New nowadays! We have New Art - ', 'A New Journalism - ', 'A New Political Economy - ', 'A New Morality - ', 'A New Sex!'[25] Elsewhere, there was much talk of New Fiction, New Publishers, New Markets, even the New Town Type. In June *Punch* featured predictably satirical portraits of 'The *New* School' of 'Passionate Female Literary Types',[26] and throughout the year parodied various women writers, particularly George Egerton as Borgia Smudgiton, author of 'She-Notes'.[27] It is surely significant that these 'She-Notes' were accompanied 'with Japanese *Fin de Siècle* Illustrations by Mortarthurio Whiskersly', obviously also targetting Aubrey Beardsley. 'More She-Notes' by IÒPna, author of 'A Yellow Plaster', clearly a take-off of Iota, appeared later in the year.[28]

On a more serious note, Matthew Arnold's 1887 article, 'Up to Easter',[29] dealing primarily with the Irish question, is particularly revelatory of the negative implications of the epithet. The article was, in fact, an answer to W.T. Stead's 'The Future of Journalism' which had appeared in the *Contemporary Review*[30] and which had advocated a much more personal approach to the profession, a topic to which I shall return at greater length in chapter three. By applying the term 'new' to what he considered a different kind of journalism, Matthew Arnold highlighted its pejorative opposition to *old* journalism. As usual, what was traditional, tried and

---

22 Ascribed to Margaret Wynman (Author of 'My Flirtations') *Woman Holiday Number* 1893, pp. 3-10.

23 In modern French '*nouveau'* applied to, say, philosophers is by no means complementary, as in the English use of *nouveau riche*.

24 *The Illustrated London News* (September 8, 1894), p. 296.

25 *The New Woman* (1894, repr. Oxford, 1998), Act 1, pp. 546-551.

26 *Punch* (June 2, 1894), p. 255.

27 *Ibid.* (March 10 and 17, 1894), pp. 109 and 127, respectively.

28 *Ibid.* (November 28 and December 8, 1894), pp. 249 and 276, respectively.

29 *Nineteenth Century* 21 (May, 1887), pp. 629-643.

30 *Contemporary Review* 50 (1886), pp. 663-679. See also W.T. Stead's earlier article 'Government by Journalism', *Contemporary Review* 49 (1886), pp. 653-674.

tested was thought to possess intrinsic merit, whereas the new, like the New Woman, was seen as a revolutionary challenge and hence highly dangerous. Significantly, in an article entitled 'Fifty Years of Women's Papers and Magazines' which appeared in the 1896 *Newspaper Press Directory*, the *Lady's Pictorial*, to which Ella Hepworth Dixon contributed for over twenty years and in which her New Woman novel first appeared in serial form, was described as 'the feminine pioneer of the *new* journalism' (my italics).

Certainly some young editors and publishers such as Edmund Yates, William Heinemann and John Lane were deliberately attempting to change the literary scene radically as the latter's 'Introduction' to *The Yellow Book* revealed:

> The aim ... of *The Yellow Book* is to depart as far as may be from the bad old traditions of periodical literature and to provide an Illustrated Magazine which shall be beautiful as a piece of bookmaking, modern and distinguished in its letter-press and its pictures, and withal popular in the better sense of the word .... It will be charming, it will be daring, it will be distinguished. It will be a *book* - a book to be read, and placed upon one's shelves and read again; a book in form, a book in substance; a book beautiful to see and convenient to handle; a book with style, a book with finish; a book that every book-lover will love at first sight; a book that will make book-lovers of many who are now indifferent to books[31] (his italics).

In hindsight one may wonder if it lived up to its claims, but innovation in content and style was certainly one of its primary intentions. Interestingly, Ella Hepworth Dixon worked with all three of these editors, and would thus find herself associated with both the New Woman and the new journalism. In her memoirs, she explains that 'one of the first newspapers I wrote for was *The World*. Mr Edmund Yates, undismayed by my youth and inexperience, printed countless short stories of mine and various articles of travel.'[32] It was William Heinemann who published *The Story of a Modern Woman* in 1894, and her short story 'The Sweet o' the Year' first appeared in *The Yellow Book* in April, 1896.

The name of Oscar Wilde was also closely associated with both *The Yellow Book* and novelty, and taken together their respective negative connotations were more than doubled: 'For many years past Mr Wilde has been the real leader in this country of the "new school" in literature - the *revolutionary* and *anarchical* school which has forced itself into such prominence in every domain of art'.[33] (my italics) The new criticism, the new fiction, even the new woman, 'are all merely creatures of Mr Oscar Wilde's.'[34] Whatever one may think of his genius, it is difficult to credit the attribution of the New Woman to Wilde. Linking the New Woman with

---

[31] Quoted by Laurel Brake (London, 1994), p. 163, from Fraser Harrison, 'Introduction', *The Yellow Book: An Anthology* (London, 1974).

[32] *As I Knew Them* (London, 1930), p. 31.

[33] *Speaker* (April 13, 1895), p. 403, quoted by Hugh E.M. Stutfield, 'Tommyrotics', *Blackwood's Magazine* (June, 1895), p. 840.

[34] *Ibid*. Even Stutfield considered this 'rather strong'.

Wilde, however, particularly at the time of his scandalous trial, cast aspersions on all concerned. Precisely when much in the world of the late Victorians was being challenged as never before, the insinuation was that the overall decline in standards leading to general decadence, whether of a sexual or a political nature, as many had feared, was largely due to the New Woman. Naming her was thus not only reductive, but at the same time empowering.

The 'New Eve' was often a 'Girton Girl', educated and emancipated, like George Bernard Shaw's Vivie in *Mrs Warren's Profession* (1898), leading a much more public life than her predecessors. Throughout the century women had become more involved in debates about changes in legislation, not only concerning domestic affairs such as women's matrimonial rights and child custody, but also about more public matters such as prostitution, thus touching spheres normally considered taboo. The New Woman was likewise associated with a more rational, less restricting type of dress and freer behaviour, including cycling and smoking. Very quickly her pursuit of independence raised questions about her femininity, her fecundity and consequently the family as a whole, while her readiness to discuss such subjects as female sexuality, contraception and venereal diseases, previously considered unmentionable, attracted violent attacks, as the contemporary cartoons from *Punch* testify. On one hand the ideal self-sacrificing wife and mother had given way to a 'self-assertive, heartless, sexless *thing*' (my italics) which is how *The Athenaeum* reviewer of Ella Hepworth Dixon's *The Story of a Modern Woman* viewed one image of the typical modern woman.[35] On the other hand even more disturbing was the image of the *over*-sexed, threateningly-erotic female, castigated at great length by Hugh E.M. Stutfield in *Blackwood's Magazine.*[36] Echoing 'a most excellent wag quoted with approval by the grave and sedate "Spectator" (who) recently described modern fiction as "erotic, neurotic and Tommyrotic"', Stutfield deplored 'the writers of the physiologico-pornographic school' who produced what he termed 'neuropathic' or 'erotomaniac fiction'. Criticism, at times more virulent than this, came from both men and women. Stutfield was clearly not alone in thinking that much contemporary literature, especially among women, was 'repulsive', 'debased and morbid'.

For some then, the New Woman was associated from the outset with decadence and degeneration. Furthermore, works such as Richard von Krafft-Ebing's *Psychopathia Sexualis* (written and revised 1882-1902), Max Nordau's *Degeneration* (1895, translation of *Entartung*, 1892-3) and Cesare Lombroso's *The Female Offender* (1895, translation of *La Donna Deliquente, La Prostituta e La Donna Normale,* 1893) seemingly provided scientific evidence for the public's anxieties. Such findings were not, however, always taken seriously. In 'Degeneration and Genius' an article published in the *Psychological Review* in 1895, William James referred to *Degeneration* as 'a pathological book on a pathological subject'. Ella Hepworth Dixon's comments in the *Lady's Pictorial* testify to her own scepticism:

---

[35] (Unsigned), *The Athenaeum* (June, 1894), p. 770.

[36] Hugh E.M. Stutfield, 'Tommyrotics', *Blackwood's Magazine* (June, 1895), pp. 833-845.

> I have lately risen from the perusal of Lombroso's pseudo-scientific work, 'The Female Offender', with the pleasing conviction that I contained in my own person all the physical and mental peculiarities of the born female criminal. I forget now whether I possessed more especially the characteristics of an epileptic murderess or merely those of an hysterical and cataleptic pickpocket ... .[37]

In a less humorous vein she goes on:

> Woman, as an individual, is as essentially the discovery of the nineteenth century as the New World was of the fifteenth, or the circulation of the blood was of the seventeenth. ... I look forward with relief to that not too distant day when they shall have satisfied themselves that we are not diseased monsters, but just human beings like themselves ... .

Nevertheless, two weeks later she acknowledges Max Nordau's defence of spinsters and refers to him no longer as Cesare Lombroso's 'satellite', but as a 'German Don Quixote'.[38]

At the same time as woman's nature continued to come under close observation and, predictably, was always found to be sadly lacking, mankind as a whole was being scrutinized as never before. As several critics have suggested, it is surely not insignificant that the stereotypical, unfeminine New Woman was seen in conjunction with the effeminate dandy,[39] and that the demise of the New Woman was loudly acclaimed by *Punch* in 1895 almost simultaneously with Oscar Wilde's trials which took place in April and May of that year. For example 'A Prognosis' in May 1895 suggested that the New Woman 'won't even last out the century! She's got every malady under the sun!'[40] Some critics, however, suspected otherwise. *The Times* reviewer of Ella Hepworth Dixon's novel must have expressed both the exasperation and the fears of many in exclaiming, 'Shall we never have done with the New Woman!'[41]

---

[37] *Lady's Pictorial* (July 13, 1895), p. 49.

[38] *Ibid.* (July 27, 1895), p. 129.

[39] The following, entitled 'Sexomania, By An Angry Old Buffer', again looks back to the pre-lapsarian, or at least pre-New Woman, state with regret and, some might say, humour:

When Adam delved and Eve span
No one need ask which was man.
Bicycling, footballing, scarce human,
All wonder now, 'Which is the woman?'
But a new fear my bosom vexes;
Tomorrow there may be no sexes!
Unless, as end to all the pother,
Each one in fact become the other.

Punch (April 27, 1895), p. 203.

[40] *Punch* (May 11, 1895), p. 227.

[41] (Unsigned), 'Review of *The Story of a Modern Woman*, by Ella Hepworth Dixon.' *The Times* (June 30, 1894), p. 19.

Indeed, it seemed highly unlikely. In September of that year, Sydney Grundy's play, *The New Woman*, opened in London and rekindled reactions. As 'A Girl About Town' writes in *Woman*:

> Thanks to the success of Mr Grundy's play at the Comedy Theatre the New Woman seems to have taken a new lease of life. She was dying from sheer exhaustion; being worried to death by essayists, novelists, and facetious journalists and caricaturists, without whom she would never have been discovered in the first instance. A bad play with such a title would have killed her; a good one has just revived sufficient interest in her to suggest the question: What do you mean by a New Woman; the term seems almost as comprehensive and elastic as that of 'lady'?[42]

In reply, Sydney Grundy frankly admits, 'I did not trouble my head very much as to what is or is not meant by the term. I only know that it seemed to offer a good subject and a good title for a play ... .' The journalist comments, 'Mr Grundy smiled - a smile ... that seemed to say "It doesn't seem to matter much what I meant by a New Woman so long as people come to see my play as they are doing."' And evidently it was extremely popular with the public: towards the end of the interview Sydney Grundy mentions that the previous evening even for Mr Comyns Carr, the theatre manager, and himself there had been standing room only.

In spite of his claims that he was not 'scoffing at the modern cultured woman', the poster advertising the play reflects the caricature stereotype of the New Woman found in the *Punch* cartoons: two objects of regular popular debate - a cigarette, albeit lit at both ends, burning in one corner and a latch-key occupying a dominant space on the wall in the opposite corner - frame a rather severe female, wearing a pince-nez, who sits amidst piles of papers and books strewn across the floor. Such an image is quite the reverse of many late Victorian portraits of women reading quietly, surely emphasizing the chaos the New Woman would bring in her wake. One can also just make out the titles of two of the novels ascribed to the New Woman characters in the play: *Man the Betrayer* and *Naked But Not Ashamed*. In the play itself one of the principal male characters, Colonel Cazenove, comments, 'That's what comes of educating women. We have created a Frankenstein.'[43]

The spectre of Frankenstein or, more exactly, Frankenstein's creation, was regularly employed throughout the nineteenth century to emphasize the monstrosity of an idea, for example Tenniel's 1866 cartoon of 'The Brummagem Frankenstein'[44] when the subject of enfranchizing the working class was broached, and his 1882 cartoon of 'The Irish Frankenstein',[45] portraying Irish nationalism as a hideous brute. To assimilate the bookish woman, clearly viewed as a freak, with such threatening sectors of society was both facile and effective. The New Woman

---

[42] 'About New Women. A Chat with Mr Sydney Grundy', *Woman* (September 12, 1894), p. 3.

[43] *The New Woman*, Act 1. lines 79-80.

[44] *Punch* (September 8, 1866), p. 103.

[45] *Ibid.* (May 20, 1882), p. 235.

may have begun as a literary phenomenon, but very quickly infiltrated other spheres and consequently became even more menacing in the eyes of her detractors. Significantly, in the 1894 *Idler* article on 'How to Court the "Advanced Woman"', Dr Arabella Kenealy begins by refuting the idea that 'the true Advanced Woman' is 'that latch-key licensed, tobacco-tainted, gala contaminated Frankenstein, which, created for the purposes of trampling beneath its grotesque proportions a patient footmark of progress, strides up and down the pages of modern literature'.[46]

The New Woman, nevertheless, did have a few sympathizers. In the concluding paragraph of his review of Sydney Grundy's play, Clement Scott pleads, 'If we are to discuss the "New Woman", let her be fairly discussed.'[47] The critic's request to consider 'the earnest side of the movement in contrast to the ridiculous side of it, which has been in the hands of writers for comic journals long enough to grow stale' had, in some ways, been granted by W.T. Stead's earlier article in the *Review of Reviews*. In attempting to provide a general overview of 'one of the most notable and significant features of the fiction of the day,' W.T. Stead perhaps hoped to explain why 'it bewilders some, angers others, and interests all'.

For, indeed, what was so new? It was, after all, not new for women to write, nor was it unusual for them to be castigated for doing so. One has only to think of Southey's advice to Charlotte Brontë, warning her that 'literature cannot be the business of a woman's life, and it ought not to be'.[48] Even George Henry Lewes, usually favourably disposed towards women, had written satirically '*My* idea of a perfect woman is one who can write but won't'[49] (his italics). Nor had objections only come from men; George Eliot had also attacked 'silly lady novelists'[50] whilst Helen Taylor had bemoaned the fact that women 'cannot live ... by the pen unless by fiction or such light popular literature adapted to the ideas of publishers as is *of little use to the world*'[51] (my italics). Their motivations might, nonetheless, have been slightly different. As women of letters themselves, they might have been extra-critical of those of their sex they thought were not maintaining standards and were thus laying them all open to easy attacks of which there was never a dearth. One can in fact find important traces of such high-minded seriousness in the New Woman writers, and, in spite of fears expressed by some reactionary writers like Mrs Lynn Linton, there was often much discussion about woman's moral mission. Views of what that mission essentially was, however, were drastically divergent.

---

46 *The Idler* 6 (August, 1894), p. 209.

47 *The Illustrated London News* (September 8, 1894), p. 296.

48 Robert Southey, quoted by Mrs Gaskell, *The Life of Charlotte Brontë* (1857; repr. Harmondsworth, 1977), p. 173.

49 G.H. Lewes, 'A Gentle Hint to Writing Women', *The Leader* 1 (May 18, 1850), p. 189.

50 George Eliot, 'Silly Novels by Lady Novelists', *The Westminster Review* (October, 1856), pp. 442-461.

51 Helen Taylor, letter to Florence May, dated July 22, 1868, republished in *Sexual Equality: Writings by John Stuart Mill, Harriet Taylor Mill and Helen Taylor* (Toronto, 1994), p. 120.

W.T. Stead tried to explain the phenomenon by suggesting that what was new was that 'the Modern Woman novel is not merely a novel written by a woman, or a novel written about women, but it is a novel written by a woman about women from the standpoint of Woman',[52] echoing to some extent the words of *The Pall Mall Gazette* critic who had begun his review of *The Story of a Modern Woman* in similar terms: 'Miss Dixon's book is a subtle study, written by a woman, about a woman, and from the point of view of a distinctly clever and modern woman herself.' Stead continued:

> Many women have written novels about their own sex, but they have hitherto considered women either from the general standpoint of society or from the man's standpoint, which comes, in the long run, to pretty much the same thing. For in fiction there has not been, until comparatively recently, any such thing as a distinctly woman's standpoint.

One might argue over the validity of W.T. Stead's claims, but one cannot doubt the distinct questioning of male hegemony. Even more troubling to many readers was the fact that 'in almost every case the novels of the modern woman are preoccupied with questions of sex, questions of marriage, questions of maternity.'

As the domestic sphere came under closer scrutiny and 'other fields than matrimony (were) opening out',[53] the institution of marriage underwent a radical re-evaluation. To a certain degree New Woman heroines could still echo Lady Audley's sentiments: 'I had learnt that which in some indefinite manner or other every schoolgirl learns sooner or later - I learned that my ultimate fate in life depended upon my marriage',[54] but romantic stereotypes were being questioned as never before. Nor were these only preoccupations for women; authors of both sexes were also expressing anxieties about the importance of a man's choice of partner. 'The Woman Question is the Marriage Question',[55] writes Sarah Grand at the end of her essay on 'The New Aspects of the Woman Question'. 'The novel of the modern woman ... take(s) marriage seriously. ... Marriage is no longer a mere affair of *trousseaux* and of bridesmaids, of finding an eligible *parti*, and being provided with board and lodging for life,'[56] recognizes W.T. Stead, and it is probably in this domain that the New Woman fiction was most innovatory.

The marriage debate did raise many questions about sex and maternity, with the latter, long thought by many to be woman's highest vocation, also seen as a root of evil. Indeed, in Sarah Grand's *The Heavenly Twins* one heroine, Evadne, having discovered that she has married a man suffering from syphilis, can only remain pure

---

[52] *The Pall Mall Gazette* (June 1, 1894), p. 4.

[53] 'Why Women are Ceasing to Marry', *The Humanitarian* (July, 1899), pp. 66-67. This was an unsigned response to the article of the same name by 'our talented contributor, Miss Ella Hepworth Dixon' published the previous month.

[54] Mary Braddon, *Lady Audley's Secret* (1862, repr. Oxford, 1987), p. 350.

[55] Sarah Grand, 'The New Aspects of the Woman Question', *The North American Review* 158 (March, 1894), p. 276.

[56] *The Review of Reviews* 10 (July 2, 1894), p. 65.

in celibacy, while her friend, Edith, having contracted the disease from her husband, dies a lingering death after giving birth to a sick child. W.T. Stead in his examination of the New Woman 'meditations on marriage and motherhood', mentions the plight of 'loveless marriage' or 'monogamic prostitution', an idea already found in Daniel Defoe and Mary Wollstonecraft who had both referred to marriage as 'legal prostitution'. George Egerton likewise picks up the same term: 'marriage becomes for many women a legal prostitution, a nightly degradation, a hateful yoke under which they age, mere bearers of children conceived in a sense of duty, not love.'[57]

What typifies the New Woman fiction, then, is not simply a difference in the representation of the quest for a suitable mate, although this was an important feature, but the conventional marriage plot was much experimented with by Ella Hepworth Dixon and her contemporaries. The choices available to single women in fiction had often been limited to marriage, for whatever motivation, and spinsterhood often seen as a slow lingering dessication of body and spirit to which death, the ultimate solution, might be preferable. Indeed, in many earlier novels, such as *The Mill on the Floss*, leaving this world was a more desirable alternative to living in it alone or sharing one's life with an unsuitable mate. In the past, education had at times been a sort of compensation for wedlock as it was for Ethel in Charlotte Yonge's *The Daisy Chain*. Likewise, it could be abandoned on marriage as in Tennyson's *The Princess*. By the last decade of the century education could be seen primarily as a key to achieving greater independence, of mind and body, opening up other possibilities. The Prince might not turn up and even if he did he might not be quite what was expected. His entrance on stage was certainly no longer the cue for the final curtain.

Thirty years later, in his discussion about the structure of novels, E. M. Forster overlooks this aspect of New Woman fiction, as did many critics before and after him. He claims 'nearly all novels are feeble at the end. This is because the plot requires to be wound up. ... If it was not for death and marriage I do not know how the average novelist would conclude.'[58] At the end of the nineteenth century, the New Woman writers were, I would argue, deliberately refusing to 'wind up' their plots so neatly, and thus challenging both literary and social stereotypes. As Ella Hepworth Dixon wrote in 1899:

> It seems tolerably certain that whatever the novel of the next century is about, it will not concern itself exclusively with the gentle art of angling for husbands. Marriage as the end of everything does not appeal to our modern novelist, and the love-story pure and simple would seem to have gone clean out of fashion.[59]

---

[57] George Egerton, 'Virgin Soil', *Discords* (London, 1895), p. 155.
[58] E.M. Forster, *Aspects of the Novel* (1927; repr. Harmondsworth, 1968), p. 102.
[59] *Lady's Pictorial* (September 9, 1899), p. 353.

I shall discuss in later chapters the extent to which she put her theories into practice in her novels and short stories, but at this point it is significant that she regularly refers to 'the *privilege* of saying "No"' (my italics). Women had said 'no' to marriage before: Elizabeth Bennett, for example, in *Pride and Prejudice*,[60] had refused Mr Collins, to the reader's great relief, but Darcy, a more suitable partner, had been waiting in the wings. By the end of the century the situation was not so cut and dried. Saying 'no' to marriage could be an ostensible rejection of the institution as in *The Woman Who Did*, although I would be loath to consider this a New Woman novel. The irony, or perhaps the tragedy, here is that the daughter born out of wedlock prefers to have nothing to do with her mother and feels unable to marry as she would wish as long as her unmarried mother lives. This leads to the mother's suicide, literal self-sacrifice, thus allowing her daughter to marry in the old-fashioned way. Here the death of a New Woman 'in a pure white dress, with two crushed white roses just peeping from her bodice',[61] a bridal image if ever there was one, represents a reversal to old values with marriage the ultimate end for a woman. Saying 'no' to marriage could also be a 'no, but...' as in *Red Pottage*,[62] where although there is no marriage at the end of the narrative, the Postscript suggests 'other pages' containing 'Rachel with children around her, and Dick not far off', implying perhaps that this was not the main concern of the story, but nor was it an anti-marriage novel *per se*. Conversely, saying 'yes' did not always mean a romantic marriage of true minds and hearts, for instance Gallia's acceptance of Mark in Menie Muriel Dowie's novel[63] is motivated by considerations of eugenics. Celibacy itself might even be a positive decision, with very different implications from traditional renunciation or virginal purity. For example, Ella Hepworth Dixon's heroine Mary Erle rejects an offer of marriage from a man she does not love, preferring 'to live her own life'. She also refuses to become the mistress of the man she once loved who had abandoned her for a mercenary marriage.

I would argue that the New Woman writers were thus experimenting with many different plots and plausibilities.[64] Marriage was no longer the reward for the good girl, with death or spinsterhood for the wicked, nor would the single woman be a source of pity and ridicule; her independence might be exemplary and enviable. Nor would the heroines continue to be, to use W.T. Stead's expression, 'mere addenda to the heroes, and important only in so far as they contribute to the perfecting or the marring of the said heroes' domestic peace and conjugal felicity'.[65]

Such preoccupations were by no means restricted to fiction. Marriage is, after all, the culminating point at which private and public or, to coin a twentieth-century

---

60 Jane Austen, *Pride and Prejudice* (1813, repr. London, 1963).

61 Grant Allen, *The Woman Who Did* (1895, repr. Oxford, 1995), p. 140.

62 Mary Cholmondeley, *Red Pottage* (1899, repr. London, 1968).

63 Menie Muriel Dowie, *Gallia* (1895, repr. London, 1995).

64 See Nancy K. Miller, 'Emphasis Added: Plots and Plausibilities in Women's Fiction', *PMLA* 96 (1981), pp. 36-41.

65 (W.T. Stead) *The Review of Reviews* 10 (July 2, 1894), p. 64.

phrase, personal and political spheres meet, and so long as these spheres had been clearly defined any examination of marriage had been rather limited. With deeper investigations into the very nature of what a woman was and what her subsequent ascribed, prescribed and proscribed roles could be, the institution itself was being re-appraised. As Ella Hepworth Dixon put it, 'the theory that a wedding ceremony mended all and ended all, is one to which thoughtful Northern and Western peoples are nowadays inclined to dispute'.[66] To judge by the response published in the magazine the following month, the article had met with wide notice in the press. Ella Hepworth Dixon's claims were apparently not borne out by statistics or the Registrar General; there had, in fact, been a rise in the marriage rate in 1897, the highest since 1876. If some women were ceasing to marry, it was therefore suggested, it was most likely in the middle-classes where other fields were open to them, but these were precisely the readers Ella Hepworth Dixon was addressing. This naturally led to further fears of decadence and degeneration.

With a certain amount of self-avowed flippancy Ella Hepworth Dixon summarized the situation thus:

> It has been seriously argued - generally by masculine writers and elderly ladies who found themselves out of sympathy with the modern feminist movement - that women, nowadays, are disposed, from selfish reasons, to shirk the high privileges and duties of maternity and domestic life, to wish to compete with men, and undersell the market from motives of pure vanity, and to have so far unsexed themselves as to have lost the primordial instinct for conjugal life altogether.[67]

She goes on to suggest, however, that 'the reason why women are ceasing to marry must rather be attributed to a shifting feminine point of view, to a more critical attitude towards their masculine contemporaries,' and furthermore, 'this critical attitude among womenfolk is no doubt mostly due to the enormous strides which have been made in feminine education during the last twenty years ... .'

The effects of education had been closely examined in an earlier article by Alice A. Gordon who points out that 'the percentage of marriages among less highly educated women is greater than among university-trained maidens'.[68] More education apparently could simultaneously put women off marriage and make them less marriageable. Alice A. Gordon continues:

> It is, of course, in these days of progress an open question, that must be decided according to each woman's individuality, whether marriage is to be considered an achievement or a 'come-down'; ... . But it must be remembered that education has, in most cases, this very valuable result; it does make women more fastidious ... and obviates the necessity of their

---

66 'Why Women are Ceasing to Marry', *The Humanitarian* (June, 1899), p. 395.

67 *Ibid.* p. 391.

68 Alice A. Gordon, 'The After-Careers of University-Educated Women', *Nineteenth Century* (June, 1895), pp. 959-960.

> having to rely on matrimony as a means of support, and therefore prevents many early, uncongenial, and improvident marriages. ... All women would be glad to marry their ideal hero; but heroes are scarce, and the average man who proposes marriage to the average girl can at best offer her no wider prospect than a round of careful housekeeping, motherhood and thrift; and it must be doubted if ... a university training is adapted for developing these homely and prosaic virtues.

More provocatively Ella Hepworth Dixon was to claim 'the modern spinster's lot, in many respects, (is) an eminently attractive one.'[69] In later chapters I shall examine further her treatment of the single woman, whom she more often refers to as 'lady-bachelor' or 'bachelor-woman', in both her fiction and non-fiction.

A few years earlier in 1888 the publication in the *Westminster Review* of an article on Marriage[70] by another New Woman writer, Mona Caird, had sparked off a seemingly endless controversy. The article incidentally appeared in the 'Independent Section' of the periodical with the accompanying remark: 'The object of the Editors in introducing this department is to facilitate the expression of opinions by *men* of high mental power and culture ...' (my italics). Mona Caird had traced a short history of marriage and emphasized 'the cruelties, indignities, and insults to which women were exposed'. She acknowledged, as others had before her, that life was difficult for the single woman, and that one should not condemn mercenary marriages, but she maintained that it was totally unrealistic to imagine that everyone would find a suitable spouse. Indeed, the population distribution, as the surplus woman controversy indicated, made it quite simply statistically impossible for every woman to hope to find a mate of any sort. In 1859 Dinah Maria Craik had already pointed out that 'marriage is apparently ceasing to become the common lot, and a happy marriage the most uncommon lot of all',[71] and concluded that 'marriage ought always to be a question not of necessity, but choice'.[72] Mona Caird had none of Mrs Craik's religious beliefs or her conciliatory tones and lacked Ella Hepworth Dixon's humour. She vituperated at great length against what she saw as 'legalized injustice', declared 'the present form of marriage ... a vexatious failure', and, not altogether surprisingly, called for a 'New Order'.

Legally, in fact, by then marriage had become more attractive, or at least less restrictive, for women. Matrimonial Causes Acts had been passed in 1857 and 1878, allowing for more freedom in separating from an undesirable husband. Married Women's Property Acts in 1876 and 1882 had given married women more control over their possessions, while two other Acts in 1873 and 1886 had extended their rights to custody of their children. Nonetheless, marriage remained at the centre of much controversy, and I would suggest continues to do so. Perhaps what exacerbated the issue in 1888 was the fact that the *Daily Telegraph* opened a letters column entitled 'Is Marriage a Failure?', thus reaching a far wider public than the

[69] 'Why Women are Ceasing to Marry', *The Humanitarian* (June, 1899), p. 394.
[70] Mona Caird, 'Marriage', *Westminster Review* 130 (August, 1888), pp. 186-201.
[71] Dinah Maria Craik, *A Woman's Thoughts about Women* (London, 1859), p. 34.
[72] *Ibid.* p. 344.

more select readership accorded to eminent thinkers such as John Stuart Mill and Robert Owen who had expressed similar views about what they considered the degrading aspects of marriage without setting off such fanatical controversies. Few, however, could have foreseen that during the course of the debate the *Daily Telegraph* would receive some 27,000 letters. A selection of the letters, including a response by Mona Caird dated August 23, was then reprinted in book form, 'edited with a preface by Harry Quilter ... and containing the most important letters on the subject ... , a paper on the philosophy of marriage by Mrs Lynn Linton, and a full account of the laws of marriage and divorce throughout the Christian world ...'.[73] Other periodicals in Britain and America ran similar polls; *Pick-Me-Up* in London even offered prizes for the best answers. The responses predictably varied enormously.

The scale of interest aroused by such questions is difficult for a modern reader to appreciate, as is the character of the *fin de siècle* reading public. Most of the authors or works in W.T. Stead's list remain unknown, although over the past few years with renewed interest in the period, some have been republished. At the time, however, their enormous popularity and widespread readership were quite frankly astounding. For example, Sarah Grand's *The Heavenly Twins* sold 20,000 copies in its first week in 1893 and was reprinted 6 times during the course of the year. Even in 1895, in spite of predictions of her demise, Grant Allen's novel about a putative New Woman *The Woman Who Did* went into twenty editions, consequently producing, as such works often did, a flood of copies, parodies, and subsequent polemics.

Such popularity was in itself cause for concern in some circles. Edmund Gosse, for instance, writing in 1895 railed:

> Things have come to a pretty pass when the combined prestige of the best poets, historians, critics and philosophers of the country does not weigh in the balance against a single novel by the New Woman. Mr Swinburne and Mr Herbert Spencer, Mr Leslie Stephen and Professor Huxley - their combined 'sales' might be dropped into the ocean of *The Heavenly Twins* and scarcely cause a splash in that enormous flood.[74]

He went on to predict 'the books so hastily praised are not less hastily forgotten, and immortals cross the field and disappear forever as continuously as figures cross the disk of the magic lantern'.[75] In some ways, he was proved right since the New Woman writers did disappear for decades, but so did the men he mentions. Ironically, Leslie Stephen remains arguably the most familiar thanks largely to the Dictionary of National Biography and to his famous daughter.

In the 1890s, then, the New Woman could be seen as a serious threat both within the literary world and in the world at large. In *After The Great Divide:*

---

[73] *Is Marriage A Failure?* (1888), reprinted in *The Late-Victorian Marriage Question* Volume 1 ed. Ann Heilmann (Manchester, 1998).

[74] Edmund Gosse, 'The Decay of Literary Taste', *The North American Review* 161 (1895), p. 116, cited by Sally Ledger in *The New Woman* (Manchester, 1997), pp. 177-178.

[75] *Ibid.*

Modernism, Mass Culture and Postmodernism, Andreas Huyssen, commenting on 'Mass Culture as Woman: Modernism's Other',[76] suggests 'the notion ... gained ground during the nineteenth century that mass culture is somehow associated with woman while real, authentic culture remains the prerogative of men'.[77] In the same essay, he continues:

> The nightmare of being devoured by mass culture through co-option, commodification, and the 'wrong' kind of success is the constant fear of the modernist artist, who tries to stake out his (sic) territory by fortifying the boundaries between genuine art and inauthentic mass culture. Again, the problem is not the desire to differentiate between forms of high art and depraved forms of mass culture and its co-options. The problem is rather the persistent gendering as feminine of that which is devalued.

One can also think of shifts in the meanings of words and social concepts which are debased when ascribed to women. For example the notion of 'intuition' which used to be the highest form of knowledge has acquired the adjective 'feminine' and thus seems less reliable, or the gendering of tears, heroic in classical literature and girlish in most Western societies today, or professions such as that of secretary, which still retain a certain esteem when restricted to Secretary of State, Home Secretary, Foreign Secretary and so on, but otherwise imply occupations for women. Likewise, Nicola Thompson in *Reviewing Sex: Gender and the Reception of Victorian Novels* cites reviewers, including women, who automatically relegated female writers to the 'second rank'. Mrs Oliphant, in particular, perhaps reflecting on her own career, suggested 'women who rarely or never find their way to the loftiest class, have a natural right and claim to rank foremost in the second'.[78] Similar sentiments were echoed in the *London Review* in 1860: 'The female novelist who keeps strictly to the region within which she acquired her knowledge may never produce a fiction of the highest order, but she will be in the right path to produce the best fiction of the class in which she is most likely to excel.'[79]

The idea of a clearly delineated separate sphere for women in literature as well as in life was a recurrent contention. Much nineteenth century writing had been concerned with defining woman's rightful place, often upholding 'as obvious and natural what is partial, factitious and ineluctably social',[80] to use Penny Boumehla's useful definition of ideology. Some of the 'newness' of the *fin de siècle* writers, therefore, lies in part in their overt challenging of dominant ideologies, especially in their re-examining of the image of domesticity as an ideal for women.

---

[76] Andreas Huyssen, *After The Great Divide: Modernism, Mass Culture and Postmodernism* (Indiana, 1986), p. 47.
[77] *Ibid.* p. 53.
[78] Mrs Oliphant, 'Modern Novelists - Great and Small', *Blackwood's Magazine* (May, 1855), pp. 554-562, quoted by Nicola Thompson (Basingstoke, 1996), p. 98.
[79] Quoted by Nicola Thompson, p. 16, from Helsinger et al. (Chicago, 1983) volume 3, p. 53.
[80] Introduction, *Thomas Hardy and Women* (Sussex, 1982), p. 5.

Simultaneously, fundamental questions were being asked about the functions and aims of fiction in general. While writers such as George Moore were advocating 'Naturalism', others like Thomas Hardy, Henry James, George Meredith and R. L. Stevenson were arguing the case for or against greater realism in fiction. As if to prove proponents of separate spheres wrong, Ella Hepworth Dixon actively participated in the discussion about 'The Place of Realism in Fiction',[81] thereby demonstrating that it was not merely of concern for male writers. Dr William Barry, Alphonse Daudet, Sir George Douglas, George Gissing, W.H. Mallock, Richard Pryce, Adeline Sergeant, Frederick Wedmore, and W.H. Wilkins also expressed their opinions on the issue in the same *Humanitarian* article.

'English literature, in its higher manifestations, has always been largely realistic, from the first of the school, Chaucer ..., through Shakespeare, ... Defoe, ... Fielding, ... Jane Austen, ... Thackeray, ... down to Mr George Meredith ...,' claimed Ella Hepworth Dixon. 'Realism ... *is* truth, *la verité vraie,* as the French quaintly phrase it,'[82] (her italics) she continued, voicing the opinion of many New Woman writers. Olive Schreiner, for example, another of the novelists on W.T. Stead's list, 'the founder and high priestess of the school', according to Stead, in her Preface to the second edition of *The Story of an African Farm,* likewise advocated true-to-life representation:

> Human life may be painted according to two methods. There is the stage method. According to that each character is duly marshalled at first, and ticketed; we know with an immutable certainty that at the right crises each one will reappear and act his part, and, when the curtain falls, all will stand before it bowing. There is a sense of satisfaction in this, and of completeness. But there is another method - the method of the life we all lead. Here nothing can be prophesied. There is a strange coming and going of feet. Men appear, act and re-act upon each other, and pass away. When the crisis comes the man who would fit it does not return. When the curtain falls no one is ready ... . Life may be painted according to either method; but the methods are different. The canons of criticism that bear upon the one cut cruelly upon the other.

Fore-shadowing Virginia Woolf and D.H. Lawrence, she concludes, 'The artist must paint what lies before him.'[83] The following year Henry James reiterates similar ideas in 'The Art of Fiction'[84] where he insists on the 'sacred office' of the writer and rails against writers like Trollope who admit to 'make believe', the equivalent of Schreiner's 'stage method', implying 'that the novelist is less occupied in looking for the truth ... than the historian'.

---

[81] *The Humanitarian* (July, 1895), pp. 7-23.
[82] *Ibid*, p. 11.
[83] 'Author's Preface', signed R. Iron (London, 1883).
[84] Henry James, 'The Art of Fiction', *Longman's Magazine* IV (September, 1884), pp. 502-521.

These claims for truth can be traced back to early novel writers such as Defoe who in the Preface to *Moll Flanders* goes to great lengths to proclaim the 'genuine nature' of the story.[85] Similarly, many nineteenth and twentieth century writers upheld this same credo, concerned as much with truth as with credibility. In *Adam Bede*, for example, George Eliot writes:

> My strongest effort is to ... give a faithful account of men and things as they have mirrored themselves in my mind. The mirror is doubtless defective ... but I feel as much bound to tell you as precisely as I can what that reflection is, as if I were in the witness-box narrating my experience on oath.[86]

Over half a century later, Virginia Woolf in her essay on 'Modern Fiction' also pleads against 'falsity and pretence'.[87]

Many of the New Woman novelists would argue that this was precisely what they were doing. One reviewer of Olive Schreiner's novel commented, 'The mark of a good novel is the sense of reality which it forces upon the reader, and the book before us achieves this distinction with signal success.'[88] Nonetheless, he concedes, 'Novels which produce this effect are not likely to be wholly pleasant reading, since reality as we know it is not wholly pleasant.' Problems arose, therefore, because, as Ella Hepworth Dixon recognized, realism is 'that impalpable something which raises a book into a work of art, and not, as many honest folk seem to think (Anglo-Saxon these, and with a fine Puritanical out-look on life and literature) as another and more euphemistic name for the Nasty'.[89] As evidence of this, when Mary Erle, one of Ella Hepworth Dixon's protagonists in *The Story of a Modern Woman*, who earns her living as a writer, tries, unsuccessfully, to sell her realistic novel, she is advised to write 'a thoroughly breezy book with a wedding at the end'.[90] In a similar vein on reception of *The Story of an African Farm* in 1883 Chapman and Hall had wanted Olive Schreiner to arrange a marriage between the fictional lovers; thereby pandering to the expectations of certain readers. The British public, Mary Erle's editor tells her, 'won't stand' the harsh realities of 'actual experience'. Ironically, at the same moment the newspapers are full of divorce scandals, and sales certainly do not dwindle.

However, even amongst New Women writers there were divergencies. One of George Egerton's characters, for instance, points out that 'the woman who tells the truth ... is untrue to her sex and abhorrent to man'. She adds, 'The truth is at all times unpalatable.'[91] W.T. Stead reveals a similar reaction in his review when he comments on the same character's saying, 'Women talk to me ... they come, strip their hearts and souls naked, and let me see the hidden folds of their nature.' 'If so,'

---

85 Daniel Defoe, *Moll Flanders* (1721, repr. Harmondsworth, 1978).
86 George Eliot, *Adam Bede* (1859, repr. London, 1969), Book Second, ch. xvii, p. 171.
87 Virginia Woolf, 'Modern Fiction' (1925, repr. London, 1984), p. 154.
88 Thomas F. Husband, *The Westminster Review* 141 (1894), pp. 631-642.
89 *The Humanitarian* (July, 1895), pp. 10-11.
90 *The Story of a Modern Woman* (1894, repr. Peterborough, 2004), p. 147.
91 George Egerton, 'A Cross Line', *Keynotes* (1893, repr. London, 1983).

writes W.T. Stead, revealing an uncharacteristic antipathy, 'they had better fold them up again - the spectacle is the reverse of edifying.'

Nevertheless, W.T. Stead's quotation from Ella Hepworth Dixon's novel cited at the beginning of his article clearly indicates that greater candour was one of the salient aspects of the literature under scrutiny:

> 'It is a subject,' murmured Strange, with a slight movement of the shoulders, 'which I must admit I find painful to discuss with young ladies.'
>
> 'Ah,' said Alison, in her quiet, serious voice, 'but then I am not a "young lady". I am only a woman taking a great deal of interest in others of my own sex.'

The hypocritical wish of the male doctor, for that is Strange's profession, not to discuss 'painful' subjects, on this occasion a young woman who, seduced and abandoned by *him*, had now become a mere number in a hospital ward where she was dying from consumption after having attempted to drown herself, is not unusual in itself. On the contrary, one can well imagine few men wanting to discuss such subjects, especially with a woman they plan to marry. What is strikingly significant, however, is Alison Ives' frank response, marking her out as most definitely a New Woman heroine. The distinctions between 'lady' and 'woman' were likewise a telling and notably recurrent topic of debate, as Oscar Wilde's re-naming of his magazine from *The Lady's World* to *The Woman's World* in 1887 testified, and to which throughout her writing career, in both her fiction and non-fiction, Ella Hepworth Dixon regularly contributed, and to which I shall return. I shall also engage in a fuller discussion of Alison Ives when I examine the novel itself at greater length in chapter five, but at this point it is enough to indicate that both Ella Hepworth Dixon and W.T. Stead emphasize the notion that 'she, at any rate, was not one of those girls who have infinite complaisances for a possible husband'.[92] The composure of her reply is in stark contrast with the usual sentimental or sententious cant found in fiction, and highlights the candour which New Woman writers in general were advocating. In a later essay, 'Men's Women in Fiction',[93] which appeared in the *Westminster Review* in 1898, Edith Slater reiterated these ideas: 'the business of women is to be candid, to show themselves as they are, and perhaps, in time, men will learn to be candid and natural too'. She then adds, 'But this comes too near the *dangers* of new-womanism, and is not directly concerned with the subject (men's love of ignorance in women)' (my italics).

Alison Ives' insistence on concern for other women is also a recurrent theme in New Woman writing. In many ways it is, in fact, the *leitmotiv* of the novel as a whole, as W.T. Stead reveals from his interview with Ella Hepworth Dixon: 'The keynote of the book is the phrase: "All we modern women mean to help each other

---

[92] *The Story of a Modern Woman* (1894, repr. Peterborough, 2004), p. 161, quoted by W.T. Stead, p. 70.

[93] *The Westminster Review* (May, 1898), p. 572.

now. If we were united, we could lead the world." It is a plea for a kind of moral and social trades-unionism among women.'[94] Perhaps the notion of women leading the world was precisely what disturbed and, seemingly, continues to unsettle, but even a sense of solidarity among women, however encouraging it may be, is by no means anodyne. Moreover, Ella Hepworth Dixon's coining of the phrase 'trades-unionism' would further stress her political consciousness and give fuel to those, like Ouida, who feared links between the New Woman and the rise of the Labour movement: 'The Workingman and the Woman, the New Woman be it remembered, meet us at every page of literature written in the English tongue, and each is convinced that on his (sic) own special W hangs the future of the world.'[95]

Although some New Woman writers were considered too inward-looking by contemporaries such as Mrs Lynn Linton as well as by later critics such as Gail Cunningham, and self-absorbtion can indeed be found in some of the protagonists in the works cited by W.T. Stead, the most obvious being George Egerton's short stories, others like Ella Hepworth Dixon, on the other hand, do reveal a more outward-looking vision and a deep-rooted concern for the general betterment of their sex. In *The Story of a Modern Woman* Ella Hepworth Dixon echoes, almost *verbatim*, the sentiments of *Women and Work. A Weekly Industrial, Educational and Household Register for Women*, published by Emily Faithfull:

> To help, if possible, those who desire to help themselves, to direct those who wish to tread the path of industry and to encourage the faint-hearted, who have to fight the battle of life against overwhelming odds, is the aim and object which we have set before us.[96]

Similarly, in a letter to Havelock Ellis, Olive Schreiner showed she had broadened her scope since *The Story of an African Farm* to include all of mankind:

> I have always built upon the fact that *From Man to Man* will help other people, it will help to make men more tender to women, because they will understand them better; it will help make some women more tender to others; it will comfort some women by showing them that others have felt as they do.[97]

There were obviously enormous discrepancies between womanly ideals and the reality of most women's lives. 'The first note of the novel of the Modern Woman is the recognition of the fundamental fact that in society as at present constituted

---

[94] Quoted by W.T. Stead, p. 71.

[95] Ouida, 'The New Woman', *North American Review* 158 (1894), p. 610.

[96] *Women and Work. A Weekly Industrial, Educational and Household Register for Women* 1 (June 6, 1874), p. 4, quoted by Philippa Levine, *Victorian Feminism 1850-1900* (London, 1987), p. 91.

[97] July 11, 1884. *Letters*, ed. Rive, p. 35, quoted by Ruth Brandon, *The New Women and The Old Men* (London, 1990), p. 72.

woman has the worst of it,'[98] declares W.T. Stead in his evaluation of *The Story of an African Farm*, 'the forerunner of all the novels of the Modern Woman.' He then speaks of 'the undisputed conviction of every living male that he would regard it as a change for the worse to be born of the opposite sex', and confesses, 'speaking as a man, I always feel as if every human being born a woman owed Nature a grudge.' Earlier writers like Edgar Allen Poe and Wilkie Collins had hinted that in many Victorian interiors behind the lace curtains lurked violence, brutality, and much human misery. Others, such as R. L. Stevenson in *Dr Jekyll and Mr Hyde* (1886), had also intimated that the darkest places might not be in the outposts of Empire, as Joseph Conrad was to suggest, but in its very heart and hearth, in precisely the sphere which had been designated for women. It had been bad enough for men like George Gissing and George Moore to speak about such topics, but trouble erupted when women themselves broke the seal of silence.

For further evidence one has only to think of the vast campaigns surrounding the Contagious Diseases Acts, first imposed in 1864 and repealed in 1883. Initially, the Act had been instituted in an attempt to control syphilis, especially in garrison towns. It allowed the arbitrary examination of prostitutes, but not of their clients. Many women were involved in the repeal campaign and, as Elaine Showalter notes, it 'gave women an excuse to use some of the sexual vocabulary previously reserved for men'.[99] She then goes on to quote Josephine Butler, the leader of the campaign, 'At the very base of the Acts lies the false and poisonous idea that women (i.e. ladies) have "nothing to do with this question," and ought not to hear of it, much less meddle with it ...'. Likewise, what was considered so shocking in the New Woman fiction was 'the treatment of subjects hitherto considered immoral or contrary to good manners, in the widest sense of the words - and the disposition to place what is called the Sex-question above all others as the theme of fiction.'[100] Speaking out when silence and obedience had been considered a woman's prime virtues had always exacted pitiless retribution, as Antigone and Cordelia bear witness. In both instances it may be argued that gender is not the central issue, but their being women intensifies the drama. Speaking up about what they should not even know was a more heinous crime, and serious charges were consequently regularly brought against the New Woman.

As Mrs Oliphant pointed out, it meant that 'things are discussed freely and easily which it would a few years ago have been a shame to mention or to think of.'[101] The earlier example of Rhoda Broughton's father forbidding her to read *Cometh Up as a Flower* (1867), a novel she herself had written, naturally unbeknownst to him, is typical of the time. As mentioned in the previous chapter Ella Hepworth Dixon recounts a similar experience in her memoirs: a young man with whom she was dancing inquired if she had read the 'Town and Country Tale'

---

[98] W.T. Stead, p. 65.
[99] Elaine Showalter, *A Literature of Their Own* (1978, repr. London, 1982), p. 193.
[100] M. O. W. O. (Mrs Oliphant), 'The Anti-Marriage League', *Blackwood's Magazine* 159 (1896), p. 136.
[101] *Ibid.* p. 149.

in that week's *The World*, and then thought better of it, saying 'No, I don't think it's quite the kind of story you ought to read.' 'The obnoxious story', as she calls it, was from her own pen, but she obviously didn't wish to spoil the evening by admitting it.[102] Like many, Rhoda Broughton's father no doubt feared the mimetic effects of fiction and disliked the idea of his daughter taking as a role model the wild heroine who in particular raises doubts about standard morality and matrimony. Esther, Rhoda Broughton's heroine in *Red As a Rose is She* (1870), is equally outspoken and witty, and refuses to marry for convenience alone. Significantly, when the hero catches her reading a French novel and severely reprimands her for it, the authorial comment is 'men are always shocked that women should *read about* the things *they do*'[103] (her italics). Late Victorian society was even more shocked that women should be *writing* about such things.

The New Woman writing thus both fed on and fuelled contemporary debates. Likewise, it raised many questions to which we are still seeking answers, and many conceptual issues, particularly those pertaining to gender, woman's nature and cultural constructs, remain problematic. Instead of portraying models of accepted behaviour, for women readers in particular, as literature was traditionally expected to do, some critics saw in its questioning of domesticity and matrimony and of woman's ascribed sphere in general an attempt to undermine and destroy the very foundations of society. Even W.T. Stead, usually so well-disposed towards women, expressed a certain anxiety about 'debasing the moral standard of the ordinary woman to the level of the ordinary standard of the ordinary man'.[104] In refusing to fictionalize life, the New Woman writers upset readers' expectations. Instead of finding coherence and confirmation in literature, readers were more often left with disturbance and diversity. For others, especially those actively taking part in its production, it was considered a locus for experimentation, a forum for contrasting possibilities and plausibilities, and a focal point precisely for the purposes of raising pertinent questions about that society.

It is indisputable that during the last decade of the nineteenth century dissident voices were being heard as never before, and such voices could not always be 'ever soft,/ Gentle and low, an excellent thing in a woman'.[105] It is interesting to note that as the new journalism encouraged more signed articles, so many of the New Woman writers were speaking out in their own voices and no longer using pseudonyms as had been the custom earlier. But at this point can one speak of a 'school' as W.T. Stead does and, if so, how typical was Ella Hepworth Dixon? It could be argued that one might well produce a New Woman work or be associated with the phenomenon without necessarily sharing similar ideas on all issues. For example as some women, like Frances Power Cobbe and Josephine Butler, were campaigning for Women's Property Rights, so others, including Eleanor Marx, were calling for the abandonment of private ownership altogether. The Suffrage

---

[102] *As I Knew Them* (London, 1930), p. 31.

[103] Rhoda Broughton, *Red as a Rose is She* (London, 1870), p. 190.

[104] *The Review of Reviews* 10 (July 1894), p. 73.

[105] *King Lear*, V, iii, lines 271-272.

campaign likewise aroused very diverse opinions, even leading to a petition signed by such eminent figures as Mrs Humphrey Ward and Mrs Leslie Stephen *against* women's suffrage.

With remarkable sympathy, only displaying little indulgence for George Egerton whom he sees as presenting 'one side, and that an unpleasant one, of the modern woman': 'the untameable savage in woman',[106] W.T. Stead presents an apparently coherent picture of the Modern Woman Writer, deftly highlighting similarities in attitudes and themes. A modern reader, however, is also struck by the dissimilarities, and what differentiates the women might ultimately be more significant. I have generally preferred to call them writers, rather than novelists, because even here the latter term does not always quite fit. W.T. Stead's list actually reveals great variety in treatment, from old-fashioned three-deckers to two-volume novels to single short novels and a collection of short stories. Few, if any, of the women confined themselves to novel writing; in fact, several only ever produced one novel and then turned or returned to other genres, as did Ella Hepworth Dixon.

Indeed, within a few years of W.T. Stead's article, the New Woman novel seemed to be on the decline. By June 1897, Lady Jeune in an article on 'Women in the Victorian Era' in the *St. James's Gazette* could declare, 'Nothing is more interesting than to note the complete disappearance of all the apostles of the New Woman movement – her preachers, her literature, her drama have collapsed, and the British matron – phoenix-like – smiles serenely over her ashes.'[107] This may have been due to changes in the habits of publishing houses and libraries, but it might also have been a deliberate choice on the part of some women writers. Almost a decade earlier in a letter to Karl Pearson, Olive Schreiner had written:

> The press is manifestly becoming the governing and ruling power ... . It matters everything in the political world 'what the papers say' and who rules them. Even more clearly the novel has taken the place of other forms of art in carrying to the *heart* of the people the truths (or untruths) of the Age.[108] (her italics)

Perhaps towards the end of the century, as the divide between high and low art widened, and as campaigns for political representation increased, more women were channelling their energies into practical work, just as Ella Hepworth Dixon's fictional Alison Ives was to do. At the same time, as well as contributing to papers, periodicals, and journals of various kinds, precisely to reveal the truths and untruths of the age, some continued to experiment with different genres, even trying their hands at drama. In this respect, with her wide range of activities, Ella Hepworth Dixon appears typical of her time.

---

[106] *The Review of Reviews* 10 (July, 1894), p. 69.
[107] *St. James's Gazette* (June 21, 1897), p. 5.
[108] Olive Schreiner to Karl Pearson, October 23, 1886, *Letters*, p. 109.

Within the first quarter of the twentieth century Rose Macaulay could have one of her characters say, 'The Woman Question, sir? What woman question? I know no more of woman questions than of man questions, I am afraid. There is an infinity of questions you may ask about all human beings.'[109] While one may sympathize with Rose Macaulay's refusal to limit herself to concerns about only 'one half the human race',[110] it must not be forgotten that in the relatively short period of time that separated her comment from the 1890s much had been achieved, not least of which was women's right to vote. The New Woman and the ensuing uproar may have been relatively short-lived, and it is easy after the event to wonder what all the fuss was about, but they can no longer be simply ignored, as was the case for many decades.

Some present-day critics, such as Elaine Showalter, have suggested that the *fin de siècle* women:

> Were ravenous for a fuller life than their society offered them, famished for the freedom to act and make real choices. Their nervous disorders expressed the insoluble conflict between their desires to act as individuals and the internalized obligations to submit to the needs of the family, and to conform to the model of self-sacrificing 'womanly' behaviour.[111]

Perhaps this helps to explain much of the unhappiness, despondency, and even morbidity of which New Woman writing is often accused. However, as Gail Cunningham, another precursor of renewed interest in the period, points out, 'All the data of the New Woman novel were present in earlier fiction; it was the interpretation which so radically differed.'[112]

In our Post-Modernist phase, while rigid divisions between literature, history, philosophy, cultural studies, women's studies and the social sciences are becoming less distinct, studies in interdisciplinary fields, such as those made by Philippa Levine, Margaret Stetz and Gaye Tuchmann,[113] have contributed to increasing our understanding of previously ignored or unexplained aspects of the New Woman writer and her *milieu*. Moreover, what appears in many ways to have been a convenient construct to marginalize such writers in their day is now being reconstituted by critics such as Ann Ardis, Gerd Bjorhovde, Sally Ledger and Lyn Pykett[114] to emphasize the literary lineage of the New Woman writer. Just as some

---

109 Rose Macaulay, *Mystery at Geneva* (London, 1922), p. 84.

110 I deliberately use the expression coined by William Thompson in his 1825 *Appeal of One Half the Human Race* in part to emphasize the longevity and continuity of the discussion.

111 Elaine Showalter, *The Female Malady* (New York, 1985), p. 144.

112 Gail Cunningham, *The New Woman and the Victorian Novel* (London, 1978), p. 20.

113 See in particular Philippa Levine, *Victorian Feminism 1850-1900* (London, 1987), Margaret Stetz, *England in the 1890s: Literary Publishing at the Bodley Head* (Washington, 1990), and Gaye Tuchmann, *Edging Women Out: Victorian Novelists, Publishers and Social Change* (London, 1989).

114 See in particular Ann Ardis, *New Women, New Novels* (New Brunswick, 1990), Gerd Bjorhovde, *Rebellious Structures: Women Writers and the Crisis of the Novel, 1880-1900*

were experimenting in life, so others were experimenting in literature and can be seen as part of an aesthetic movement, fore-runners of Modernism, heralding issues which would later be developed in the works of, for example, Dorothy Richardson and Virginia Woolf. Yet again, other critics such as Ruth Brandon see the New Woman in an even broader, international context, 'as but one manifestation of that passion for fresh thinking, that search for new ways of approaching life which swept the whole of the Western world between 1880 and 1914.' [115]

To my mind the New Woman is very much a product of the urban world, a world in which Ella Hepworth Dixon was perfectly at home. As her memoirs indicate, she travelled widely, mixed with most eminent personalities of her day, and was permanently in work. Both in her life and in her writing she clearly challenged traditional representations of women, albeit in a less polemical way than some of her contemporaries. Where other New Woman writers, such as Sarah Grand, were using shock tactics to raise issues which had been denied for so long, but which had not disappeared such as double moral standards, contagious diseases, death through childbirth and so on, Ella Hepworth Dixon used much more subtle, understated means to appeal to a wide reading public.

In succeeding chapters I shall examine in detail her literary output, all of which first appeared in the periodical press. At this point, I would argue that her fine sense of irony regularly provided light relief, and hence made her work more palatable then and now to readers of both sexes. In no way, however, does this diminish her literary merit or detract from the underlying seriousness of her ideas.

(Oslo, 1987), Sally Ledger, *The New Woman: Fiction and Feminism at the Fin de Siècle* (Manchester, 1997), and Lyn Pykett, *The 'Improper' Feminine* (London, 1992) and *Engendering Fictions: The English Novel in the Early Twentieth Century* (London, 1995).

[115] Ruth Brandon, *The New Women and the Old Men* (London, 1990), p. 3.

Chapter 3

'The Bastille of Journalism'[1]

> In these degenerate literary days, when there is not so much a 'mob of gentlemen who write with ease' as an army of ladies who employ the pen as a means of living or as a weapon of warfare, it is inevitable, I suppose, that the standard of literary excellence should not be high.[2]

These opening lines of Ella Hepworth Dixon's weekly column in the *Lady's Pictorial* of April 9, 1898, would at first sight appear somewhat surprisingly to be echoing the worst fears of her more conservative contemporaries. The elite, masculine, world of *belles-lettres* had been infiltrated by the 'fairer sex', to the detriment of both. As discussed in the previous chapter, such anxieties about degeneration and falling standards were by no means restricted to the publishing world. Nevertheless, recent studies by Margaret Beetham, Peter Keating, and Margaret Stetz[3] amongst others have amply demonstrated that throughout the last decades of the nineteenth century journals became the prime site of debate about changes in society. The phenomenal increase in the number of periodicals in general as well as those aimed primarily at a female reader brought to public notice issues which many might have preferred to keep private. Although few of the journals lasted, their influence, albeit fleeting, cannot be denied. Moreover, they reflect the dynamism and the divergencies of their time.

---

[1] Ella Hepworth Dixon's own phrase from 'The Modern Way: A Social Causerie', *Westminster Gazette* (January 14, 1925), p. 6. See Appendix 1 for a limited chronology of Ella Hepworth Dixon's literary output. Whilst every effort has been made to trace and identify her contributions to the numerous periodicals for which she wrote, this has not always proved possible. At the beginning of her career, as was the custom, many articles and short stories were simply unsigned. Likewise, during the First World War many propaganda articles were anonymous. Where in doubt I have preferred to abstain from ascribing work erroneously to her pen. Moreover, on some occasions, as with the *Woman Christmas Number* of 1894, material is simply missing from the otherwise rich resources at Colindale; at other times, as with *The World* July-December, 1892, the material is unfit for use.

[2] *Lady's Pictorial* (April 9, 1898), p. 520.

[3] See in particular Margaret Beetham, *A Magazine of Her Own?* (London, 1996), Peter Keating, *The Haunted Study* (London, 1989), and Margaret Stetz, 'New Grub Street and the Woman Writer of the 1890s' in Nikki Lee Manos and Meri Jane Rochilson (eds), *New Approaches to British Fiction of the 1890s* (London, 1994).

An overview of 'Fifty Years of Women's Papers and Magazines' in the 1896 *Newspaper Press Directory* begins by mentioning the astounding increase from 'only four periodicals and magazines purporting to be especially for women' … to 'close on fifty'. 'Nothing ... is more astonishing than the extraordinary increase during the last few years in the number of papers and periodicals devoted to the interests of women,' declares the author of another article entitled 'Journalism for Women During the Reign' published in *Woman* on the occasion of Queen Victoria's Jubilee.[4] The article continues:

> A dozen years ago, at least two-thirds of the existing papers had not come into existence. Women who could afford it bought *Queen*. The rest, for the most part, did without a paper, perhaps scarcely felt the lack of one. At the present moment there are papers which cater specially for every type of woman; the rich, the poor; the educated, the ignorant; the serious, the frivolous; the 'advanced', the conservative; the intelligent, the empty-headed; every sort of woman from the duchess to the shop-girl ... is separately appealed to, and a weekly journal has become absolutely necessary on both sides the hearth ... .

Nor did women restrict their reading solely to periodicals specifically designed for them. As Wilhelmina Wimble a little later in *The Lady's Realm* remarked, 'When Mr Yates started *The World*,[5] and described the new weekly as a "journal for men *and* women", he introduced a *revolutionary* element into the standpoint of the Press towards the weaker sex'[6] (my italics). She adds:

> He was the first to recognize the importance, when catering for a society more than half of whose members were women, of taking the interests of this larger section into consideration. The impulse he gave has widened and spread ever since, until there is scarcely a paper now that does not provide matter specially attractive to the feminine sex - that, in short, has not somewhere its 'LADY'S REALM'.

By the end of the century, the woman reader had clearly become a force to be reckoned with. Moreover, as Wilhelmina Wimble notes:

> The necessity having been admitted of attracting women as readers, the natural development followed of getting women to write for women. This recognition by the Press of the feminine point of view is part of the movement for giving to women a greater share in life generally.[7]

---

[4] (Unsigned), *Woman* (June 16, 1897), pp. 33-37. The Queen had actually reigned for sixty years, but so rare an occurrence was this that no better word could be found.

[5] *The World* began in 1874.

[6] Wilhelmina Wimble, 'Incomes for Ladies: Journalism', *The Lady's Realm* (August, 1897), pp. 467-468.

[7] *Ibid.*

The fourth estate, therefore, provided many women with both a voice or, to return to Ella Hepworth Dixon's article and to use her telling metaphor, an arm and a livelihood. Wilhelmina Wimble actually uses more imperialistic language, commonly employed in such discussions, referring to 'the great continent ... of the opportunities Journalism offers to women'. Small wonder, then, as Ella Hepworth Dixon had remarked in an earlier 'Pensées de Femme', that the woman writer had detractors: 'I have always been led to suppose, by a perusal of the so-called humorous papers, that if there was one thing on earth which the average man loathed, it was a female writer.'[8] In the 1898 article cited at the beginning of this chapter she writes:

> It is humiliating for the sex to be told at a public dinner, and by no less an authority than the literary critic of the *Daily Telegraph*,[9] not only that we cannot spell, but that we cannot punctuate our sentences. Then, to make matters worse, the editor of a woman's penny paper has written a little book to tell us how to succeed in journalism - a book in which he duly notes the woman-journalist's unbusiness-like habits, her irresponsibility, and - her tendency to devastating headaches!

As if to complete the discrediting picture of the woman journalist, she adds, 'Every now and then one meets a male scoffer who "wants to know" why women do not even edit their own papers?' This 'deplorable fact' had already been pointed out by Evelyn March-Phillipps in her 1894 evaluation of contemporary 'Women's Newspapers' in the *Fortnightly Review*: 'Almost all these journals are edited by men. One would think women should know best what will please women, but as editors we are told they are deficient in the capacity which grasps a business situation ... .' She then points out, however, that 'many are sub-editors, and manage special departments, and on every paper, I think I may say, the bulk of the work is done by women'.[10] The phenomenon was also discussed in a later interview with Mrs Meynell, the newly elected President of the Women Journalists' Society, published in April 1898 in *The Humanitarian*. To the question, 'Do you think that it arises from the incapacity of women to edit successfully, or from the fact that women work more amicably under a man's guidance?' Mrs Meynell replied, 'I should think it is merely accidental. Men happen to have the money to float papers and the control is naturally taken by them. Probably, when women have more money and amass fortunes, the order of things will be reversed.'[11]

Ella Hepworth Dixon's response, with no mention of her own remarkable achievements, but with typical force and irony, is rather different:

> Well, some of us find it more stimulating to edit *your* papers. And with Mrs Beer in the editorial chair not only of the *Sunday Times*, but of *The*

---

[8] *Lady's Pictorial* (July 4, 1896), p. 33.
[9] W.L. Courtney.
[10] *Fortnightly Review* LXII (1894), pp. 661-670.
[11] *The Humanitarian* (April, 1898), pp. 229-235.

> *Observer*; with Miss Flora Shaw installed as Colonial editor of *The Times*; with Mrs Crawford as French political correspondent of the *Daily News*, and purveyor of piquant 'tips' to *Truth*; with Mrs Meynell's subtly feminine powers of analysis delighting us week by week in the *Pall Mall Gazette*; with all the great newspapers awaiting the final word of Madame de Novikoff on foreign politics; with the *Fortnightly*, the *Contemporary*, and the *Nineteenth Century* full of feminine writers: I do not think any one can seriously contend that women have failed in journalism. (her italics)

On such evidence, it is difficult to disagree with her. It seems all the more astounding then that Arnold Bennett, for he must be the un-named editor to whom Ella Hepworth Dixon refers, should have published when he did, early 1898, the similarly un-named 'little book', *Journalism for Women*, subtitled 'A Practical Guide'. What makes it even more surprising is that in December the previous year his own 'penny paper', *Woman*, had started a series on 'Women Editors of London' beginning with Mrs Woodhull-Martin of *The Humanitarian* and concluding with Mrs Beer of *The Sunday Times*,[12] and had earlier that same year produced a glowing picture of 'the excellence of modern journalism for women' in the above-mentioned article, 'Journalism for Women During the Reign'.

Echoing to some extent Evelyn March-Phillipps, this survey logically describes changes in the periodical press which had taken place over the sixty years of Queen Victoria's rule. If earlier journals, such as the *Ladies' Own Magazine*, are condemned as 'vapid and inane productions', the author concedes, 'at the present time two points about women's journalism are salient: First, the intellectual and common-sense policy of high-class women's papers, compared with the state of affairs in the past ... and second, the important position now held by women in journalism.' Whilst the conclusion again comments on the fact that 'very few weekly papers for women are edited by women', photo-portraits of some of the eminent women editors mentioned by Ella Hepworth Dixon illustrate the article, thus corroborating her claims. Incidentally, a picture of Ella Hepworth Dixon herself, described as 'Editor of *The Englishwoman*' although by then she no longer held that position, appears in the centre of the first page of the article, flanked by Mrs Beer and Miss Gillian Debenham, editor of *Judy*, a comic paper. The article is unsigned, not unusual in itself, but it might well have been written by Arnold Bennett, as, under various pen-names, was a considerable portion of the magazine, including reviews of his own work. It contradicts, however, much of what he writes in his Guide where he does indeed chastise women for being unreliable and irresponsible, and accuse them of inattention to detail, with sloppy spelling and punctuation, and a general lack of restraint. Such apparently glaring discrepancies require some explanation, or, 'truly', to quote from another 'Pensées de Femme', 'the inconsistency of the stronger sex is sometimes of a nature to make the gods laugh'.[13]

---

[12] *Woman* (December 22, 1897), p. 15 and (August 10, 1898), p. 12, respectively.
[13] *Lady's Pictorial* (July 6, 1895), p. 5.

To a certain degree, the concluding sentences of Arnold Bennett's Guide shed some light on the matter:

> A vast number of women engaged in journalism, I verily believe regard it as a delightful game. The tremendous seriousness of it they completely miss. ... Therefore, my final words to the outside contributor ... are these: Journalism is not a game, and in journalism there are no excuses.

This is highly reminiscent of 'the breadwinning-in-earnest point of view' which was put forward in two earlier articles published in *Woman*, in a new series entitled 'What Women May Do', and in which the author insists:

> From the first let me say I am not going to encourage every girl and woman who occasionally pens an essay or a short story, with or without the satisfaction of seeing it in print, in the belief that she is a journalist. I have not space to deal with amateur journalism, out of which a large number of women make a very small number of pounds per annum, and from which they appear to have no ambition to soar into the higher flights of the profession. It has been said by American newspapers gifted with lively imaginations that there are over a thousand women journalists in London. My own necessarily extensive experience has taught me that there are some thirty or so of women efficient, all-round journalists; about fifty more who write well on special subjects, of which they have a special knowledge, and perhaps a couple of hundred who contribute occasional articles to the daily and weekly press, or are content with penning descriptions of balls, bazaars, and suburban and provincial festivities for ladies' fashion papers. The class that I could wish to see very much augmented is that which I have classified as 'all-round' journalists.[14]

The article begins on a rather apologetic note: 'It is a subject ... that has been written upon almost *ad nauseam*', but it was clearly a controversial topic and hence of continued interest. In the following week's article, the author reiterates the claim to be 'writing for the few and not the many. The supply of women who *dabble in* journalism, and who aspire only to write for women's papers and women's columns far exceeds the demand ... '[15] (my italics). A letter from 'Another Man Editor' which had appeared previously in the same magazine also raised doubts both about women's motivations and the quality of their writing. The editor in question, having apparently been 'compelled in several cases to substitute men for women, because the prime object of the paper is to cater for the reader not the writer', concludes, 'What I find is that an inordinate number of women are taking up journalism not because they are especially fitted for it, but because they "must do something".'[16]

---

[14] 'What Women May Do, 1 - Journalism', *Woman* (March 23, 1892), pp. 3-4, signed 'The Editor'.

[15] 'What Women May Do, 1 - Journalism, Continued', *Woman* (March 30, 1892), pp. 3-4.

[16] *Woman* (July 10, 1890), p. 5.

The topic had again been treated in another article published in *Woman*. This time it was signed 'Sarah Volatile', one of Arnold Bennett's numerous pseudonyms, and bears many similarities to his Guide. In both this article and the Guide much praise is bestowed upon J.M. Barrie's fictional journalist, whose pen-name is appropriately Noble Simms, and the advice he gives to the young hero, an aspiring writer in *When a Man's Single*. At the same time Roy Devereux and Mrs Meynell are cited as 'the two finest women journalists now working in London'. According to the author:

> Any woman with brains, health, fierce determination and a fair education can become a competent journalist if she chooses to put herself in hard training for one or two years. But not otherwise. And I would recommend no woman in search of a livelihood to turn to journalism unless she has either a natural talent for the business, or friends of the Press who are willing to help her.[17]

Journalism was, thus, to be considered a serious vocation not, as many thought, a mere hobby for amateurs or simply another way of making ends meet. Basically, by means of his Guide, Arnold Bennett might be credited with attempting to encourage a more disciplined, business like attitude in women writers, and hence defending his own profession, much as W.T. Stead had advocated in his earlier *Contemporary Review* article.[18] Nor was this in any way a sexist attitude. In April 1898 in *The Humanitarian* interview with Mrs Meynell, Sarah A. Tooley describes the Women Journalists' Society as 'a society of professional workers - not of irresponsible amateurs', and also argues that women 'do not take the same pride in their profession as men seem to do'. On this note of essential professionalism, Ella Hepworth Dixon would certainly agree with Arnold Bennett. The source of their differences, therefore, lies elsewhere. Moreover, such divergencies of opinion were not only indicative of conflicting ambiguities within the literary world; they were also revelatory of larger, more general debates about woman's changing place in society.

From the mid-Victorian period onwards, there had been increasing concern about the growing numbers of women seeking employment. In the late 1850s the Langham Place Circle became particularly active in drawing attention to the plight of such women, and to this end began publishing the *English Woman's Journal* with Bessie Rayner Parkes as editor. In 1859 the Society for Promoting Employment of Women was also set up with the specific aims of both training and finding work for women. Another publication, *The Year-Book of Women's Work*, which, as its name implies, concentrated entirely on this subject, first appeared in 1875. This was edited by Louisa M. Hubbard who in the same year also started the monthly *Woman's Gazette - or news about work*, which changed its name to *Work and Leisure* in 1880 and remained in circulation until 1893. Numerous articles in

[17] 'How Women May Make Money X – Journalism', *Woman* (February 5, 1896), p. 8.

[18] W.T. Stead, 'The Future of Journalism', *The Contemporary Review* 50 (1886), pp. 663-679.

the periodical press, similar to the above-mentioned series in *Woman,* also appeared. Significantly, many of the papers aimed at the gentlewoman also contributed to the discussion of 'What Women May Do'. The *Lady's Pictorial*, for example, from its début in 1881 ran a series called 'Woman's Work', but this was generally restricted to the home, especially the kitchen, school, or occasionally the medical domain, and then only in the lower echelons. From time to time lucrative employment such as painting on silk or china, making pottery or jewellery or perhaps music was advocated, but on the whole woman was still regarded primarily as nurturer or nurse.

It will be noted that most, if not all, of these activities could still be carried out within the confines of the home and remain hobbies rather than jobs. This fundamental distinction between mere pastime and paid employment, which Arnold Bennett emphasized in his Guide, was a subject which Ella Hepworth Dixon treated at length in her novel, *The Story of a Modern Woman*, and to which, not surprisingly, given her own need to earn a living, she regularly returned in her non-fiction, as in the *Lady's Pictorial* when she comments on the 'amazing revolution' of Woman demanding 'to be paid proper wages for work performed ...'.[19] Nor was she alone in raising further questions about equal pay for equal work. *Winter's Weekly* likewise regularly advocated that a woman should 'by all means do all the work she can get to do, but let her insist on being paid at the same rate as a man would receive'.[20] It goes without saying that such concerns about women's wages were not always motivated by a desire for greater equality; it was often feared, as is mentioned in *The Humanitarian* interview with Mrs Meynell, that, in accepting lower wages, women were underselling men and hence ruining the market in general, not only in the field of journalism. Somewhat predictably, W.T. Stead apparently did pay his women contributors the same as the men. On several occasions[21] Ella Hepworth Dixon recounts a discussion of the topic with George Meredith. For example in her 'Pensées de Femme' of June 29, 1895, she writes:

> Is Lovely Woman in the future ... going to 'foot the bill'? This question seems at the present time to be agitating the souls of many worthy citizens, who see in the present emancipation of their sisters and daughters, *the thin end of the revolutionary wedge.* (my italics)

Later in the same article, she continues:

> We were talking, not so long ago, in the famous chalet which gives on Box Hill, of this very question of the wage-earning woman. I have it on no less an authority than that of Mr George Meredith that men will never have any

[19] *Lady's Pictorial* (November 16, 1907), p. 834.

[20] *Winter's Weekly* (November 10, 1894), p. 5.

[21] For example *Lady's Pictorial* (February 26, 1910), p. 300 and (December 23), 1916, p. 888, *Westminster Gazette* (November 4, 1925), p. 8, and *As I Knew Them*, p. 162.

> real respect for women until those women can and do earn as much money as a man. To have money is beside the question.[22]

With a flippancy often adopted when dealing with serious subjects, she concludes, 'So adieu to a life of luxurious ease, matrons and maids of the twentieth century; gird your loins for the battle and thank heaven when ... you can earn enough to support a husband in the luxury in which he has been brought up!'

Many of the suggestions for earning a living put forward in the periodical press, however, even for salaried posts, would hardly allow such independence. In September 1884 the *Lady's Pictorial* began another series about 'Ladies' Employment'. Whilst recognizing that there were governesses enough and that the telegraph offices were full, few alternatives were offered: nursing, teaching, and various clerkships. The following year the same magazine embarked on a sequence of articles entitled 'Woman: her position, her prospects, her duties and her doings', which basically dealt with legal and political affairs rather than paid employment, although it did raise the question of housework being considered unpaid labour, a debate which is still raging over a century later. In April 1887 an article about literary ladies discussed the difficulties of finding a publisher and earning money from one's writing. In 1888 a series on 'Women at Work' could still only suggest jobs in typewriting, shorthand, telegraphy, the post office, book-binding, or matchbox-making.

Throughout the 1890s, with increasing numbers of educated women looking for work, the topic continued to receive considerable attention. *Winter's Weekly*, for example, from December 1893 until April 1894 ran a series also entitled 'Women at Work' which, besides the mother's help and the trained nurse, included slightly more unusual employments such as the lady furniture dealer or 'In a West-End Costume Department'. *The Ladies' Field*, which had originally circulated for a nine-month period from October 1896 until June 1897, included a weekly column on 'Women Workers' when it reappeared in March 1898, offering both advice and news, but with few interesting suggestions of meaningful work. Even as late as 1899 a series in *Woman at Home* on 'Profitable Employment for Educated Women' could still only propose a relatively limited range of occupations such as the running of tea or luncheon rooms, teaching gymnastics, dressmaking, dispensing, superintending a laundry. It is worth noting that *The Englishwoman*, the magazine of which Ella Hepworth Dixon was editor when it began in 1895, later set up an employment agency in its pages. By then it appears that employment agencies regularly placed advertisements in papers, but apparently these often led to abuse and mismanagement, as a warning published in *Woman* would testify. *The Englishwoman* is singled out as setting up 'an agency on novel lines ... (which) it is to be hoped may save many ladies from falling into the hands of the managers of what might very fitly be called "Agencies for the Pillaging of Gentlewomen!"'[23] Some observers, including Ella Hepworth Dixon, would argue that it was not until

---

[22] *Lady's Pictorial* (June 29, 1895), p. 969.
[23] *Woman* (August 16, 1899), p. 16.

World War I that the situation changed. For example,'All prejudices and hard-and-fast rules about what is "women's work" and what is not have already gone by the board,' wrote Ella Hepworth Dixon in 1916 in an article entitled precisely 'Women Must Work And Men May Weep'.[24] Two years later in 'Too Much Leisure' in the same magazine she added, 'In three years all the old prejudices and shibboleths have been swept away ... , and the Young Person, who has proved her strength in the Great War, is now to step forward with something like an equal chance with her brother.'[25]

Journalism, it will be remarked, was rarely included in such surveys of possible employments for women, or merited separate treatment altogether. In February 1890 writing on 'Journalism for Women' in *Woman*, Mabel Collins claimed:

> The pretty old-world theory, that a woman's place is the domestic hearth, has had to give way before the facts of life, as is, indeed, the fate of most theories. Now the only question is the choice of a vocation for those many women left outside of domesticity. ... The rich woman who has no hearth to tend can choose a vocation; there are many occupations and studies, any one of which can absorb a life-time. But a woman who has to become of necessity a breadwinner in her own right has to choose a profession or a business.[26]

Nevertheless, even if some might agree in theory with her, or with Ella Hepworth Dixon's principle that 'most women of to-day prefer to disburse for their own expenses, experiencing at once a thrillingly new sensation, and asserting by this simple means the economic independence of the sex',[27] not everyone considered journalism an appropriate means to this end. The editorial in *Winter's Weekly* of September 22, 1894 entitled 'Shall Women Work?' reveals some explanation:

> It is strange that this subject should engross so much of men's attention as seems to be the case, judging from the vivid correspondence now appearing in a contemporary, and still more strange that the question should be put in these words. It ought to be 'Shall women work for wages?' or 'Shall women work for money?' For when was the time that women did *not* work ...? ... If a woman is the happy wife of a man who is able to provide for all her wants, and those of her children, why, she must work differently to the woman who is left a widow with half a dozen youngsters and has not bread to put into their mouths. If a woman is one of those to whom marriage does not happen to come, and is without property, and desires to avoid dependence, she must work, if she is physically able, to find herself food and raiment.
>
> But why all this spluttering over it? Nobody splutters about the women who make nails or the women who go hoeing potatoes and turnips, what is

[24] *Lady's Pictorial* (December 23, 1916), p. 888.
[25] *Ibid.* (December 14, 1918), p. 682.
[26] *Woman* (February 15, 1890), p. 2.
[27] *Lady's Pictorial* (June 29, 1895), p. 969.

> vaguely called field-work - oh, dear no! ... But let a widow woman in a higher sphere of life take to journalism, or novel-writing, or the study of medicine, or any other profession by which she can make a decent living, and at once there is an outcry from the unapproachable men that she is taking the bread out of their mouths. The very same men will complacently let women clean their doorsteps or their boots, or endanger their lives cleaning windows. But these are occupations which men do not wish to keep for themselves - they are women's work![28] (her italics)

Clearly, woman was encroaching on man's territory, and, as mentioned in the previous chapter, some men of letters such as Matthew Arnold who were seeking to differentiate between literature as a vocation and literature as a business or a trade would view the influx of women as a sign of further degradation. Hence Ella Hepworth Dixon's references in her 'Pensées de Femme' to 'degenerate literary days' and to the alleged falling standards of literary excellence.

It should be mentioned that even for men the world of journals was regularly looked down upon. In J.M.Barrie's *When a Man's Single*, so admired by Arnold Bennett, a short exchange between the hero's beloved and her mother is revelatory:

> '... he is evidently to be a newspaper man all his life.'
> 'I wish you would say journalist, mamma, ... or a literary man. The profession of letters is a noble one.'
> 'Perhaps it is, ... but I can't think it is very respectable.'[29]

But 'what is that subtle line of demarcation which divides the Press from literature proper?' asks Sarah A. Tooley in *The Humanitarian*,[30] and then goes on to mention some of 'the profession's most distinguished members' such as Addison, Johnson and Steele as well as contemporaries such as W.T. Stead who are 'proud to be called journalists'. 'Conventional distaste at being called journalists', nevertheless, was regularly expressed by both men and women inside and outside the profession. In discussing means of making and saving money, George Bernard Shaw's Mrs Warren puts 'a turn for music, or the stage, or newspaper-writing'[31] in the same category, thereby casting aspersions on its respectability. Mabel Collins cites the example of a naval officer 'of the old school of thought and feeling' who, having fallen in love with a lady journalist, asks her to give up her newspaper work, much as the dancer in Ella Hepworth Dixon's 1908 play, *The Toyshop of the Heart*, is expected to abandon the stage after her wedding. The naval officer's comment is telling: 'I can understand a lady taking up her pen when she has *some fancy* she

---

[28] 'Editor's Thoughts', front page of *Winter's Weekly* 182, Volume VII. For the week ending September 22, 1894. Edited by John Strange Winter (Henrietta Eliza Vaughan Stannard).

[29] J.M. Barrie, *When a Man's Single* (1888; repr. London, 1923), p. 188.

[30] Sarah A. Tooley, 'Women in Journalism. An interview with Mrs Meynell. (President of the Society of Women Journalists)', *The Humanitarian* Volume XII, Number 4 (April, 1898), pp. 229-235.

[31] *Mrs Warren's Profession*, Act II. (1898; repr. London, 1947).

wants to express *prettily* - but *newspaper* work!' (my italics). A similar opinion is echoed by Mary Erle, one of Ella Hepworth Dixon's heroines in *The Story of a Modern Woman*, when she declares, 'Aunt Julia ... thinks I am given over to the Evil One since I've become a journalist.'[32] J.A. Middleton, writing in *The Humanitarian* on 'Women Journalists of the Past',[33] might well conclude 'that the woman of a hundred years ago could wield her pen as readily and as forcibly as the woman journalists of today', but he nonetheless recognizes that 'in the popular mind' 'the woman journalist is so essentially modern, so completely associated with the New Woman Movement', and hence, although it is not openly articulated, an anathema. Even as late as 1903 in *The Daily Mirror*, when incidentally it was still aiming to be a woman's daily, an article on 'The Woman Journalist' laments that 'there is an undoubted tendency with the debutante in this work toward the dead blight of "new womanism" which it is difficult to escape'.[34]

As John Strange Winter acknowledged, such discussions were by no means limited to the feminine press. In June 1893 *Blackwood's Magazine* published 'The Experiences of a Woman Journalist', a rather depressing account of a young woman who had come to London 'to look for work on a newspaper'.[35] The reaction of a contributor to the *St. James's Gazette* suggests that such narratives were by no means rare:

> Is it not about time that we had a little respite from the 'Experiences of Lady Journalists', fresh editions of which are now appearing almost daily? A pleasant change might be afforded by the experiences, say, of a 'lady laundress' – or perhaps a gentleman journalist might thrill us with his reminiscences.[36]

Apparently no respite was granted. The *Sunday Times*, for example, in March 1894, in the heyday of the New Woman, in turn published a long article on 'Employment for the Ladies'.[37] After a rather long preamble, the 'real subject of this paper' is revealed to be 'woman's work on the Press'. Whilst declaring that 'our sisters of the pen are doing splendidly, and that scores (it may be hundreds) of ladies are earning livelihoods suitable to the estate of gentlewomen with the assistance of the ink-stand', in conclusion the author suggests 'this article is written in a less lively strain than usual. The reason may be that the struggle for existence amongst the "poorer sex" is a very serious matter indeed. Not only serious to women but serious (in spite of the "equality of the sexes" nonsense) to men also.' Evidently the 'equality of the sexes nonsense', in spite of its parenthesis, was matter

---

[32] *The Story of a Modern Woman* (1894, repr. Peterborough, 2004), p. 144.
[33] *The Humanitarian* (September, 1899), pp. 193-196.
[34] 'Quex', 'The Woman Journalist', *The Daily Mirror* (November 10, 1903), p. 8.
[35] (Unsigned, but in fact Charlotte O'Conor Eccles), *Blackwood's Magazine* CLIII (June, 1893), pp. 830-838.
[36] (Unsigned), *St. James's Gazette* (June 28, 1893), p. 12.
[37] 'How Things Are Done (By the Author of "Written on the Spot" and "Green-Room Recollections")', *Sunday Times* (March 11, 1894), p. 4.

for concern. Having said, 'it seems to me a pity to suggest any distinction between the sexes so far as journalism is concerned', the writer nonetheless maintains 'certain portions of a newspaper fall *naturally* to the pens of our lady scribes' (my italics). As in many such commentaries, the author then attempts to distinguish between the journalist and the reporter, expressing doubts 'that our sisters will make their way' as the latter. It is particularly interesting to note that he refers to 'a clever novel now appearing in "a ladies' paper" in which sketches of editors are introduced. The authoress evidently knows her subject, and I think, on the whole treats her models without injustice.' This must refer to Ella Hepworth Dixon whose *Story* was then appearing in serial form in the *Lady's Pictorial*.

The article clearly indicates, as would Arnold Bennett amongst others, that there were domains which were more suited to the woman writer than others. Mabel Collins' article had also raised this issue in a second anecdote concerning 'a genial, chivalrous gentleman' who was also 'the editor of a great country paper'. Having spoken 'on the subject of "women as journalists" with a well-known woman newspaper writer' and told her 'It is not your sphere', when he found he wanted a 'light hand' on his paper, he 'offered the lady a staff appointment'. Obviously, as long as women knew their place and kept to it, they could be admitted into the world of journals.

Herein lie perhaps the deep-rooted causes of disagreement between Arnold Bennett and Ella Hepworth Dixon. In spite of certain disclaimers, as the very title of his Guide indicates, the former would appear to be upholding the gender-based distinctions regularly advocated outside the world of journals. Ella Hepworth Dixon, on the other hand, as I hope to show in a close evaluation of her work, understandably resisted such stereotyping in theory and in practice. It is surely significant that she did not limit herself to working for women's periodicals alone, and her contributions to magazines for general readership were not restricted to the ladies' pages. In her memoirs she claims to have been educated and treated on an equal footing with her brothers, and, perhaps logically, in adulthood saw no reason to modify her habits. In a *Westminster Gazette* article written towards the end of her life she still railed against the idea of 'an artificial cleavage between the two sexes'.[38]

Nevertheless, to judge from the numerous articles on the subject of women and the press which were published during the 1890s, Ella Hepworth Dixon was expressing a minority opinion. Even amongst women writers this idea of separate spheres within the profession was regularly upheld. *Winter's Magazine*, for example, ran a six-part series from November to December 1893 on 'How to Become a *Lady* Journalist' (my italics). It seems surprising that the need was felt to specify gender, especially by a writer such as John Strange Winter. Moreover, many of her comments, such as describing women writers' work as 'amateurish' and 'infantile',[39] show no tenderness towards her sex, and foreshadow many of Arnold Bennett's criticisms. Unlike the latter, however, she even provides practical

---

[38] 'The Modern Way: A Social Causerie', *Westminster Gazette* (January 14, 1925), p. 6.
[39] *Winter's Magazine* (December 2, 1893), p. 79.

exercises for the 'budding journalist', as would several journals over the next few years.[40] From October 1896 to September 1898 *Atalanta* ran a series entitled 'School of Journalism' which provided practical advice for beginners in the field. This included various writing exercises for which prizes were offered and the best articles were then published. In his chapter on 'Novelists and Readers', Peter Keating points out that by the last decades of the century 'literary advice had become a marketable commodity', leading to the extensive 'publication of literary handbooks, manuals, guides, reference works and periodicals'.[41] It is almost as if the etiquette manuals of the beginning of the century had been resuscitated to different ends. A particularly interesting example is W.T. Stead's 'How to Become a Journalist' which was originally published in January 1891 in *The Young Man*, and republished the following year in a collection of his essays entitled *A Journalist on Journalism*. It is worth noting that in this enthusiastic defence of the profession no distinction is made between men and women journalists.

Coincidentally, at the same time as Arnold Bennett published his Guide, *The Woman at Home* asked well-known writers such as Mrs Humphrey and Miss Ella Curtis 'Is Journalism a Desirable Profession for Women?'[42] and lengthy extracts appeared in *Woman* at the same time as Arnold Bennett's Guide was reviewed.[43] Mrs Humphrey's defence of a certain sisterly solidarity would certainly find an echo in Ella Hepworth Dixon, whilst a genuine pride and pleasure in the work would meet with general agreement, but on the whole the responses given tend to reinforce the notions of distinctive spheres expounded by Arnold Bennett and John Strange Winter.

Significantly, in most evaluations of woman's place in the press, a need was felt to stress the femininity of the female writer, as Ella Hepworth Dixon herself does in her description of 'one of the prettiest parties' given by the Society of Women Journalists. She begins:

> Ungallant suspicions have been so frequently cast upon the social and domestic capacities of the writing-woman, that even a misogynist might have rejoiced to see how 'John Oliver Hobbes' and the Society of Women Journalists refuted such calumnies by giving one of the prettiest parties of the season at Stafford House ... .[44]

Likewise, in the *Woman* series on 'Women Editors of London' much was made of their maternal and domestic capabilities, and in the *Lady's Pictorial* series on 'Lady

---

[40] I am indebted to Fred Hunter for drawing my attention to the number of guides for aspiring young journalists including Frances Low's *Press Work for Women: A Textbook for the Young Woman Journalist* (London, 1904).

[41] *The Haunted Study* (London, 1989), p. 71.

[42] *The Woman at Home* (March, 1898), pp. 534-538.

[43] *Woman* (March 15, 1898), p. 18.

[44] 'Pensées de Femme', *Lady's Pictorial* (July 4, 1896), p. 33.

Journalists'[45] which began in November 1893, whether describing Mrs Crawford, Miss Emily Faithful, Mrs Roy Devereux, Mrs Meynell or Ella Hepworth Dixon, emphasis was always placed on their 'womanliness', their 'unvarying kindness and courtesy', 'their unimpeachable taste' and their overall refinement. Each written biography was accompanied by a photo-portrait, revelatory of various types of literary women, from the motherly to the austere, from the downright dowdy to the elegantly refined, Ella Hepworth Dixon falling into the last category. (The photograph on the cover is taken from this article.) At the same time, contrary to the opinions of Arnold Bennett and the *Daily Telegraph* literary critic, W.L. Courtney, referred to in Ella Hepworth Dixon's 1898 'Pensées de Femme' cited at the beginning of this chapter, the women writers were presented as being 'thoroughly hard-working', 'indefatigable', possessing 'untiring energy as well as reliability', 'polished literary style' and 'a most conscientious regard for accuracy'.

The overall introduction to the series thus gives a rather glowing picture, but nevertheless suggests a distinctive feminine role in the press:

> As journalism as a suitable profession for ladies has happily long passed from the vague and uncertain region of theory into that of successfully accomplished fact, and, more especially, as it is now universally admitted that there are many special branches of journalistic work which women can take up more effectively than men, of which such a periodical as the *Lady's Pictorial* itself is a conspicuous proof, we have peculiar pleasure in presenting our readers on this and the next page, with a first series of portraits of lady journalists, to whose ability and industry the public owe a vast amount of information and entertainment. ... Journalism for women is by no means restricted, as many suppose, to the chronicling of the latest vagaries of fashion or the newest movements in the more or less frivolous circles of society ... . Art and literature, philanthropic effort, political and social movements of the first importance, foreign travel, and exploration of little-known nooks and corners of our great cities at home, tentative talks with men and women who have helped to make history in the serious or lighter meaning of the word, notable events, and people in every class and circumstance of contemporary society - these are the worlds and entities which the lady-journalist has made her own, and which, with a courage and a patience which are essentially womanly, she has persisted in her work, living down prejudice, and in the end winning a success which has not only meant securing an honourable and remunerative profession for the individual, but the opening up of a new and fitting field for educated and intelligent women-workers for all time.

In spite of the claim that the woman journalist was no longer restricted in her scope, the topics mentioned still remain largely geared towards interests typically associated with a feminine press. An earlier unsigned article in *Woman* had

[45] 'Lady Journalists', *Lady's Pictorial* (November 11, 1893), p. 734, (November 25, 1893), p. 823, (December 9, 1893), pp. 928-929, (December 23, 1893), p. 1020, and (February 10, 1894), pp. 176-177.

indicated as much, and prefigures many of the issues raised in *Journalism for Women*, and may even have been written by Arnold Bennett:

> There can be no doubt as to the increasing opportunities which journalism as a profession offers to a bright, clever woman, but I am not among those who are disposed to believe that the newspaper of the future is to be altogether the work of the ladies, and I may perhaps be permitted to point out where, according to my experience, *their true sphere* in journalism lies, and how they may best fit themselves for it.[46] (my italics)

The writer maintains 'A woman's sphere in journalism generally lies far away from the office or composing-room ... ', and continues:

> I am of course assuming that a woman's *aspiration* in journalism is limited to the work which is most congenial to her sex and habits. In America, lady journalists enjoy a somewhat wider range than at present they care to adventure upon in England, and editors send young women to break the record in globe-trotting, or commission them to personate thieves and lunatics, in order to furnish racy descriptions of the inner economy of prisons and mad-houses for the delectation of their readers. Work of this kind is hardly, however, what English ladies have in mind when they talk of Journalism for Women. (his italics)

Without going quite as far as her American sisters, Ella Hepworth Dixon certainly resisted such restrictions. In her memoirs, for example, when describing her early journalistic activities, she describes trying 'a 'prentice hand on travel articles' for Edmund Yates' *The World* including 'one about a leper hospital at Molde in Norway, which I visited with the ship's doctor in the role of an English nurse, no outsiders being permitted.'[47] The article was in fact entitled 'A Leper's Paradise',[48] and Ella Hepworth Dixon therein recounts how, having toyed with the idea of calling herself 'Dr Janet, of Harley Street', the title of a famous New Woman novel by Arabella Kenealy likewise discussed by W.T. Stead in his *Review of Reviews* article on 'The Novel of the Modern Woman', she was finally admitted as 'Sister Diavolina', surely a passing reference to Sarah Grand's *The Heavenly Twins*, also discussed in the same article, where the boy twin is named 'Diavolo'. Nor was this the only occasion on which she had fun with names. In 'One Doubtful Hour', originally published in 1897 in *The Christmas Number of Lady's Pictorial*,[49] she names the boat on which the protagonists travel back from India 'John Oliver Hobbes', then the President of the Society of Women Journalists.

She appears, however, to have been an exception in undertaking such journalism. Even in 1903 when *The Daily Mirror* began and was initially intended

---

46 'Women as Journalists by a Man Editor', *Woman* (July 3, 1890), pp. 3-4.

47 *As I Knew Them* (London, 1930), p. 161.

48 *The World* (July 4, 1894), pp. 31-32.

49 *The Lady's Pictorial Christmas Number* (1897), pp. 16-21.

to be a paper for women,[50] and on which it should be remarked Ella Hepworth Dixon was offered a prime position, Mary Howarth in her first editorial was still promoting a rather conservative role for women in the press world. This may in part be due to the fact that *The Daily Mirror* needed to justify its existence by being different from other dailies. After claiming that it was to be more than just a newspaper, the editor insists that it was to be dedicated to the daily life as opposed to the weekly or monthly organization of women and, sounding remarkably like any other woman's magazine, would concentrate on topics such as the family, dress, the 'house beautiful', gardening, health, cooking. The next article, incidentally in French, entitled 'Heureuse et Utile', welcomes the appearance of a newspaper dedicated to women 'qui, *tout en s'abstenant autant que possible de la politique*, cherche uniquement à instruire et amuser la femme'[51] (my italics). Yet, Ella Hepworth Dixon in an earlier 'Pensées de Femme' had specifically mentioned changes, not only in women as writers, but also as readers, thus providing perhaps some explanation as to why *The Daily Mirror* in its original format encountered such limited success:

> The type of woman whose study of the morning papers was restricted solely to the births, deaths, and marriages is, I fear, as extinct as the dodo. She was probably an amiable person, but she has not survived the storm and stress of the end of the nineteenth century. The journalistic world caters for another woman - a woman who has a life, a career, and possibly a fortune of her own, and who looks at the human comedy more and more with a man's eyes.[52]

This description reads rather like a self-portrait. The 'journalistic world' did provide Ella Hepworth Dixon with a career, if not a fortune,[53] and allowed her to express her views on the 'human comedy'. It is interesting to note that in February 1899, a week after dealing with 'The Literary Life' in its 'Women Workers' page *The Ladies' Field* had initiated a 'New Experiment' - 'to widen this column in its scope, and throw it open for the discussion of many hitherto untouched questions', including 'suffrage for women'. Entitled 'Women in Parliament' it clearly substantiates Ella Hepworth Dixon's claims.

Her obituary in *The Times*[54] described her as being 'born to journalism'. One is tempted to add 'and dying in it', since she was still contributing articles on a wide range of topics to magazines well into her seventies, up until the last year of her life. The last signed articles I have found so far were published in *The Empire Review*: 'Ladies' Clubs' appeared in Volume XLIX (1929), and 'The New Egypt' in Volume LIII (1931). Indeed, everything she ever published, including her

---

50 *The Daily Mirror* started on November 2, 1903 and short articles by Ella Hepworth Dixon appear in the issues of November 2, 4, 6 and 12.

51 Jules Hedeman, 'Heureuse et Utile', *The Daily Mirror* (November 2, 1903), p. 10.

52 *Lady's Pictorial* (April 9, 1898), p. 520.

53 On her death in January 1932 the net value of her Personal Estate was £996.

54 *The Times* (January 13, 1932), p. 14.

famous New Woman novel, appeared first in the periodical press. Unlike her heroine, however, so successful was Ella Hepworth Dixon in competing in what remained largely a man's world that, albeit for a very short time, she became that *rara avis* a lady Editor of a woman's magazine. One can begin to see more clearly why she would take umbrage at the comments of Arnold Bennett and others like him.

In her memoirs Ella Hepworth Dixon discusses her début in the profession with typical self-deprecation. 'My first editors were (sic) Edmund Yates, of *The World* … . He was an old friend of my people, and was most kind to my youthful efforts.'[55] Elsewhere she describes him as 'undismayed by my youth and inexperience, (he) printed countless short stories of mine and various articles of travel.'[56] She adds, 'A series of short stories was running in the paper called "Town and Country Tales". They had to be what nurses used to call "owdacious". Mine were terribly "knowing".' In the *Lady's Pictorial* 1893/4 overview of Lady Journalists she was credited with 'some thirty "Town and Country Tales" for *The World*'. Very few of these are signed, however, making it difficult to ascribe them with certainty to her pen. So far I have only identified two which carry no signature as hers. 'Number Twenty-Nine'[57] bears too many similarities in both style and content to the chapter entitled 'Number Twenty-Seven' in *The Story of a Modern Woman* not to be by the same author. The doctor of the title, described as 'a bland and fashionable ladies' physician', is the type of character Ella Hepworth Dixon reworked into a more sinister form in Dr Dunlop Strange in her novel, and 'Full-stop or Period'[58] must also be by Ella Hepworth Dixon, making it her earliest identifiable work. In her autobiography Louise Jopling recounts sending a telegram to a suitor in India with the wording 'Don't come. Too late.' which the Indian Babu transcribed as 'Don't come too late'. She then adds, 'The ambiguity of the message gave Miss Hepworth Dixon the idea for a short story in "The World", in which I was amused to find the facts more or less represented.'[59] Indeed, the story begins with the exact words of the telegram.

Edmund Yates died in May 1894, but the journal remained much as it had been and Ella Hepworth Dixon continued to contribute the occasional travel article, signed simply with her initials, for example 'Algiers Up-to-date'[60] and 'The Cold, White Ends of the North'[61] in 1893, 'On An Unknown Island'[62] about Palma in 1894 and 'In the Footsteps of Sterne'[63] in 1895, followed in 1896 by another article about Scandinavia.[64] From 1894 she also regularly contributed a short story to the

[55] *As I Knew Them* (London, 1930), p. 161.
[56] *Ibid.* p. 31.
[57] *The World* (April 15, 1891), pp. 29-32.
[58] *Ibid.* (October 6, 1886), pp. 17-18.
[59] *Twenty Years of My Life* (London, 1928), p. 66.
[60] *The World* (August 30, 1893), pp. 22-23.
[61] *Ibid.* (September 27, 1893), pp. 24-25.
[62] *Ibid.* (May 16, 1894), pp. 26-27.
[63] *Ibid.* (August 7, 1895), pp. 24-25.
[64] *Ibid.* (September 9, 1896), pp. 25-26.

annual *Christmas Number*[65] and signed such stories with her full name. In 1898 her sister Marion also contributed a short story, 'Supper for Two',[66] and the following year Ella Hepworth Dixon made her last contribution, as far as I have been able to ascertain, entitled 'The Head Upon the Charger'.

Her very first signed story to my knowledge is 'Dr Patmore's Patient' which appeared in the *Sunday Times* in January 1888,[67] and was, to employ her own expression when relating the event in her memoirs, 'an extraordinary experience':

> They then published, every week, one or two complete stories, and on this particular occasion, Mr Haddon Chambers and I had each written one. The printers saw fit to put our stories side by side: a column of Mr Haddon Chambers ... and a column of mine ... . The result was diverting, but quite incomprehensible. When I went down on Monday to air my grievance with the editor,[68] all I got was the reply: 'My dear young lady, no one would have read your story if it had been printed properly. As it is, all the Clubs in London are talking about it!' [69]

It certainly did her budding career no harm, for over the next few months Ella Hepworth Dixon contributed several 'Chats with Celebrities' to the *Sunday Times*. Not all the 'Chats' are signed, but her signature appears on those with Frederic Cowen, Frederick Goodall, R.A., Mrs Hodgson Burnett, and John Strange Winter.[70] At the end of the same year she contributed, and signed in her own name, a short story, 'A Winter Idyl', to *The Lady's Pictorial Christmas Number*, and thus began a long collaboration with that magazine, which only ended in March 1921 when it became part of *Eve*. Simultaneously, she also worked with Oscar Wilde on *The Woman's World*. Again, she mentions this in her memoirs, and thereby reveals a less familiar aspect of her editor: 'At one time Oscar Wilde edited a magazine of splendid appearance called *The Woman's World*, and I have a most flattering letter from him about a story I contributed to it called "Murder or Mercy",[71] to which he gave the unstinted praise which is so rare in Editors.'[72] It was in fact entitled 'Murder - or Mercy? A Story of Today', and indeed deals with a topic of ongoing interest. It also contains some embryonic elements which Ella Hepworth Dixon would later rework into *The Story of a Modern Woman*. Following an accident which leaves her crippled, the heroine, Alison Bligh, asks her lover, a well-reputed doctor, to practise euthanasia on her, which he does, but then neglects his own health as a result of the severe mental shock and dies after catching diphtheria from

---

65 'The White Death' (1894), 'The World's Slow Stain' (1895), 'Its Own Reward' (1896), 'A London Episode' (1897).

66 *Christmas Number of The World* (November 17, 1898), pp. 57-59.

67 'Sunday Times Feuilleton', *Sunday Times* (January 29, 1888), p. 8.

68 The editor from 1887-1890 was Phil. Robinson.

69 *As I Knew Them* (London, 1930), p. 164.

70 Frederic Cowen (March 18), p. 7, Frederick Goodall, R.A. (April 1), p. 8, Mrs Hodgson Burnett (April 15), p. 7, and John Strange Winter (May 6), p. 7.

71 *The Woman's World* (October, 1888), pp. 466-469.

72 *As I Knew Them* (London, 1930), pp. 34-35.

a patient. Ella Hepworth Dixon also contributed a few 'interviews at home' of some personal friends when Wilde decided to end the series. 'People,' he wrote, 'are beginning to tire of the silver ink-pots, the Persian rug, the brass paper-weight, the palms in pots ... .' She recognizes, 'He was right. Made attractive at first by Edmund Yates in *The World*, this kind of journalism had become passably absurd.' Nevertheless, in spite of Ella Hepworth Dixon's disclaimers, this is precisely what, according to several of the overviews of the feminine press, many other women journalists were still writing and what Mary Erle's editor asks her to do in *The Story of a Modern Woman*. Moreover, *The World* continued to publish such articles well into this century, and to this day they are still a prominent feature in certain magazines.

Ella Hepworth Dixon's name also appears on two articles in Oscar Wilde's magazine of 1889, 'Women on Horseback'[73] and 'On Cloaks'.[74] In comparison with her later work, these are relatively long, not the 'titbits' which became so popular at the *fin de siècle* and which would become the mainstay of her output over the next few decades with weekly columns in several journals, including the *Lady's Pictorial, The Ladies' Field, The Sketch* and *The Westminster Gazette*. Both articles deal ostensibly with fashion, a woman's subject *par excellence*, but they immediately reveal their author's individual treatment of such topics and her wider interests. 'On Cloaks' gives a historical overview including many literary references, while 'Women on Horseback', ultimately promoting a rational form of riding dress, shows the writer's engagement in contemporary debates, rational dress being much under discussion at the time. Ella Hepworth Dixon concludes:

> Very fortunately for women's health and happiness, public opinion upon the subject of exercise and athletics of all kinds has undergone a complete revolution during the last ten or fifteen years; and the woman who can take a five-barred gate, or succeed in being 'in at the death', gains as much masculine respect and admiration nowadays as the girl who turns out senior wrangler or writes 'the book of the season'.

Significantly, the two articles attracted the attention of the magazine reviewer in the *St. James's Gazette. The Woman's World* was not systematically mentioned in the monthly overview of magazines, and it may be a simple coincidence that Ella Hepworth Dixon contributed articles at the appropriate time. On the other hand, the reviewer's comments emphasize her appeal to readers of both sexes:

> Mr Oscar Wilde and his enchanting fashion plates combine to make *The Woman's World* attractive; and there is much in the magazine which, primarily intended for feminine delectation, is of quite equal importance to such persons as husbands and brothers. Of such are Miss Hepworth Dixon's

[73] *The Woman's World* (March, 1889), pp. 227-233.
[74] *Ibid*. (August, 1889), pp. 509-513.

> paper about 'Women on Horseback' and Miss Evelyne Moore's brightly written article about Angelica Kaufmann.[75]

And:

> *The Woman's World* is a capital magazine for a married man to buy. He tells his wife he got it entirely for her sake; but he may always find some very good reading for himself … . Miss Ella Hepworth Dixon gives a very learned and amusing, plentifully illustrated article on 'Cloaks in Europe' (sic) from the days of Frédégonde, the wife of Chilpéric, down to the time when our mothers were young.[76]

Within the next few years Ella Hepworth Dixon's name had become a selling point for journals, indicative of the general shift away from anonymity in the press. For example, the advertisement[77] for *The Special Winter Number of 'Woman'* of 1891 declared, 'Every Story, Article, and Illustration will be the work of a Woman' and specifically mentioned 'A short story by Ella Hepworth Dixon', the only other named author being Mrs Edward Kennard. After the success of *My Flirtations*, *The Special Holiday Number of 'Woman'* in 1893 used her pen-name in its advertisement:

> This number will be full of LIGHT LITERATURE suitable to the season, BEAUTIFULLY ILLUSTRATED, and printed on good paper. AMONG OTHER SPECIAL FEATURES there will be a ROMANTIC STORY by MARGARET WYNMAN, Author of 'MY FLIRTATIONS', entitled 'LIKE TO LIKE'.[78]

Ella Hepworth Dixon is, incidentally, the only writer mentioned by name, whilst the advertisement for the 1894 *Christmas Number*[79] announced 'A Special Feature will be a Four Page Supplement illustrating ... Types of the World's Women', and placed her real name first in the list of contributors of 'four complete stories'.

After this, her direct contributions to *Woman* ceased. She was, however, interviewed in the series 'My Faith and My Work' in 1896 following Roy Devereux, Mrs Andrew Dean, Alicia Ramsay and Mrs Meynell. As usual, Ella Hepworth Dixon is self-mocking:

> The intelligent reader - or I have written in vain - will perceive that it is a becoming sense of modesty which forbids me to accept complacently, and without a protest, the flattering invitation of *Woman*. When it came to the

[75] (Unsigned), Review of March Magazines, *St. James's Gazette* (March 1, 1889), p. 7.
[76] *Ibid.* (July 29, 1889), p. 6.
[77] This advertisement appeared on several occasions in *Woman,* for example on October 21, 1891, p. 16, and on January 13, 1892, p. 2.
[78] *Woman Holiday Number* (1893), pp. 3-10.
[79] Unfortunately, a copy of this *Christmas Number* is not to be found in the otherwise very full collection of *Woman* at Colindale.

point, had I any Faith, or had I any Work which was worth wasting honest printer's ink on?

As a matter of fact, it may be time enough twenty years hence - if the gods permit that one should live so long - for me to give a *compte rendu* of 'my Faith and my Work'. At present, so poor an assortment of literary baggage have I, that it is only a kind of journalistic joke that I can permit myself to join the eminent company in the present symposium.[80]

She had also earlier received high praise from the pen of the *Woman* literary critic:

Her two first books have been among the most successful publications of the past few years. ... Miss Hepworth Dixon is much sought after by editors because she writes carefully, punctually, and honestly, never 'scamping', and having only one quality of work; and her clear bold handwriting is a thing of joy to printers.[81]

The notion that she was 'much sought after by editors' is borne out by Ella Hepworth Dixon's own testimony in her memoirs in the chapter on editors where she describes being approached by several eminent editors such as the first Lord Burnham: 'One day I received a little letter from him saying he had read everything which I had written, and asking me to contribute regularly to the *Daily Telegraph*. The result was a number of travel articles, which were more popular in the late Victorian era than now.'[82] So far, however, I have been unable to find any such articles bearing her signature. She also devotes an entire chapter to Lord Northcliffe and describes how Sir Alfred Harmsworth sent for her when he envisaged setting up the *Daily Mirror*. In the same section she relates 'a thrilling moment' at a dinner party given by William Heinemann when her host called out, 'Have you heard that Alfred Harmsworth is buttonholing everybody he sees to say you are the only journalist who knows how to write?'[83] Elsewhere she notes, 'Mr Arnold Bennett was editing a weekly paper called *Woman* when I met him first and I often wrote short stories for its columns. He was a gay and kindly editor, and made his contributors "play up".'[84] In spite of their differences of opinion, therefore, there seems to have been no long-standing animosity between the two.

By the beginning of 1895, after the success of *The Story of a Modern Woman* which I shall discuss in a separate chapter, Ella Hepworth Dixon had other, more pressing, professional commitments which could explain her absence from the pages of *Woman*. In the above-mentioned 'My Faith and My Work', she concludes:

I suppose that every scribbler, some time in his life, aspires to be an editor. - When Messrs F.V. White and Company proposed last year to start a new magazine, *The Englishwoman*, and offered me the editorial arm-chair, I sank

80 *Woman* (September 23, 1896), p. 8.
81 *Ibid.* (December 5, 1894), p. 5.
82 *Ibid.* p. 163.
83 *Ibid.* pp. 140-143.
84 *As I Knew Them* (London, 1930), p. 178.

> into it with much satisfaction. And then, for some six or seven months, life became a whirl of proof-sheets, process blocks, and printer's devils; of processions of youths armed with portfolios; of young ladies in *pince-nez,* coming vaguely in search of 'work'; ... .[85]

'Number 1 of *The Englishwoman* edited by Ella Hepworth Dixon' was advertised as 'ready early in March'. The publishers, F.V. White and Company, obviously invested in a fairly large publicity campaign as advertisements for the new journal appeared in several magazines including *The World* and *The Sketch*,[86] as well as on hoardings, or so Ella Hepworth Dixon recounts in her memoirs. She also relates how William Heinemann, who apparently liked to be consulted on the literary projects of his authors, met her 'with this reproach: "I see your name on all these advertisements and you've never told me you've accepted an editorship."'[87]

The advertisements for *The Englishwoman* promised:

> An Illustrated Magazine of Fiction, Fashion, Society, and the Home.
> Stories by the Most Popular Authors of the Day.
> Articles of General Interest and Interviews with Celebrities, Profusely Illustrated.
> Monthly Prize Competitions.
> Exhaustive Articles on Every Topic Connected with the House and Home.

Such a description would fit many a woman's magazine and it is difficult to envisage exactly how, except perhaps by the name of its editor, it was going to differentiate itself from others of its type. As critics both then and now have pointed out, competition for women's readership, whether of one penny weeklies, threepenny or sixpenny monthlies, was fierce. The *St. James's Gazette* review of Ella Hepworth Dixon's magazine, for example, noted, 'The monthly magazines continue to multiply exceedingly.'[88] Interestingly, directly below the advertisement for *The Englishwoman*, *The World* published the following announcement for another:

> New Ladies' Paper. One Penny Weekly.
> *The Ladies' Gazette.*[89]
> Fashion - Society - The Home.
> Coloured Plate with Every Number.

In January 1895, just two months before *The Englishwoman*'s entry into the world of journalism, in its long-running series on 'Journals and Journalists of To-Day', *The Sketch*, somewhat coincidentally, published an interview with Mr.

[85] *Woman* (September 23, 1896), p. 8.
[86] *The World* (March 6, 1895), p. 33 and *The Sketch* (March 13, 1895), p. 333.
[87] *As I Knew Them* (London, 1930), p. 188.
[88] (Unsigned), 'The Englishwoman', *St. James's Gazette* (March 14, 1895), p. 4.
[89] *The Ladies' Gazette* began in 1895 and disappeared in 1899, a year before *The Englishwoman.*

Gibbons of the *Lady's Pictorial*[90] which began with the question, 'How on earth do all the ladies' papers manage to live?' The response, not surprisingly, was, 'They don't *all* live' (his italics). This might to some extent explain *The World* reviewer's rather reserved reception of *The Englishwoman*: 'Starting with the doubt that there is place for yet another sixpenny magazine after the pattern of the *Strand*, there is little to be said for *The Englishwoman* save that it is neither better nor worse than the rest.'[91]

Two other periodicals to which Ella Hepworth Dixon had contributed regularly by 1895 were more generous in their appraisal. Since she apparently remained on good terms with all three, such differences of opinion cannot necessarily be attributed to personal loyalties or animosities. The review in *Woman*,[92] signed 'Barbara', perhaps another of Arnold Bennett's pen-names, simply mentioned the 'new sixpenny monthly for women, edited by Ella Hepworth Dixon' and listed some of her illustrious contributors. The critic in the *Lady's Pictorial*,[93] which, as an even more direct rival, might have felt more threatened, went to greater lengths, again drawing attention to Ella Hepworth Dixon's appeal to both men and women readers:

> Miss Dixon may honestly be congratulated alike upon the quality, quantity, and judicious variety of contents of the first number of this new candidate for the suffrages of women-readers. Indeed, so discreetly has she blended all the best features which we are accustomed to look for in high-class magazines of the day, that there is no reason why, despite its title, she should not find plenty of readers amongst both sexes. There is nothing namby-pamby on the one hand and nothing coarsely audacious on the other in the pages of *The Englishwoman*, Rosa Matilda and the Newest Woman being conspicuous by their absence ... . Fashions, furniture, books, plays, sport, and feminine topics generally are dealt with by ladies who have made such subjects their speciality, and the magazine, which is fully and artistically illustrated, is excellent value for the sixpence asked for it.

Subsequently, in its book reviews the *Lady's Pictorial* regularly referred to its competitor and expressed unstinting praise especially for Ella Hepworth Dixon, although it has to be said that the *Lady's Pictorial* continued to pay compliments to the magazine even after Ella Hepworth Dixon had left. For example, '*The Englishwoman* has not a dull line in it this month, and the accomplished editor has, it would seem, the enviable gift of being able to keep the balance between the Englishwoman who advances and her sister who lags behind ... .'[94] Such comments recall the motto of *Woman*: 'Forward! but not too fast.' By all accounts, Ella

[90] 'Journals and Journalists of To-Day XXXIII Mr Gibbons and the "Lady's Pictorial"', *The Sketch* (January 30, 1895), p. 23.

[91] (Unsigned), 'Reviews and Magazines', *The World* (May 8, 1895), p. 30.

[92] 'Book Chat', *Woman* (April 3, 1895), p. 7.

[93] (Unsigned, but usually Miss Curtis, better known as 'Blue Stocking'), 'Books of the Day', *Lady's Pictorial* (March 23, 1895), p. 414.

[94] *Lady's Pictorial* (May 4, 1895), p. 657.

Hepworth Dixon was taking no risks in her periodical. '*The Englishwoman* ... is as bright this month as summer sunshine ought to be ... like one of those delicious fruit salads there is a little of everything that is "nice" in it', wrote the reviewer in June and concluded, somewhat excessively, '*The Englishwoman* is worth double its price.'[95]

The Englishwoman actually remained in circulation for five years, a relatively respectable life-span in those days for a journal of its type. In her memoirs Ella Hepworth Dixon describes the much shorter shelf-life of *The Daily Mirror* in its original format:

> I was duly engaged, as leader writer ... to be paid at the handsome rate of something like £1500 a year, but alas for human hopes, nobody wanted a woman's daily paper in London, and very shortly after Alfred Harmsworth had turned the *Daily Mirror* into the first illustrated morning paper, with the extraordinary success we know. With this devastating change went the feminine leader-writers and staff. These lightening surprises were then the joke of Fleet Street. [96]

As a point of comparison, it is worth noting that in the *Ladies' Field* series on Women Workers an article on 'The Literary Life' in February 1899 mentioned £150-200 as an average income for women journalists, with a rare number earning 'anything from £300 to £500'.

It has long been assumed that Ella Hepworth Dixon remained editor of *The Englishwoman* throughout its five year existence. Her name, however, only appears until Volume I Number 6, August 1895. Volume II Number 7 still bears the names of F.V. White and Company as publishers, but thereafter the journal was published by Simpkin, Marshall, and Company, and no editor's name is given. In February of the following year Ella Hepworth Dixon was already writing of her experiences as an editor in the past tense: 'Once upon a time, when I was an Editor, I hugged a long-cherished dream. In the periodical which, for a brief period, I was privileged to direct, it was my ambition to have a certain fully-illustrated article - "Cats of Celebrities and Celebrated Cats".'[97] Furthermore, by her own account, in the article on 'My Faith and My Work' in *Woman* in September, 1896, the experience as editor was short-lived:

> Owing to circumstances over which I had no control, in half a year *The Englishwoman* had changed publishers; and nowadays, if my work is of a less responsible and exciting nature, my waste-paper basket, at least contains only such MSS. of my own as I find necessary to reject myself.[98]

---

[95] *Ibid.* (June 1, 1895), p. 841.
[96] *As I Knew Them* (London, 1930), pp. 141-142.
[97] *Lady's Pictorial* (February 1, 1896), p. 142.
[98] *Woman* (September 23, 1896), p. 8.

Contrary to general belief, then, Ella Hepworth Dixon's collaboration with *The Englishwoman* was curtailed long before the demise of the journal in 1900. Moreover, it is very difficult to evaluate how much influence, both direct and indirect, she ever had in the magazine since there was no editorial as such. Her own signature never appears, but almost all the articles were signed and visibly Ella Hepworth Dixon employed the pens of members of her own family, especially her sister Marion, who wrote the regular book reviews, 'Under the Lamp', and contributed a short story, 'A Desperate Remedy'.[99] Described as a 'capital story in dialogue' by the *Lady's Pictorial* reviewer, it is very similar in style to some of Ella Hepworth Dixon's own stories. It begins, for example, 'I'm going to marry him, did I tell you?' which is reminiscent of the opening lines of Ella Hepworth Dixon's 'The World's Slow Stain', her contribution to *The Christmas Number of The World* that year: 'I'm going to marry a man who jilted me ten years ago.' This seems to suggest the sisters were strongly influencing each other. A certain S.W. Hepworth Dixon also signed an article on 'The Trafalgar Bicycle Club'[100] in the series on Ladies' Clubs in London. This could be the sister-in-law Sybil to whom Ella Hepworth Dixon dedicated her memoirs, but so far this is the only occurrence I have found of the signature and have no evidence that Sybil wrote. There was an older Hepworth Dixon sister who did write, but her name was Edith and she had died in 1879.

However brief her occupation of the 'editorial arm-chair', Ella Hepworth Dixon seems to have suffered no loss of credibility in the profession, and her name is even cited as a point of reference in the 1896 *Newspaper Press Directory* article on 'Fifty Years of Women's Papers and Magazines'. In evaluating *The Woman at Home*, the author comments, 'This purported to be a valuable medium for thoughtful women, but, unfortunately falls far short of this ideal, which was much nearer being attained to by the *Englishwoman*, under Miss Ella Hepworth Dixon's editorship, which came out last year.'[101] Nor does she herself express the slightest trace of bitterness or disappointment. In her memoirs in the introduction to the chapter on editors she merely notes, 'Having been an editor myself, I understand the trials, the unutterable boredom, the delirious excitement, the difficulty of "suffering fools gladly", the delight of pouncing on the right man or woman for one's purpose, which make the experience of such a personage.'[102]

With less hindsight, the *Woman* interview, published so shortly after her departure from *The Englishwoman*, would testify both to her continued enthusiasm and her lack of rancour. This may in part be explained because so many other opportunites were available to her. Personifying the energy and tireless productivity so often mentioned in the contemporary overviews of women in the world of journals, Ella Hepworth Dixon, whilst still at the helm of *The Englishwoman*, had

[99] *The Englishwoman* Volume 1, Number 3 (May, 1895), pp. 198-202.
[100] *Ibid*. Number 5 (July, 1895), p. 372.
[101] (Unsigned), *Newspaper Press Directory* (1896), p. 13.
[102] *As I Knew Them* (London, 1930), p. 161.

already begun[103] a weekly column with the *Lady's Pictorial*. This was the most long-standing arrangement of her life, since, albeit with short interludes and a few changes of name, it lasted well over twenty years. From June 1895 until December 1906 her column was entitled 'Pensées de Femme', described in 1898 in *The Woman at Home*'s overview of 'Two Great Ladies' Papers'[104] as 'a column of bright "Pensées de Femme" upon current topics'. This article also provided portraits of some of the members of the Editorial Staff, including Ella Hepworth Dixon. Interestingly, she is the only one of the five journalists represented who did not have a *nom-de-plume*, perhaps again insinuating that the name did count for something with the public. In January 1907 her column was renamed 'In a Looking-Glass' and the sections became shorter. Amongst the 'New Features for 1908' advertised on the front page of the last *Lady's Pictorial* of the year was '"Hors D'Oeuvres" by Ella Hepworth Dixon', although by the first issue of January 1908 it had changed to 'Soufflés', and was advertised as such, perhaps because *The Sketch* also ran a column by the other name. The following year saw another change, this time to 'Social Etchings', and so it remained for two years, after which it no longer bore a regular title, each contribution being named individually. In March 1921 the magazine amalgamated with *Eve*, and Ella Hepworth Dixon's contributions ceased.

She had, in fact, been collaborating with the *Lady's Pictorial* from the earliest days of her career, and, beginning with 'A Winter Idyl'[105] in 1888, made regular contributions, signed in her own name, to the *Lady's Pictorial Christmas Number*. Significantly, the *Christmas Number* in 1894 was entitled 'Seven Stories by Modern Women', surely, like W.T. Stead's article in the *Review of Reviews*[106] earlier that year, intentionally echoing the title of her celebrated novel. Besides her short story, 'A Man of Pleasure', the collection consisted of stories by Marie Corelli, Violet Hunt, Iota, Clo. Graves, Clara Savile-Clarke and Mrs W.K. Clifford. In the *Sketch* interview,[107] published whilst Ella Hepworth Dixon was still only an outside contributor of 'literary matter', the editor of the *Lady's Pictorial*, Alfred Gibbons, had cited her as one of the 'leading English lady journalists'. In her memoirs, she writes equally highly of him:

> Another editor with whom I had long dealings was Mr Alfred Gibbons of the *Lady's Pictorial* - which had an enormous vogue in Suburbia, and belonged partly to the Ingram group of weekly newspapers. Curt and kindly, he was a man of innate good taste and perception, and was celebrated for getting

---

103 *Lady's Pictorial* (June 22, 1895), p. 955.

104 (Unsigned), *The Woman at Home* (April, 1898), pp. 561-565. The second article on *The Gentlewoman* (pp. 566-570) was signed by J. S. Wood, the editor at that time.

105 *The Lady's Pictorial Christmas Number* (1888), pp. 25-27.

106 (W.T. Stead) 'The Book of the Month: The Novel of the Modern Woman', *Review of Reviews* 10 (July 2, 1894), pp. 64-74.

107 'Journals and Journalists of To-Day XXXIII Mr. Gibbons and the "Lady's Pictorial"', *The Sketch* (January 30, 1895), p. 23.

> useless contributors out of the editorial room more swiftly than any other editor in London.[108]

Alfred Gibbons' response to the request *Woman* had made of 'editors of several of the best women's papers' in its overview of 'Journalism for Women During the Reign',[109] 'to state succinctly the leading principle or principles upon which their journals are conducted' perhaps explains why their working partnership was so long-standing:

> The *raison d'être* of the *Lady's Pictorial* is two-fold. It chronicles ... upon the one hand, every movement and every incident of importance which makes for the progress of woman, in the best sense of the word, and records sympathetically everything which tends towards the improvement of the status and the enlargement of her natural talents and acquired capabilities; while on the other hand, it depicts by pen and pencil that lighter, but equally important side of woman's life, in which she contributes to the well-being of others, as well as pleases herself, by the adoption of all that is newest and most charming in dress; by playing her part in the social side of life as hostess or as guest, and by assisting in a score of ways in advancing the interests of benevolent institutions, and bringing together, to their mutual advantage, all classes of Society.
>
> Recognizing that both the lighter and the graver side of woman's life have their proper place and their due influence, the *Lady's Pictorial* opens its columns equally to the purely fashionable, and as some may deem it frivolous phase of society, and to that earnest zealous section that aims at the intellectual and material progress of women, the amelioration of their condition as a body, and the eventual emancipation of the sex from all disabilities imposed upon them as women, and their due establishment upon an equality with men in all the essential conditions of industrial, professional and social life.

This sounds much like a general credo for Ella Hepworth Dixon's own literary career. A high regard for her own sex and a desire for greater justice for women undoubtedly permeates her entire output. Moreover, her capacity to combine the 'frivolous' and the 'zealous' is a particularly distinguishing feature of her writing. This enabled her to treat even the most delicate or thorny subjects with wit, thereby making it difficult to accuse her of being a 'shrieking sister' or a 'wild woman'. In her overview of the Queen's rule in 1897, for instance, she writes:

> It is the women, in all probability, who are most concerned with the coming era, and who will look back with most curiosity to the past - especially to the condition of their sex when Queen Victoria mounted the throne. Early Victorian ideals permitted small outlet for feminine energy. ... It is within

[108] *As I Knew Them* (London, 1930), p. 162.
[109] *Woman* (June 16, 1897), pp. 33-37.

> the bounds of possibility that, sixty years hence, the world may be a more reasonable world for a woman to live in … .[110]

In her professional capacity she regularly discussed the issue of equality between the sexes and complained that 'there is … , and will always be, much nonsense written about women'.[111] For example, 'The world has hitherto liked to suppose - for it is socially convenient to do so - that *all women* have a vocation for the celibate life. It is a foolish theory, and leads to much perplexity and scandal'[112] (her italics). Occasionally, therefore, she displayed a certain suspicion of male pens. 'I had high hopes of the clever lady who is writing the *Dies Dominae* articles in the *Saturday Review*', she declared, but sadly disappointment set in:

> Has one got to inform so observant a person as the writer of those articles that the rivalry of women is the outcome of economic conditions, of artificial training, of false conceptions of life, and is by no means a fundamental trait of the softer sex? ... One begins to suspect that the signature in the *Saturday Review* may conceal, not a modern feminine personality, but that of some estimable elderly gentleman saturated with the archaic ideas of the sixties.

A little later[113] she remarked:

> Irate masculine critics have sometimes accused me of cultivating too high a standard for my sex. I have been told again and again that my ideas are Utopian, and that I have altogether too favourable an opinion of 'the monstrous army of women'. Well, I must admit the accusation. Charming, intelligent, humorous women - the women, in fine, whom I am proud to call my friends - are such 'good fellows!' It is a real pleasure for me to gossip, week by week, to women in *Lady's Pictorial.* Every now and again I get an agreeable note, I hear an appreciative phrase, which tell me I am in touch with many of my readers. It is a privilege, indeed, not to be lightly regarded, that of being able to catch the ear, to put, as it were, one's finger on the pulse of so large a feminine public. In all that makes for progress, for sanity, for purity, for health, I am with them heart and soul.

She was thus ever ready to defend her sex, as in her first 'Pensées de Femme',[114] yet her esteem and sympathy did not blind her to certain shortcomings in women and she was equally ready to take them to task if the occasion demanded it. At the same time as she took up her pen to defend spinsters or bachelor women, her preferred term, and so-called superfluous women,[115] so she expressed a surprisingly modern concern for the married state. As in her fiction, marriage is rarely idealized,

---

110 *Lady's Pictorial* (June 26, 1897), p. 944.
111 *Ibid.* (April 4, 1896), p. 465.
112 *Ibid.*
113 *Ibid.* (December 26, 1896), p. 966.
114 *Ibid.* (June 22, 1895), p. 955.
115 For example *Lady's Pictorial* (March 11, 1899), p. 339, and *The Sketch* (March 10, 1913), p. 355 and (March 25, 1914), p. 385.

but she does occasionally as in *The Sketch* of December 13, 1911, speak of the 'New Camaraderie' between man and wife, much like that described between the main protagonist and her husband in 'A Scribbler's Comedy', first published in *Pall Mall Magazine*[116] in 1895. Later, at the time of Cecily Hamilton's *Marriage as a Trade*,[117] Ella Hepworth Dixon draws attention to other factors: 'If marriage is indeed a trade, then women who intend to enter it should be specialized still more, rather than less, for at present most of them go into it with the most amateurish notions of their high responsibilities and duties.'[118] Her celebrated *Humanitarian* article, 'Why Women are Ceasing to Marry',[119] raises issues about child-bearing and caring which remain problematic. To judge by the response published in the magazine the following month, the article had met with wide notice in the press, which was not unusual for Ella Hepworth Dixon. Many of her articles such as the first in *The Daily Mirror* in November 1903 and later in the *Westminster Gazette* in November 1921 would also set off a series of reader-responses. Whether this was intended is difficult to say since many journals started actively encouraging the participation of readers, a feature which still persists.

In the fifth of the series on Lady Journalists in the *Lady's Pictorial*, and, incidentally, the one featuring Ella Hepworth Dixon, a comparison is made between 'the new school of journalism ... which has developed into a social power in the land' and the few women journalists of the past, including the Honorable Mrs Norton, Miss Harriet Martineau and Miss Frances Power Cobbe:

> A wide gulf exists between these ladies, who turned out severe and critical essays, political leaders, reviews of books dealing with science, philosophy, and ethics, and the modern journalist, who is expected to be ubiquitious, rushing from place to place with notebook and pencil, looking up every subject discussed alike in drawing-room and kitchen. The triad of clever ladies catered for the few, but the modern journalist never throws her care for the many off her mind.[120]

I would argue that Ella Hepworth Dixon's 'care for the many' was particularly salient in her coverage of the Suffragist movement. In an early 'Pensées de Femme' in 1895, when there had been yet again talk of the Government granting women the Franchise, she put forward arguments similar in essence to those advanced by George Bernard Shaw in *Mrs Warren's Profession*:

> Man, so far as one can judge, is an eminently practical being. ... He has his own ideas - sufficiently bewildering ones - about what is fit and proper for woman to do. She may toil in a white-lead factory or at the pit's mouth, but not in a printing office; she may exhibit herself *au naturel* in living pictures

[116] *Pall Mall Magazine* V (1895), pp. 286-294.
[117] Published in 1909 by Chapman and Hall, London.
[118] *Lady's Pictorial* (July 17, 1909), p. 108.
[119] *The Humanitarian* (June, 1899), pp. 391-396.
[120] *Lady's Pictorial* (February 10, 1895), p. 176.

> or in a glass tank, but she may not paint from the living model in art-school; she may take dangerous leaps on a trapeze, but she may not ride a bicycle; she may write novels, but she must ignore the half of life; she may stump the country at election time, but she must not say her say about a corroding evil of modern life.[121]

As time passed and the vote continued to be withheld, she would frequently return to the topic, but from slightly different perspectives. In 1908, for instance, she comments, 'It is a strange fact that in this argument about the franchise most of the logic is to be found on the spindle side, and most of the unreasoning prejudice and the perfervid emotion is to be found among the masculine protagonists.'[122] And then again, in one of her *Sketch* articles on 'The Sex which Needs Defending', she would add, 'In these days of strained political relations between men and women I often find myself defending those delightful and illogical specimens of humanity who wear tall hats, starched collars, and trousers.'[123]

As she confessed, she was never a militant herself:

> I, for one - though I sat on many platforms, wrote insidiously, but not blatantly, in favour of the franchise, and once 'demonstrated' in the back seat of a motor-car - admit with humiliation that I have never 'burned for my faith' at all. Which is a shameful thing.[124]

Nevertheless, she always showed tremendous respect for those who were, while castigating those who actively campaigned against voting rights for women. For example:

> Because excellent Mrs Blank, seated placidly in her mansion at Streatham, with a panting motor at the door waiting to convey her to an Anti-Suffrage meeting, has no political ambitions, it is, I take it, at least unfair that she should in any way try to prevent her more public-spirited sisters from attaining the object for which they have made so many and such heroic sacrifices.[125]

In one of her later *Sketch* articles she expressed relief that:

> Mrs Mary Gawthorpe's suggestion that sympathisers with the Suffragists must starve in order to vote has met with scant response. I do not see why a considerable portion of humanity should inflict permanent injury upon themselves because a Government has shown itself perfidious. Some of us would prefer that recalcitrant Man should suffer the torments of hunger and

---

[121] *Ibid.* (July 6, 1895), p. 5.
[122] *Ibid.* (December 12, 1908), p. 1114.
[123] *The Sketch* (November 29, 1911), p. xii.
[124] *Westminster Gazette* (June 30, 1926), p. 8.
[125] *Lady's Pictorial* (April 10, 1909), p. 566.

> thirst rather than that the women-folk should go on enduring these horrors.[126]

Even after the franchise had been 'triumphantly attained',[127] she continued to point out the injustices and vagaries of the vote. In 1923 in her weekly *Westminster Gazette* column she bemoans, 'I have been pursuing this phantom vote since 1918',[128] and then recounts, in typical humourous vein, her lack of success, basically due to her not being a property owner. Still disenfranchised, she returned to the topic a few years later in the same journal and expressed her disgruntlement with less humour.[129]

In fact, politics frequently recurred in her *Westminster Gazette* contributions, further demonstrating her belief that a woman journalist need not restrict herself to a narrowly defined sphere. It is true that Ella Hepworth Dixon rarely wrote about subjects such as science or philosophy, or topics often gendered male such as legal or medical matters. Nor did she undertake the investigative type of journalism such as Harriet Taylor Mill had done in the *Morning Chronicle* in the 1840s.[130] But nor did she limit herself to the typically female. Domestic concerns such as housekeeping, cooking, furnishing, health and hygiene are largely absent from her prose, and when they are present they are very often given a different slant. What might ostensibly begin as an article on fashion, as in her earlier mentioned contributions to the *Woman's World*, would lead to a commentary on humanity in general. For example, in one of her *Sketch* articles, which were nearly always accompanied by very ornate fashion plates, she writes:

> There are persons who maintain that this ascendancy of John Knox's 'monstrous regiment of women' is due, in large degree, to the changing, baffling, complicated aspect of their clothes. Were they dressed, it is alleged, always in plain homespun, they would neither allure not intimidate, and their specious arguments could be more easily refuted. Naturally enough, even the most modern woman is reluctant to abandon so lethal a weapon, so that we perceive the most intellectual women interested in changing waist-lines and ... gorgeous in purple and fine linen.[131]

Likewise a piece on gardening, which had become such a popular hobby, gave her the opportunity to extrapolate: 'The modern garden ... has become so intimate and personal a thing as to be a revelation of character, a kind of Futuristic picture of the Soul.'[132] Other topics such as travel, current affairs, literature, music, eminent men

---

[126] *The Sketch* (October 16, 1912), p. 61.
[127] *Lady's Pictorial* (September 28, 1918), p. 332.
[128] *Westminster Gazette* (December 6, 1923), p. 7.
[129] *Ibid.* (June 30, 1926), p. 8.
[130] See in particular Ann P. Robson and John M. Robson (eds), *Sexual Equality: Writings by John Stuart Mill, Harriet Taylor Mill and Helen Taylor* (Toronto, 1994).
[131] *The Sketch* (December 13, 1911), p. l.
[132] *Ibid.* (July 31, 1912), p. 125.

and women, also gave Ella Hepworth Dixon the possibility to make more general remarks on contemporary issues. During the Boer War, from March 3 until May 19, 1900, she wrote weekly articles for *The Ladies' Field* on 'The Way of the War', and, besides her early interviews with celebrities at home, from January to July 1914 she wrote a monthly page entitled 'The Woman's Progress' for *The Illustrated London News*, the series being interrupted by the outbreak of World War I.

As mentioned at the beginning of this chapter, it is not always possible to identify authorship. In her memoirs, she claims to have reviewed William Heinemann's play, *The First Step*, for *The Illustrated London News*, but the only review I have found is unsigned.[133] Likewise she recounts being asked to replace George Bernard Shaw as music critic for *The World* at the Leeds Music Festival, but so far I have been unable to trace her article. It may have been in October 1892 and, unfortunately, the collection of *The World* July-December 1892 at Colindale is unfit for use. Many articles, such as wartime propaganda for the *Manchester Guardian* and the *Daily Mail* series on 'Women's Part in the War' or 'What Women are Doing', were logically anonymous, although the signatures of other notable women writers such as Cecily Hamilton, Elizabeth Robins, Evelyn Sharp and Netta Syrett, did occasionally appear.

Throughout her long career Ella Hepworth Dixon produced a wide variety of articles for journals of all sorts, including general dailies as well as specifically women's weeklies or monthlies and was appreciated by readers of both sexes, not necessarily for the same articles or for the same reasons. Simultaneously, she continued to contribute short stories to special editions of several periodicals, including *The World* and *Lady's Pictorial*, until the beginning of the twentieth century. When *The Ladies' Field* began again in March 1898 she had a weekly column entitled 'A Woman's Ways' which, with an interruption during the Boer War, lasted until March 1902. After this she continued to write the occasional piece such as the first 'Diary of a Londoner' in October 1901, which became a regular feature written by Claudia Carew, or 'The Lost Art of Self-Control' in March 1904. She then used practically the same name, 'Woman's Ways', when she began writing for *The Sketch* in February 1907. Her collaboration there lasted until November 7, 1917 when she was sixty. Interestingly, her articles did not appear as part of the woman's page, again testifying her appeal to a general readership.

On the whole, Ella Hepworth Dixon's contributions to magazines such as the *Lady's Pictorial*, *The Ladies' Field* and *The Sketch* were anecdotal in nature, consisting of a series of short 'tit-bits', so in vogue at that time. Over the years, her pieces tended to become shorter and even more pithy. Several reviewers of her novel commented on its 'sketchy' nature, too, suggesting perhaps that even in her longest work of prose the fragmentary style suited her pen. The *Sunday Times* critic, for example, writes, 'This novel has the merit of introducing a number of *sketches* of modern metropolitan life', the reviewer in *The Graphic* comments on 'the *sketches* of a certain side of society in which the authoress displays a striking

[133] *The Illustrated London News* (March 2, 1895), p. 263.

faculty for quick, shrewd and independent observation', whilst L.F. Austin in *The Illustrated London News* also noted that 'the book is rather a series of detached *sketches* than a coherent whole' (my italics).

In the eyes of a certain public, Ella Hepworth Dixon may have embodied the New Woman, as discussed in the preceding chapter, but she was far-removed from some of the excessively serious women writers such as Sarah Grand, or those like George Egerton who were writing in a more febrile, rather neurotic way. Unlike some of her contemporaries, she generally displayed an optimism which may ultimately have proved unfounded, but which offered some relief from the jeremiads which were also being written at that time. Moreover, she usually managed not to take herself too seriously, mocking her shortsightedness and indulging in a certain amount of self-parody. She even makes fun of lady dramatists at a time when she must have been working on her own play.[134] This might explain why, to judge by her ubiquitious signature and her own accounts in her memoirs, she was so much sought after. Indeed, she would appear to have worked with most of the leading editors and publishers of her time and on the whole seems to have benefited from a mutual respect and understanding.

Journalism thus provided Ella Hepworth Dixon with interesting, purposeful work, which enabled her to promote, in theory and in practice, the cause of other women and to remain an independent bachelor woman herself. It was also a source of valuable background material for some of her fiction. *The Story of a Modern Woman* is the most obvious example, but the world of journalism and literature is also at the heart of several of her short stories. She may even have started a trend. In 1894 the *Sunday Times* reviewer of her novel pointed out that 'so far as we know the career of the heroine is new to fiction',[135] but two years later in July 1896 M.F. Billington in her overview of 'Leading Lady Journalists', which somewhat surprisingly makes no mention of Ella Hepworth Dixon, commented, 'Fiction has made heroines of us, and the "lady journalist" has figured in more than one recent play or burlesque.'[136] Over the next few years several works of fiction centering on a journalist heroine did indeed appear. In 1895 George Paston published a short story entitled 'A Lady Journalist'[137] in which the lady journalist of the title is in fact rather dubious, since she persuades her fiancé to write for her. In the course of the story he loses both his job and fiancée, and she marries the editor. In 1899 George Paston then published a full-length novel, *A Writer of Books*, whose female protagonist, Cosima Chudleigh, is a more interesting character altogether, and echoes to some extent Mary Erle's experiences in Grub Street. The other most notable series on lady journalists are Cottrel Hoe's 'Jennie Baxter, Journalist' in the *Windsor Magazine* from December 1897 to November 1898, later published in book form and signed by the author's own name, Robert Barr,[138] and Annie S.

[134] *Lady's Pictorial* (October 5, 1907), p. 512.
[135] *Sunday Times* (June 3, 1894), p. 2.
[136] *Pearson's Magazine* 11 (July-December, 1896), pp. 101-111.
[137] *English Illustrated Magazine* (January, 1895), pp. 65-73.
[138] Published in 1899 by Methuen and Company, London.

Swan's 'Journal of a Literary Woman in London' in *Woman at Home* from April 1901 to September 1902. As the title suggests, this consists of a series of stories told by Miriam Carter, and includes several descriptions of literary women. For example Kitty Ford, 'journalist for the latest ladies' paper', is described as an 'odd little figure in a very limp and soiled white nun's veiling frock peering through her shabby lorgnette at the smart guests'. Jennie Baxter, on the other hand, is 'always most beautifully attired', has a strong sense of her profession, but is tired of relying on a 'fitful income', and, as the story unfolds, reveals admirable enterprise.

It has often been suggested that in her fiction Ella Hepworth Dixon, like many New Woman writers, deliberately darkened the image of the woman writer or the artist in general. It cannot be denied that her most famous work, *The Story of a Modern Woman*, certainly does not glamorize the life of an aspiring artist or journalist. Not all contemporary critics considered it entirely exaggerated or necessarily pessimistic. The *Sunday Times* reviewer, for example, suggested that Mary Erle's success in journalism 'should be encouraging to ladies who find themselves by stress of circumstances, or from love of literary pursuits, anxious to work for their own living',[139] an idea shared by the critic in *The Graphic,* who thought 'her experiences … will thus be found of interest by thousands of other Mary Erles'.[140] *The Sketch* critic also noted 'the habits of editors are sketched with that disrespectful playfulness which distinguishes the feminine attitude towards Fleet Street',[141] further evidence of which is found in some of Ella Hepworth Dixon's short stories. For example in 'A Scribbler's Comedy'[142] the heroine, 'John Bathurst', even gets the better of a male editor. In spite of his misgivings about 'the presence of women in newspaper offices', so charmed is he by this 'radiant vision ... illuminating the dingy newspaper office', so unlike his usual impression of lady journalists 'in pince-nez and waterproofs', that he favourably reviews her 'volume of short stories illustrative of the New Revolt', and is even ready to offer her a column on the Woman Question. The title of this story was changed to 'A Political Comedy' when it was republished in the 1904 collection, and the emphasis was then placed not so much on the writing as on the politics, and then not those of 'John Bathurst' herself, but of her husband, perhaps indicative of a shift in Ella Hepworth Dixon's own concerns, or the interests of her reading public. In other short stories Ella Hepworth Dixon portrays women novelists, as in 'The Goddess from the Machine'[143] which focuses on an accomplished novelist who wins the love of young man, or 'The Plain Miss Pendleston'[144] which also demonstrates the powers of an older woman novelist over a younger more sensational fiction writer.

[139] *Sunday Times* (June 3, 1894), p. 2
[140] *The Graphic* (June 16, 1894), p. 715.
[141] *The Sketch* (June 27, 1894), p. 476.
[142] *Pall Mall Magazine* V (1895), pp. 286-294.
[143] *The Lady's Pictorial Christmas Number* (1896), pp. 1-5.
[144] *Lady's Pictorial* (November 23, 1901), pp. 937-940.

In 'The World's Slow Stain'[145] the heroine, though not a professional writer, had produced a successful novel out of her suffering.

I would argue, therefore, that in her fictionalizing of the literary world Ella Hepworth Dixon portrays different types of women writers, but because her short stories are much less well-known than her novel, it is the image given in the latter which dominates. Nevertheless, in her memoirs on occasions Ella Hepworth Dixon also reveals that she, too, had not always enjoyed quite the success we are elsewhere led to believe. She admits that in the 'gay nineties' when she 'spent a winter Season in New York', she 'was *prudent enough* to conceal the fact that (she) had ever written for any journal. A "newspaper woman," over there, had no social standing whatever'[146] (my italics). By 1900, however, the situation must have changed for she contributed at least one signed article to the *New York Independent.*[147] Nor should it be forgotten that male writers such as J.M. Barrie, George Gissing, and Henry James were also writing in their fiction about the difficulties inherent in the press world. There are, for example, interesting similarities between Ella Hepworth Dixon's 'What Women Worship'[148] and Henry James' 'The Death of the Lion', the first story in the first volume of *The Yellow Book*, where the destructive powers of the press are a central issue. In 'Condemned'[149] and 'Like to Like',[150] Ella Hepworth Dixon also treats the theme of the influence of the fourth estate, and, especially in the latter story, again seems to be drawing on her own experiences with editors.

In her memoirs she writes:

> English editors, if not quite so much hail-fellow-well-met as American specimens of the genus, are invariably courteous and kind. A woman editor, like a woman doctor, is usually more stiff and uncompromising. When I was in New York, I used to dine with Mr. and Mrs. Ballard Smith, and he was then the editor of *The New York World* (in the 'nineties a paper with an enormous circulation). In the middle of dinner the telephone bell would ring, and Ballard Smith would rise unconcernedly from the table, give his orders down the 'phone (possibly something of epoch-making interest) and stroll back to the table quite unperturbed. 'If you were the Editor of a great London daily,' I said to him, 'you would certainly array yourself in more frills!'[151]

I have not found a fictional representation of a woman editor in her work, but in 'Like to Like' Ella Hepworth Dixon reworks this anecdote into fiction. The story features a certain Jefferson Tuck, an unassuming proprietor and editor of the *New York Standard.* The first person female narrator tells him, '"Mr Tuck, if you were

[145] *Christmas Number of The World* (November 21, 1895), pp. 59-61.
[146] *As I Knew Them* (London, 1930), p. 100.
[147] 'London in Khaki', *New York Independent* (July 26, 1900), pp. 1794-1796.
[148] *Woman* (June 3, 1891), pp. 14-16.
[149] *Ibid.* (April 9, 1891), pp. 15-16.
[150] *Woman Holiday Number* (1893), pp. 3-10.
[151] *As I Knew Them* (London, 1930), p. 161.

the proprietor and editor of a great London paper you would take yourself so much more seriously. Why, you would be pompous and important." And he only replied, with that humorous twinkle of his: "Well, Lady Jane, I believe you. That's just what their papers are.'"[152]

In both her fiction and her non-fiction, Ella Hepworth Dixon raises questions about the world of journals. In a telling 'Pensées de Femme', cited in the Foreword, she perhaps foresees the growing intrusion of a certain form of journalism. After the publication in *Woman* of an interview with Mr Cecil Rhodes' nurse, she writes 'who shall predict what early indiscretions of the great, the good and the famous may not be given to an eagerly expectant world?'[153] In the same article she also expresses misgivings that her own writings will be judged 'the drivellings of a fogey, the maunderings of a benighted intelligence, were they to survive to the enlightened scrutiny of the women of a century hence'. I hope to have shown that much would have been lost if the Superintendent of the British Museum reading-room had been proved right in his claim that 'newspapers ... as a rule are printed on such bad paper that, with the corrosive qualities of the ink and the acids in the paper, they may be expected to crumble gradually into dust and nothingness', and access to Ella Hepworth Dixon's innumerable contributions to such a variety of periodicals were no longer possible. Journalism was first and foremost her livelihood, and, since all her fiction initially appeared in periodicals, it is impossible to imagine her career outside the world of journals. At the same time, her experiences also chronicle an era when journalism, especially journalism for women, in spite of, and perhaps partly because of, its detractors, was flourishing. Towards the end of her life and career in the *Westminster Gazette* in January 1925, she writes:

> These modern days are certainly the opportunity of the Women. For the first time they can, and do, compete with men ... . One of the last citadels to fall was the newspaper office. Here prejudice reigned supreme ... . Today the Bastille of Journalism has fallen.[154]

Her choice of metaphors surely reflects the revolutionary nature of the phenomenon.

---

[152] '"Like to Like;" A Story of Two Continents', *Woman Holiday Number* (1893), p. 3.

[153] 'Pensées de Femme', *Lady's Pictorial* (February 8, 1896), p. 173.

[154] 'The Modern Way: A Social Causerie', *Westminster Gazette* (January 14, 1925), p. 6.

Chapter 4

Short Stories of Modern Women

As discussed in the previous chapter, the *fin de siècle* saw many changes in the world of publishing. The growing circulation of journals and their ever-increasing variety created both a need and an outlet for non-fiction articles as well as for fiction, with a gradual shift away from serialized novels in favour of shorter complete works. Many of the New Woman novelists made regular contributions to periodicals, and in this respect Ella Hepworth Dixon was no exception. In fact, her first book in print, *My Flirtations* (1892), was the compilation of a series of twelve individual sketches originally published in the *Lady's Pictorial* earlier that same year with one new addition, her novel first appeared in serial form in the same magazine, and her volume of short stories, entitled *One Doubtful Hour and Other Sidelights on the Feminine Temperament* (1904), contained works which had all appeared previously, in some cases in a slightly different form, in journals such as *The Ladies' Field*, *Lady's Pictorial*, *Pall Mall Magazine*, *The World* and *The Yellow Book*. Together with occasional articles, including music and art reviews, they mark the beginnings of her literary career.

Clearly, for the novice author the short story can be, and often was, a means of apprenticeship, and for this reason might appeal to many débutant fiction-writers. Some critics, however, such as Elaine Showalter, Hélène Cixous and Luce Irigaray have argued, by drawing similarities between women's lives and women's writing, and suggesting that women actually write differently because of their physical experiences of the world, that the short story is a medium ideally suited for them, particularly those writing at the end of the nineteenth century. A phenomenal number of short stories were indeed then written and published by women. George Egerton, author of perhaps the most famous collections of short stories of the *fin de siècle*, *Keynotes* (1893) and *Discords* (1894), admitted, 'I was a short-story, at most a long short-story writer. ... The long book was not my pigeon ... .'[1] Nevertheless, it would be unwise to use this as evidence to gender the short story. Not only were many of the major male writers, including Joseph Conrad, George Gissing, Henry James, James Joyce, Rudyard Kipling, Robert Louis Stevenson, and H.G. Wells producing fine examples of the genre, but also, as I hope to show with close

1 'A Keynote to *Keynotes*', *Ten Contemporaries: Notes Toward Their Definitive Bibliography*, ed. John Gawsworth (Terence Armstrong) (London, 1932), p. 59, quoted by Martha Vicinus in her Introduction to the Virago edition of *Keynotes and Discords* (London, 1983), p. xiv.

reference to the work of Ella Hepworth Dixon, not all women were writing in the same vein all of the time. A somewhat distorted vision, therefore, is given if one focuses only on the gender of the author.

Critics such as Walter Allen, Clare Hanson, Peter Keating, Derek Stanford and Patricia Stubbs[2] have more usefully set the literary phenomenon in its historical context, drawing attention to social and economic conditions in general. Whether concentrating on the genre itself or the *fin de siècle* period as a whole, all echo Somerset Maugham's idea that 'the rich abundance of short stories during the nineteenth century was directly occasioned by the opportunity which the periodical afforded'.[3] Clare Hanson in particular further highlights links between the Art world and literature, tracing the influence of artistic movements such as Impressionism on the writing of fiction, especially that of the Modernists and, I would add, their fore-runners like Ella Hepworth Dixon. It is worth remembering that, like Elizabeth Bowen much later, she initially intended to pursue a career as a visual artist before turning to writing, and I would argue that her prose often reveals the trained viewpoint of a painter.

Significantly, these recent critics also reappraise the stature of the short-story. What is regularly seen as a minor literary form, 'a novelist's by-product', to use Clare Hanson's phrase, is shown to lend itself to even greater experimentation than the novel, and, far from being a novelist manqué, 'the short story writer needs to be more of a writer, more of an artist, more of a dramatist',[4] according to Frank O'Connor. Nadine Gordimer in turn declares that 'short-story writers see by the light of the flash; theirs is the art of the only thing one can be sure of - the present moment. Ideally, they have learned to do without explanation of what went before, and what happens after this point.'[5] In one of her *Sketch* articles published during the First World War, a time when apparently 'the short story ... attained instant popularity', Ella Hepworth Dixon writes of the 'real sense of fleetingness and fragility', and suggests that 'existence is only an impression, perhaps an illusion.'[6] These descriptions are particularly appropriate for George Egerton's stories which are almost invariably narrated in the present tense with the emphasis often falling on 'A Psychological Moment', as one of her stories is called. Ella D'Arcy likewise writes rather impressionistic stories in the same vein, as the titles of her collections *Monochromes* (1895) and *Modern Instances* (1898) suggest. In 'The Elegie', the first story in *Monochromes*, for example, Ella D'Arcy describes the hero's

---

[2] See in particular Walter Allen, *The Short Story in English* (Oxford, 1981), Clare Hanson, *Short Stories and Short Fictions* (Basingstoke, 1985), Peter Keating, *The Haunted Study* (London, 1989), and Patricia Stubbs, *Women and Fiction: Feminism and the Novel 1880-1920* (Brighton, 1979).

[3] W. Somerset Maugham, *Points of View* (London, 1958), p. 150.

[4] Frank O'Connor, *The Lonely Voice: A Study of the Short Story* (Cleveland, 1962), pp. 22-23.

[5] Nadine Gordimer, 'South Africa' in 'The International Symposium on the Short Story', *Kenyon Review* 30 (1968), p. 459.

[6] 'Woman's Ways', *The Sketch* (August 15, 1917), p. viii.

'curiosity to probe sensations',[7] which could almost be a *leitmotif* for her own writing as well as for that of George Egerton. In the same story she also writes of a woman artist, Flore Vasseur, who 'obtained by illegitimate methods a brilliancy of coloring as unrivalled as it was transitory'.[8] This desire to capture by whatever means the intensity of emotions in precise moments of transition and their forcible lack of fixity clearly prefigures Modernist writings such as Virginia Woolf's 'moments of being', D.H. Lawrence's 'tremulations on the ether' and James Joyce's 'epiphanies'. The subtitle of Ella Hepworth Dixon's own collection of short stories would also imply that she was working in the same mode. I hope to show that this was merely one aspect of her writing and that her themes and style were more varied than the majority of her contemporaries.

In the 1896 article on 'My Faith and My Work' in *Woman* Ella Hepworth Dixon mentions spending 'some toilsome years practising the art of story-telling in the newspapers and magazines'.[9] An earlier review of her life and work in the same magazine in December 1894 notes 'a little more than ten years ago her short stories first began to appear among the "Town and Country Tales" in *The World*, and she has since been a constant contributor to that paper.'[10] Not one such tale, however, bears her signature, and it was only after the success of her novel that she signed stories in *The World*'s Christmas Numbers from 1894 to 1899. Elsewhere, nevertheless, in the *Lady's Pictorial*, the *Sunday Times*, *Woman*, and *The Woman's World*, her name appears in full from 1888 onwards. The first occurrences I have found are for 'Dr Patmore's Patient' in the *Sunday Times*, 'Murder – or Mercy?' in *The Woman's World* and 'A Winter Idyl' in *The Lady's Pictorial Christmas Number*, all in 1888.

It is interesting, therefore, to note the 'black gauze veil of Anonymity', to use her own expression employed in 'My Faith and My Work', over the series of sketches which constituted her first book. Her *Times'* obituary[11] ascribes two novels to Ella Hepworth Dixon, but in her memoirs she calls *My Flirtations* her first book,[12] and describes *The Story of a Modern Woman* as 'my first (and only) novel',[13] so I prefer to consider the former as 'short fiction'. *My Flirtations* had previously been published anonymously in serial form in the *Lady's Pictorial* from January 23 to April 30, 1892, and in book form they were ascribed to Margaret Wynman, the first person narrator usually called Peggy. As far as I have been able to ascertain Ella Hepworth Dixon's choice of pseudonym has no deeper significance other than adding to the overall whimsical tone of the writing and being especially fitting for a woman who does indeed set out to win a man, as was expected of all women. *The Sketch* reviewer's opinion that 'it is fitting that her

7 'The Elegie', *Monochromes* (London, 1895), p. 63.
8 *Ibid.* p. 49.
9 'My Faith and My Work', *Woman* (September 23, 1896), p. 8.
10 'Marjorie', *Woman* (December 5, 1894), p. 5.
11 *The Times* (January 13, 1932), p. 14.
12 *As I Knew Them* (London, 1930), p. 35.
13 *Ibid.* p. 187.

name should have more than a suspicion of allegory'[14] would support such a claim. The critic in the *Lady's Pictorial*, however, suggests an almost wilful desire to confuse or arouse curiosity:

> It is not for me to say whether the owner of the clever pen, and the observant eyes, is not already known to the world under another name. In fact, I have my own strong suspicions as to the sex of the writer, and I should not be at all surprised to learn that the pseudonym hides the identity of a well-known literary man. The secret, of course, remains hidden in the breast of the Editor, but I feel sure that my opinion is not without foundation.[15]

In her memoirs Ella Hepworth Dixon claims, 'As it had a foolish title (suggested for publishing reasons) I never owned to its authorship ... .'[16] In the 1896 *Woman* article, she expressed similar embarrassment, although it is difficult to evaluate the veracity of her feelings:

> The booklet bore the egregious title (need I say a 'publisher's title'?) of *My Flirtations*, and had clothed itself, unbeknown to the author, in a cover of violent pink, on which some person who will be for ever hateful to me had designed, with considerable archness, a silver fan. Oh, that title; oh, that cover; oh, that silver fan! What have I not suffered from the very thoughts of you?

It might be argued that a 'considerable archness' is a regular feature of her work, and from the outset in serial form the sketches were entitled *My Flirtations*. Perhaps significantly when *My Flirtations* came out in America, the cover was changed from pink to green with a gold design on it. Her distaste, however, was not shared by all: the critic in *Woman*, for instance, described it as 'prettily bound'.[17] Modern readers may judge for themselves as the British Library possesses an original copy.

Letters exchanged between the author and the publishers of the book, Chatto and Windus, reveal no mention at all of any desire to change the title. On the other hand, they continually express concern about 'what name is to be given on the title page'. A day after offering Ella Hepworth Dixon thirty-five pounds[18] for the reproduction of her 'social sketches entitled *My Flirtations*', Andrew Chatto wrote to her sister, Marion, on the subject:

---

[14] L.F.A., 'The Book and Its Story: "*My Flirtations*"', *The Sketch* (February 8, 1893), pp. 90-91.

[15] 'Blue Stocking' (Miss Curtis), *Lady's Pictorial* (October 15, 1892), p. 583.

[16] *As I Knew Them* (London, 1930), p. 35.

[17] 'Book Chat', *Woman* (November 30, 1892), p. 13.

[18] As a point of comparison, Gissing had earned £ 150 for *New Grub Street*, a three-volume novel published the year before *My Flirtations*, but his earlier books had only earned him fifty pounds each.

> I had not noticed that 'My Flirtations' were published anonymously, and was under the impression that your sister would put her own name to a publication of the sketches in book form. I would always advise authors to secure to their own names any popularity that may attract to a success, by always publishing in their own names - most pseudonyms are open secrets. - But this is not a point I would press in opposition to your sister's wishes, if on consideration she decides to adopt some other pen name.[19]

This might suggest that Marion Hepworth Dixon was acting as an agent for her younger sister. Both sisters are mentioned in the *Lady's Pictorial* series on Lady Journalists which appeared from November 1893 to February 1894, but the fact that the elder sister is mentioned second would imply that she remained, without doubt, less famous than her sibling. In her memoirs, when discussing the success of *The Story of a Modern Woman*, which she had dedicated 'To My Sister Marion', Ella Hepworth Dixon mentions being invited out a great deal with her sister, perhaps as chaperons for each other. Marion Hepworth Dixon was better known as an art critic, as her regular articles in, for example, the *Magazine of Art* and *The Studio* would testify,[20] but she also produced works of short fiction, and even contributed two short stories to *The Yellow Book*: in Volume IV 'A Thief in the Night', described as 'gruesome in the extreme' by the critic in the *Lady's Pictorial*,[21] and 'The Runaway' in Volume XIII.

In the next letter to Ella Hepworth Dixon, apologizing for being unable to pay royalties, but offering half the profits from an American edition, the publisher writes, 'The question of anonymity we shall be pleased to leave to your decision.'[22] By August, however, Ella Hepworth Dixon is asked more urgently, 'Perhaps you could give us a choice of two or three pseudonyms, should you still not like to use your own name, though we should of course prefer this latter.'[23] Andrew Chatto generally preferred writers to use their own names, but perhaps there was also a certain prestige associated with the name of Ella Hepworth Dixon's famous father, although by then he had been dead for thirteen years, in which case it might well be the origin of Mary Erle's editor in *The Story of a Modern Woman* paying not so much for the quality of her first piece of work, as for her father's name. '"The name, of course," went on the editor, "... the name counts for *something*. Your late father's name carries weight with a *certain* section of the public"'[24] (her italics).

---

[19] Chatto and Windus archives. Letter dated April 28 (1892). All the correspondence between Chatto and Windus and Ella Hepworth Dixon cited in this chapter is to be found in the University of Reading Archives and Manuscripts Department.

[20] See Appendix 4 for a limited list of Marion Hepworth Dixon's writings.

[21] *Lady's Pictorial* (February 2, 1895), p. 158.

[22] Chatto and Windus archives. Letter dated May 11 (1892).

[23] *Ibid*. Letter dated August 9 (1892).

[24] *The Story of a Modern Woman* (1894, repr. Peterborough, 2004), p. 108. Incidentally, in line 11 of 'Ulysses', the poem by Tennyson from which Mary Erle selects her father's favourite maxim for the inscription on his gravestone, the hero proudly declares, 'I am become a name'.

Similarly, in *My Flirtations* it is the fame of the heroine's father as a member of the Royal Academy which attracts some suitors as much as, if not more than, her own charms.

Chatto and Windus' insistence on her own name might also indicate that Ella Hepworth Dixon had already begun to make a name for herself. Indeed, by October 1891, the name 'Ella Hepworth Dixon' obviously had some attraction for the public as 'The Special Winter Number' of *Woman* advertised 'Every Story, Article, and Illustration will be the work of a Woman', and included 'A Short Story by Ella Hepworth Dixon'.[25] Furthermore, after *My Flirtations*, 'Margaret Wynman' also became a selling point. For example 'The Special Holiday Number' of *Woman*, 1893, advertised as one of its 'special features' 'a ROMANTIC STORY by MARGARET WYNMAN, Author of "MY FLIRTATIONS"'.[26] And, in spite of Ella Hepworth Dixon's protestations, when *The Story of a Modern Woman* first began to appear in serial form it was signed 'Ella Hepworth Dixon, ("Margaret Wynman", Author of "My Flirtations")'.[27] It is interesting to note that in the later exchange of letters between Ella Hepworth Dixon and Grant Richards before the publication of *One Doubtful Hour* the publisher expresses reservations about the financial success of a collection of short stories 'even with your name'.[28] Interestingly, this time all the transactions took place without the intervention of Marion Hepworth Dixon.

Undoubtedly *My Flirtations* was received enthusiastically. Barbara in *Woman*'s 'Book Chat' begins, 'A prettily bound and exceptionally clever and amusing little series of sketches is *My Flirtations*, by Margaret Wynman ... ',[29] and adds, 'This little volume ... is much better worth reading than many more pretentious volumes.' Ella Hepworth Dixon herself gives most credit for the success of the book to 'the delightful illustrations by Mr (now Sir Bernard) Partridge of Punch'.[30] The critic in *The Saturday Review* in part agreed with her: '*My Flirtations* has in Mr Bernard Partridge a sympathetic illustrator, who in his own line is unrivalled.'[31] In fact, Bernard Partridge had provided the illustrations for the original serialized version of *My Flirtations*, and regularly illustrated Ella Hepworth Dixon's short stories in *Lady's Pictorial*, especially those published in the Christmas Numbers. In a letter dated 28th April, 1892, Andrew Chatto had informed Marion Hepworth Dixon that if her sister accepted his publication offer he would 'arrange to obtain

[25] The advertisement appeared several times in the pages of *Woman*, for example October 21, 1891, p. 16 and January 13, 1892, p. 2.

[26] Likewise this advertisement appeared on several occasions, for instance in *Woman* (June 7, 1893), p. 14.

[27] *Lady's Pictorial* (January 6, 1894), p. 6.

[28] Letter dated January 18, 1904. All the correspondence between Grant Richards and Ella Hepworth Dixon cited in this chapter is to be found in the 'Rarebooks and Special Collections' library, University of Illinois, Urbana-Champaign.

[29] 'Book Chat', *Woman* (November 30, 1892), p. 12.

[30] *As I Knew Them* (London, 1930), p. 35.

[31] (Unsigned), *The Saturday Review* (October 8, 1892), p. 419.

the illustrations from "The Lady's Pictorial"'. Notwithstanding, however charming they might be, if 'the little volume ... had a vogue among such formidable critics as Heads of Oxford Colleges and the like', as the author claims, it was not only because of the pictures. Robert Ross, friend of Oscar Wilde and a 'universal favourite in London' according to Ella Hepworth Dixon in her memoirs, declared in his review 'a new humorist had arisen,' an opinion shared by several others. 'The older humour is not dead after all - at least the announcement was premature,' affirms the critic in *The Saturday Review*, 'and the lady who writes under the name of Margaret Wynman has vindicated her sex from the old charge of having no appreciation of humour, old or new. *My Flirtations* is one of the most amusing books we have come across for a long time.' The *Lady's Pictorial* reviewer also praises *My Flirtations* as:

> Distinctly good work. It would have been so easy to vulgarize the subject, but Miss Wynman is not vulgar. She is satirical, too, without being bitter; amusing without being farcical; frivolous without being flimsy; observant without being hypercritical, and quite as ready to pick holes in herself as in her admirers![32]

This highlights one of the distinguishing features of Ella Hepworth Dixon's work in general. Both in her fiction and non-fiction, especially in her later weekly contributions to the *Lady's Pictorial* and *The Sketch*, Ella Hepworth Dixon regularly displays a fine sense of humour, sometimes at her own expense. In the 'Foreword' to *As I Knew Them* she claims, 'I possess what Meredith says is a test of a sense of humour: I thoroughly enjoy a joke against myself',[33] and, as mentioned in chapter one, promptly tells of a young man being enamoured of her portrait, but fleeing when he catches sight of the flesh and blood woman 'grubby with oil-paint' and 'dressed in an unbecoming jersey'. Her passing references on several occasions in her fiction, as in *The Story of a Modern Woman* and 'A Scribbler's Comedy', to 'a female journalist, who wore a waterproof and a pince-nez, ... with a superior expression'[34] may likewise reveal a certain self-mockery.

On other occasions, nevertheless, her intents are more serious. One of the principal characters in *The Story of a Modern Woman*, Alison Ives, suggests that a sense of humour is 'what women ought to cultivate above all other things, especially the poorer classes'. 'With a keen sense of the ridiculous, they would never fall in love at all; and as to improvident marriages, they simply wouldn't exist.'[35] George Egerton, likewise, perhaps unexpectedly, ocasionally advocates a humorous approach to courting and marriage. In 'A Conjugal Episode', a story from *Flies in Amber* (1905), she declares, 'it is in human mating that the true spirit of comedy may be found sitting cheek by jowl with tragedy.' She continues:

---

32 'Blue Stocking' (Miss Curtis), *Lady's Pictorial* (October 15, 1892), p. 583.
33 'Pensées de Femme', *Lady's Pictorial* (June 25, 1898), p. 963.
34 *The Story of a Modern Woman* (1894, repr. Peterborough, 2004), p. 129.
35 *Ibid*. p. 74.

> Unfortunately for those immediately concerned, it is the comedy that is obvious in the consideration of the unions of their acquaintances, whilst the tragedy grips them in their own. I take an interest in marriages. A sense of humour, coupled with a nice curiosity as to human motives, may lead an observer at times into singular company, and add a fresh *conte drôlatique* to his (sic) collection of conjugal episodes.[36]

Ella Hepworth Dixon returns to this theme in her 1899 article in *The Humanitarian* on 'Why Women are Ceasing to Marry': 'Now that we have educated our womenfolk into a sense of humour - and there is no surer test of breadth of mind - this wifely meekness (married ladies ... looking up to their spouses with admiration tempered by awe) is no longer possible.'[37] At the end of the article she predicts, with questionable accuracy:

> It would seem certain that if woman continues to cultivate her faculties and her sense of humour - to exercise, in short, her feminine prerogative of deliberate choice in the great affair of matrimony - that the standard of human felicity will be steadily raised, and the wedded state will shine forth in a different light to that in which it stands revealed to many thoughtful persons to-day.[38]

Although it is, as usual, remarkably difficult to gauge the author's tone, terms such as 'the great affair of matrimony' and 'the wedded state' suggest undercurrents of irony resonant in the last lines of *My Flirtations*:

> *Womanlike*, my sister throws down the 'Twentieth Century', and we bend curiously over the box as the maid lifts gingerly out a garment of shimmering white and silver from under a layer of tulle. *Symbols of the Eternal Feminine*, those lengths of glittering satin flaunt themselves over the sofa and along the floor, lighting up the dim little room with their sumptuous whiteness, while, like a June cloud, the foam of tulle floats for an instant in the winter dusk.
>
> It is my wedding gown. (my italics)

The series of 'flirtations' thus ends with the traditional betrothal, and yet, as *The Sketch* critic points out, 'there is no apparent reason why she (Margaret Wynman) should like Mr Ford well enough to marry him'. In a later article Ella Hepworth Dixon provides a possible answer, worthy of the pen of Oscar Wilde or Noel Coward: '"You never marry the man you like, of course," said a clever and charming matron to me the other day; "you just look round, after a time, and accept the least objectionable person you know".'[39] In *My Flirtations* one suspects Ella Hepworth Dixon is playing with readers' expectations as well as deliberately

[36] 'A Conjugal Episode', *Flies in Amber* (London, 1905), pp. 103-104.
[37] 'Why Women are Ceasing to Marry', *The Humanitarian* 14 (1899), p. 392.
[38] *Ibid*. p. 396.
[39] 'Pensées de Femme', *Lady's Pictorial* (June 11, 1898), p. 883.

making fun of those of her own sex who, to her mind, take themselves too seriously. At the same time she is distancing herself from the polemics of the marriage debate. More than merely a means of entertainment, humour can thus be a shield as well as a weapon.

For many women of the period, however, the tragic elements were no laughing matter and far outweighed the comic. Much of the writing by women such as Olive Schreiner, Mona Caird and Ella d'Arcy concentrated on the more solemn aspects of such issues, leading their detractors to accuse them, with some justification, of being too introspective and morbid. It might be argued that during the course of her career Ella Hepworth Dixon, too, became increasingly more serious. She never again quite attained the lightness of touch which permeates *My Flirtations*, except perhaps in her memoirs. On the other hand, although some topics such as maternity[40] are never treated in jest, she generally did manage to strike a balance between drawing attention to society's injustices to women and, with the help of a few comic interludes, pointing out humanity's weaknesses in general. This helps to explain why *My Flirtations* was greeted with such enthusiasm by readers of both sexes. In the opinion of *The Saturday Review* critic the work 'is something quite fresh. ... there is none of that terrible sameness too common in fiction and real life.' There is certainly no hint of morbidity or degeneration which some contemporary critics feared were infiltrating the inner fibres of society. As *The Sketch* comments 'Miss Wynman's adventures in the labyrinth of love are set down with not a little sparkle, an agreeable flavour of malice and a keen appreciation of the foibles of certain masculine types.'[41]

In this respect Ella Hepworth Dixon's sense of humour is of the Wildean variety, where wit and irony are employed to make fun of social mores. For example, when describing an outing with suitor number VI, Dr Styles, a country practitioner, Margaret Wynman, anticipating Ernest/Jack Worthing, declares, 'Life ... would be tolerable if it were not for its pleasures, and possibly English summers would be less dreary to look back upon were it not for the inevitable picnic.'[42] In fact, several of Margaret Wynman's devotees do seem to epitomize elements of the effeminate *fin de siècle* dandy, either in their speech or behaviour. Comments by the critics suggest that much fun must have been had in certain circles speculating on Ella Hepworth Dixon's possible real-life models, including Oscar Wilde and Richard Le Gallienne. Interestingly, the chapter which did not appear in the pages of the *Lady's Pictorial* deals with Duncan Clive, an actor/manager, 'the most daringly thin disguise of an actual personality', according to *The Sketch* critic.[43]

---

[40] In agreement with Alice Meynell and with uncharacteristic vehemence, Ella Hepworth Dixon expresses her dislike of the Victorian attitude to motherhood, exemplified in the works of Dickens where 'for a woman to bear a child is a humorous episode'. *As I Knew Them* (London, 1930), p. 121.

[41] Signed L.F.A. 'The Book and Its Story: *My Flirtations*', *The Sketch* (February 8, 1893), pp. 90-91.

[42] *My Flirtations* (London, 1892), chapter VI, p. 64.

[43] *The Sketch* (February 8, 1893), pp. 90-91.

VAL REDMOND.

Figure 4.1 Val Redmond, suitor number V, *My Flirtations*

This may in part suggest the real reason for her wish to remain anonymous.

Margaret Wynman's first admirer, Gilbert Mandell, 'the artistic suitor', considered by *The Saturday Review* to be 'one of the most successful of types':

> Was a middle-sized man of thirty-four, with rather pink cheeks, and a slightly bald forehead. His hands were fleshy and white, and had exquisitely pared and polished nails. A manicure usually attended to his hands. He always had the latest scandal; and sometimes, when he was going to say something specially malicious, he hesitated a little in his speech, not from false shame, but because he was so delighted with what he was going to say. For the rest, he was always beautifully dressed, and generally affected fashions that were coming in.[44]

Elsewhere he is described as 'an example of that extremely modern mixture, a man of fashion and a critic'.[45] He tries to cultivate her mind, but when he finally 'alluded in a roundabout sort of way to an organ he was pleased to call his heart',[46] she realizes it is impossible to continue the relationship. This is also partly for snobbish reasons since his father had made his money in drains, but he, too, is in many ways a snob, so one feels no sympathy when his advances are rejected and he takes himself off abroad.

Val Redmond, suitor number V (figure 4.1), which the *Lady's Pictorial* critic thought 'perhaps the most successful in the book', is of a similar type and has even more of the dandy about him:

> He was curiously pretty, incredibly malicious, and indisputably 'smart', with a nice house in Sloane Street, where he entertained a great deal, and a little following of young gentlemen who copied his neckties and buttonholes, and whom one saw giggling together in corners and calling each other pet names.[47]

Whereas Gilbert Mandell had, according to Christina, the narrator's sister, shown 'a depraved taste for schoolgirls', Val Redmond liked the society of 'elderly dames', particularly Countesses, Duchesses and Ladies. The affair was, therefore, never very promising and was appropriately 'hastened by gossips, and ... killed with a *mot*' from Christina's notoriously acid tongue. Peggy Wynman and Val Redmond nevertheless remain on dining-terms.

Claud Carson, suitor number VII, is also a favourite with the ladies and a further variation on the theme of the affected artistic type; *The Sketch* reviewer even suspects 'a rather audacious portrait from life':

> All heads were turned in the direction of the young poet as he stood talking to the Royal Duchess, his beautiful eyes fixed on her face, while

---

[44] *My Flirtations* (London, 1892), chapter I, p. 8.
[45] *Ibid.* p. 10.
[46] *Ibid.* p. 11.
[47] *Ibid.* chapter V, p. 48.

> occasionally, with a pretty, fatigued movement, he raised a white, graceful hand and pushed back the lock of blonde hair from his forehead.[48]

He ends up marrying his landlady's daughter, 'as poets generally do' according to Christina.

As one might expect, Ella Hepworth Dixon also makes fun of other types of various ages and aspirations such as the Oxford scholar, Frank Harding, suitor number IV, who eventually goes off to the colonies, or the Hon. Julian Clancy, number VIII on the list, who is only interested in celebrities, or yet again number XI, René Lavasseur, a French gentleman painter who is 'swallowed up' by Paris, or the dashing man in uniform, Tony Lambert, devotee number II, who has to marry money in order to maintain the family estate. 'We all know Tony,' declares 'Blue Stocking' in the *Lady's Pictorial*. 'He generally comes not from Sheffield, but from Woolwich, and he is always "thoroughly pleased with himself, his regiment, and his belongings".'[49]

Nor is it only men who are targeted. Women also come under close scrutiny, especially the pretentious provincials, painters of water-colours and readers of Rider Haggard and Edna Lyall. By means of a pithy phrase or two, Ella Hepworth Dixon reveals a great deal about her contemporaries' daily lives, from their courting rituals and motivations to their entertainments, including music-halls and opera, *Samson and Delilah* at Covent Garden and Ibsen's *Hedda Gabler*, as well as social shams and intellectual snobberies. Very little escapes her sharp eye for significant detail and by the end of the thirteenth 'flirtation' the reader is left with a fairly comprehensive collage of the domestic and public life of a certain class in late Victorian England.

Even the traditionally sacrosanct icons, the home, the family, and marriage are treated with a certain cynicism. Margaret Wynman describes herself as 'a middle-class damsel of modest dowry' who engages in husband-hunting, not so much as a necessity as one might expect, but as a sport. Her sister, Christina, who 'doesn't care for young men', and is 'brutally cynical; but then she is clever', even likens her heart to a frame in which she temporarily places the picture of the man of the moment. George Egerton uses the same image in her short story 'An Empty Frame' in *Keynotes*, but with greater poignancy, this time to indicate constancy. A frame stands empty on the middle of the bedroom mantel-board and is filled with the picture it once held by the mind's eye of the female protagonist, now married to another. Ella D'Arcy, on the other hand, introduces a variation on the stereotypical flirt in her short story, 'The Pleasure Pilgrim', who even has an alpenstock 'decorated with a long succession of names, which, ribbon-like, were twisted round and round it, carved in wood'. 'They are not the names of the peaks she has climbed, or the towns she has passed through; they're the names of the men she has fooled. And there's room for more,'[50] the host warns his young male guest. Lulie

[48] *Ibid.* chapter VII, p. 79.
[49] *Lady's Pictorial* (October 15, 1892), p. 583.
[50] 'The Pleasure Pilgrim', *Monochromes* (London, 1895), pp. 183-184.

Thayer is further described as an 'adventuress, but an end-of-the-century one. She doesn't travel for profit, but for pleasure. She has no desire to swindle her neighbour, but to amuse herself,'[51] very much like Peggy Wynman. Ella D'Arcy's story, however, has a more sinister outcome as ultimately the heroine shoots herself, some say unintentionally, merely to frighten her lover, others say to prove her love, and yet another claims it was her one final histrionic gesture.

Like Lulie Thayer, and many a literary heroine, Peggy Wynman has a close female confidante,[52] but Christina does not play the role of the typical gooseberry. It is to her that the heroine turns if she wants 'to get out of a scrape', not to her mother, 'who would not be of the faintest use under such circumstances'. She had married at seventeen and has 'no patience with her daughter's philandering'. Peggy's comment is, 'It must be like eternally dining off roast mutton to marry at seventeen, and settle down dully and respectably for the rest of your natural life.' In an earlier short story, 'A Winter Idyl',[53] which contains several elements reworked in *My Flirtations*, including two sisters, one more knowing and far more flirtatious than the other, their chaperon aunt was also married at eighteen, much to the scorn of the narrator: 'People married infants in pinafores, with inky fingers, in those days.' Such a flippant reaction to marriages of the sort, which were clearly not uncommon, was not shared by everyone. For example, one of George Egerton's more harrowing stories, 'Virgin Soil' from *Discords* (1894), also deals with a young woman who was married at seventeen and who comes back five years later to accuse her mother of rearing her in ignorance, not innocence, and then selling her into marriage, 'a legal prostitution, a nightly degradation, a hateful yoke', an issue frequently discussed by New Woman writers. Ella Hepworth Dixon's aim throughout *My Flirtations* is primarily to amuse, as she admits in the above-mentioned 'My Faith and My Work' interview in *Woman* in which she refers to it as 'frivolous'. In *My Flirtations* therefore she passes over the more serious implications of such practices, although she does treat such topics with more gravity elsewhere.

As it is, Peggy Wynman is clearly more knowledgeable than many girls of her age, and her cynical sister Christina, whose interests vary from Socialism to vegetarianism to 'Under-payment of Feminine Labour', would seem to be even more aware of the world and have all the makings of a notorious New Woman. Their father is a Royal Academician which allows Ella Hepworth Dixon to make a few scathing remarks about the English Art world, a theme to which she would return with more seriousness later in her novel and at regular intervals in her non-fiction. As mentioned earlier, it is the father's celebrity which attracts many young men, but he assumes relatively little responsibility for his daughters except in drawing the line at Peggy's posing for a portrait of Delilah, although she has

---

[51] *Ibid*. p. 182.

[52] Ella Hepworth Dixon often bases her stories on two sisters of different personalities as in 'A Winter Idyl', 'An Idyl of the Engineers', 'It's Own Reward', 'A Suburban Tragedy', and 'The Fortune of Flora'.

[53] *The Lady's Pictorial Christmas Number* (1888), pp. 25-27.

already posed as, predictably, the madonna, a nun and a bacchante. Parental control is, therefore, minimal and what there is, is laughable. This might pyschologically explain why Peggy finally accepts a mature older man, a wealthy stockbroker, as otherwise he is described as being devoid of any surface charm, except perhaps his silence, and his being visibly 'born to be henpecked' and having 'the *cachet*, the unmistakable appearance of a *husband*'[54] (her italics).

My Flirtations is thus an entertaining comedy of manners, but it can also be read as a social document, revealing much about *fin de siècle* middle-class society and contemporary affairs such as emigration, the cult of the metropolis as opposed to the provinces, the better divorce laws in the United States, and higher education for women. At times Ella Hepworth Dixon employs expressions like 'trembling chords', or 'Symbols of the Eternal Feminine', or the 'primeval one', which are more commonly associated with writers such as George Egerton and Ella D'Arcy whose stories are regularly concerned with attempting to identify what they see as the very essence of Womanhood. It is difficult, however, not to suspect Ella Hepworth Dixon of satire when she writes of Woman's 'untamed spirits', her 'witch-like elements' or her 'divine fibre', especially in a work such as *My Flirtations*. In this aspect she has more in common with contemporary male wits such as Oscar Wilde or Max Beerbohm than fellow women writers. In examining her other short stories I hope to show different sides to her writing.

Before the publication of *My Flirtations* Ella Hepworth Dixon had contributed many individual stories to several magazines during the 1880s. She continued to write short works of fiction for periodicals, including *Ladies' Field*, *Pall Mall Magazine*, *Woman* and *The Yellow Book*, as well as *The Lady's Pictorial Christmas Number* at regular intervals throughout the 1890s and the early years of the twentieth century, the last story so far found being 'The Capture of Miss Cohen', published in the *Pall Mall Magazine* in February 1907.[55] It was only in 1904, however, that a collection of her stories appeared in book form. The collection was published by Grant Richards and dedicated to Eugénie Phillips 'whose friendship was of the rare and exquisite kind.'[56] This may have been 'simply a commercial exercise',[57] as Peter Keating suggests was fairly common at that time and which could 'involve complicated negotiations'. A rejection letter dated 'August 28, '3' from Andrew Chatto indicates that Ella Hepworth Dixon had tried to publish a collection of short stories earlier and had remained in contact with her original publishers even though she had declined their offer for the publication of her novel. It is not absolutely clear if this is 1893 or 1903, but it is catalogued with correspondence from 7. 3. 93 - 4. 12. 93, which would indicate that Ella Hepworth Dixon took her affairs into her own hands rather soon after the success of *My Flirtations* and no longer relied on her sister's intervention. Another letter dated

---

[54] *My Flirtations* (London, 1892), chapter XIII, p. 154.

[55] *Pall Mall Magazine* (February, 1907), pp. 229-234.

[56] *As I Knew Them* (London, 1930), p. 68.

[57] *The Haunted Study* (London, 1989), p. 41. For further details about the publication of short story collections the whole of chapter one is particularly interesting.

July 17, 1903 from the publisher Grant Richards suggests that she had been asked to make certain revisions, and a note from the author explaining that three of the stories had been re-written does indeed appear in the frontispiece. On the whole, however, the adjustments appear to be minor, often simply a question of details such as dates or names. Another letter dated January 21, 1904 indicates that a different title, 'The Pity of It', had been considered, but Ella Hepworth Dixon had preferred 'One Doubtful Hour', the title of one of the stories, and, as the other had already been used, her choice was kept. The addition of 'And Other Sidelights on the Feminine Temperament' clearly reflects Peter Keating's claim that there was a tendency to give collections a greater degree of formal unity. It might be argued that the short story collection, such as James Joyce's *The Dubliners*, constitutes a subgenre of its own. Interestingly, Virginia Woolf's *Mrs Dalloway* was initially intended to be a series of stories entitled *Mrs Dalloway's Party*.

All of the stories in Ella Hepworth Dixon's collection are therefore predictably concerned with women and women's lives, and offer fascinating examples of many of the pre-occupations of what has been dubbed New Woman fiction. As discussed in chapter two, throughout the *fin de siècle* period many New Woman writers were challenging the myths of romantic love and marital expectations, and consequently experimenting with variations on the traditional marriage plot in their fiction. Few accepted marriage as an end in itself, but Ella Hepworth Dixon is rarely as categorical as, for example, Olive Schreiner or Ella D'Arcy in condemning all marriages as doomed or necessarily oppressive for women. Like George Egerton, she also occasionally adopts a male persona and thus raises questions about the implications of marriage from a man's point of view. She tends to display a rather practical, open-minded approach, developed at greater length in her *Humanitarian* essay on the subject:

> If young and pleasing women are permitted by public opinion to go to college, to live alone, to travel, to have a profession, to belong to a club, to give parties, to read and discuss whatever seems good to them, and to go to theatres without masculine escort, they have most of the privileges - and others thrown in - for which the girl of twenty or thirty years ago was ready to barter herself for the first suitor who offered himself and the shelter of his name.[58]

Ella Hepworth Dixon is here raising subtle questions about the motivations for marriage and suggesting that it may no longer be so necessary or attractive, and consequently spinsterhood is no longer an anathema. Ella Hepworth Dixon's own unmarried state may naturally have made her more indulgent of spinsters both in her fiction and her non-fiction. In an earlier story, 'Wyllie's Wife',[59] described as 'a most exciting story of Monte Carlo' by the critic in *Woman,* one of the characters, Miss Pollexfen, referred to as 'smart', 'with her thirty obvious years, her dyed

---

[58] 'Why Women are Ceasing to Marry', *The Humanitarian* 14 (1899), p. 394.

[59] *The Lady's Pictorial Christmas Number* (1891), p. 17. It was not, however, included in the published collection.

bronze hair, her caustic tongue, and an air of assurance,' exclaims, 'Old maids? ... Bosh! There are only lady-bachelors nowadays. Who is going to marry when they can have such a good time single?' Obviously, such liberty is limited to a certain class, as she declares she 'can always *buy* ... a *little* husband any day' (my italics), but the implications of such statements are far-reaching. The ageing spinster, for example, is no longer a subject of ridicule, but can even allow herself to cast aspersions on conventions. Unlike some of her contemporaries, however, Ella Hepworth Dixon, largely thanks to her satirical tone, manages to express such ideas in ways not to outrage her readers. As the reviewer in *The World* notes, 'Miss Hepworth Dixon takes on the whole a sombre view of life for women, but she is not a morbid writer, and she has the excellent gift of humour controlled by good taste and imparted in good English.'[60]

In 'The Fortune of Flora',[61] for instance, the intervention of a rather eccentric maiden aunt, Aunt Charlotte, a pleasant variation on the stock old maid figure, saves the situation. Unlike her younger sister who had married and whose 'fortune had long ago been swallowed up in her husband's embarrassments', she is 'a spinster of original turn, with a handsome dependence of her own',[62] a wily woman of the world, very much the New Woman who smokes and travels widely, even to darkest Africa. The story this time begins 'on the eve of the adventure of matrimony' for a young couple, with each party expecting financial support from the other. When the newly-weds in turn secretly seek the aunt's advice she takes them under her wing and eventually leaves them her fortune. At first a certain mystery shrouds their occupations: the wife has no idea what the husband's work is and he has no idea that she works at all. What is important is that both husband and wife are equally willing to seek paid employment outside the home which leads to a better, more equal conjugal relationship within. There is a cheerful note throughout the story which again belies the often held notion that woman writers were incapable of presenting anything but morbid images.

Nevertheless, the title story in the collection, 'One Doubtful Hour',[63] is of a kind to leave readers 'harrowed or disquieted',[64] according to the reviewer in *The Illustrated London News*. Ella Hepworth Dixon's 'merciless truth of ... observation' highlights the typical double standards in attitudes and expectations of men and women, 'the one doubtful hour' having extremely different signification for the male and female characters. The duality of viewpoints is emphasized from the first lines. The characters are introduced simply as 'a man and a woman', but while he was 'grizzled', well past his youth, forty-three or four, we learn very shortly 'just the right age', she, albeit much younger, in her early thirties, is described as 'faded'. Their speech also differentiates them, but in an unusual way:

---

[60] P. and Q., 'Pages in Waiting', *The World* (July 5, 1904), p. 32.
[61] Originally published in the *Lady's Pictorial* (November 22, 1902), pp. 850-853.
[62] *Ibid.* p. 851.
[63] Originally published in *The Lady's Pictorial Christmas Number* (1897), pp. 16-21.
[64] (Unsigned), 'A Reviewer's Miscellany', *The Illustrated London News* (August 20, 1904), p. 260.

his is formal, hers is full of 'that particular military slang' one would more likely expect of a masculine character. Then, more significantly, while 'with a little sigh of pleasure' he announces, 'Why, we're almost home', she doesn't 'seem to look forward to getting back to England with as much pleasure and interest.' 'Home isn't always the happiest place,' she replies and 'suddenly realized that she had said the wrong thing'.

Indeed! Wasn't home supposed to be woman's sphere, the ideal place where her influence could be felt most? The colonel later admits 'she was still associated, in his mind, with home, and green parsonage gardens, and the narrow convenances of the upper middle class.' He, too, had let his imagination get the better of him; she is never of that class. Sadly, 'home! This word meant to Effie a dining-room in a mildewy crescent in Westsea, her mother's bedroom contiguous to their one living-room, a damp bedroom of her own built in the garden; an attic for the two little sisters.' To make matters worse, 'on the drawing-room floor lived Major Harkness, with his wife and ever-increasing young family'. The 'sordid economies' of the lives of so many were very different from the colonel's expectations: a short stay with his sister in Ryde and then 'a nice house, with a moderate rent, in Earl's Court'.

Not that Effie had not dreamt about home in conventional terms as:

> A snug little sitting-room of her own, doing fancy work by the fire while her husband read the newspaper. Her smiles would not have been forced; they would have come naturally enough then. She would like, above all, she thought, to have had a baby of her own, a baby with dimpling, creasy wrists, and little feet which kicked. She would like to have felt a child's fat arms locked round her neck ...

Fulfilling that dream, however, was not so easy. 'It was one of the eternal ironies of life that, in pursuit of this ideal, she had been obliged to dance and giggle, and say audacious things for exactly twelve years.' In an earlier story, 'A Man of Pleasure',[65] Ella Hepworth Dixon evokes the same theme. The heroine, Stella Magnus, still unmarried at thirty, initially described as 'an egotistical, self-reliant, self-analytical woman', recalling her own first ball, muses, 'How long ago it all seemed. ... Twelve years! An eternity in the short space in which a woman is young and admired. With a pang she felt herself suddenly middle-aged, ...' She is obviously far more independent, both financially and emotionally, than Effie, but nevertheless time and social pressures have taken their toll on her, too. Thus, 'regularly Effie appeared at the balls - those five-shilling dances which form the marriage-market. But how tired Effie was of balls! She had been to so many in her life, had danced so unceasingly in pursuit of an ever-vanishing husband.' Later in the story Ella Hepworth Dixon speaks of the 'old, old tragi-comedy; the degrading, unceasing pursuit of the possible husband....', and later still reiterates the 'eternal

---

[65] *The Lady's Pictorial Christmas Number* (1894), pp. 17-19. This story was not included in the re-published collection, but Ella Hepworth Dixon gives this title to the novel written by the heroine in 'The World's Slow Stain', a story I shall examine later.

tragi-comedy' of a 'woman, made desperate with disappointment' snatching 'at this straw of happiness like one who is drowning. With worn, cheap smiles and inviting eyes, she essayed to make herself desirable.' As if this were not enough, the prey in question is only too aware of the situation and sees 'she had, for all the world, the air of a lean and hungry huntress, and moreover, although he was too gallant to acknowledge it even to himself, that of a hungry huntress of men'.

The story reaches a climax when both realize their mis-apprehension, with the man's earlier recognition heightening the pathos. Colonel Simpson can hardly be considered a blackguard or an arch villain; to himself, to Effie and to the reader he appears a decent enough man. I would suggest that the reader's sympathies lie more with Effie largely because, although Ella Hepworth Dixon provides partial viewpoints of both protagonists, it is so much more difficult for Effie to fit the mould society has prepared for her. She is expected to find a husband and live happily ever after, but is scorned and shunned if she goes about this in an active rather than a passive way. The 'doubtful hour' takes on a further significance for the reader, since Ella Hepworth Dixon does not specify exactly what happened. Seemingly, Effie has again 'said the wrong thing', 'something silly'. She then sees 'that mixture of astonishment, disgust, and, yes, repulsion' on the colonel's face. Superficially, 'he had saved the situation' and 'she kept on smiling', until she could find refuge in the cloakroom and wait for him to leave. In the wet and dark she subsequently scurries back to the sacrosanct home, where she gases herself as the wife upstairs gives birth to yet another girl.

Such a summary might smack of melodrama, yet style and tone throughout are subdued. Almost echoing the 'professional tone' of the doctor who both examines the corpse and delivers the baby, Ella Hepworth Dixon finely juxtaposes death and birth: 'Effie lay on the bed, silent, inert, still dressed in her black ball-gown', as 'a shrill feminine voice on the stair' declares, 'Yes, it's a girl - a very fine little girl'. This conclusion lends itself to several interpretations. One might argue that this serves to accentuate the continual round of human affairs, and that in providing a new-born child Ella Hepworth Dixon refuses to end with total closure. To my mind the last image of Effie strongly recalls that of Herminia Barton, another 'woman who did', albeit rather differently. The latter suffers because she attempted to defy the constraints of society, whereas the former was desperately trying to conform to those very same demands. There is, therefore, greater pathos in Effie's situation and, without polemics or sensationalism, Ella Hepworth Dixon moves the reader far more than Grant Allen. The reviewer in *The Illustrated London News* clearly shared this impression: 'a suffering woman, mean and petty as her egoism may be, is a tragic figure when she is vivisected for us in this fashion'.[66] Later, in a letter written to the author during the war Frances Hodgson Burnett complimented Ella Hepworth Dixon on the style and content, 'the real and the human', of the story. 'If you could write something as simply poignantly human as that of the girl who made

[66] (Unsigned), 'A Reviewer's Miscellany', *The Illustrated London News* (August 20, 1904), p. 260.

her last desperate throw - in vain ... it would be immense. Not a thing of blood but of soul.'[67]

Effie is the eldest of three fatherless daughters living with their mother in restricted circumstances, all trying to find a suitable partner. She is, however, 'past thirty' and has 'a slightly morbid temperament' which helps to explain her suicide, common enough in *fin de siècle* literature, if not in life, too. Effie has clearly learnt her lessons well and behaves very much like Mary Erle in *The Story of a Modern Woman* when she hears that the man she has been waiting for is to marry someone else, 'she made an effort - an effort which completely prostrated her next day - to look smiling, calm, imperturbable. Why, the very fabric of civilization was based on that acquiescent feminine smile.'[68] Interestingly, this scene takes place at the theatre while Effie's is at a ball, emphasizing the public repercussions of private disappointments. Yet, even in the privacy of home, 'especially in her own house', 'a woman ... should always smile. It was on that acquiescent feminine smile that the whole fabric of civilization rested.'[69] Ella Hepworth Dixon's repetition of these phrases would suggest a preoccupation with such behaviour, and, indeed, it was a theme to which she returned regularly in both her fiction and non-fiction. For example, she devotes a whole 'Pensées de Femme' to the topic:

> Not the least tiresome of the conventions of Society is the one which ordains that we should always be smiling when we appear in public. It is a rule, to be sure, which is applied with special rigour to feminine persons … . A woman, however tired or worried or preoccupied she may be, is expected to be for ever 'wreathed in smiles' … .[70]

As in her novel, she also emphasizes the physical and mental cost, 'an outlay of energy, a disbursement of vitality, which should by rights be expended on worthier subjects'. In the above-mentioned story, 'Wyllie's Wife', the heroine, the unhappy wife of the title, likewise alone at a masked ball, declares, 'It was like life ... a crowd of people, and yet one wore a mask, and no one knew what one was really like.' Women were continually called upon to wear masks appropriate for every occasion. Ella Hepworth Dixon constantly appeals, if not for the disappearance of the mask, at least for greater understanding and compassion for what might lie behind it. When, for example, Effie sees the colonel enter the ball-room, she feels 'it would never do ... for Colonel Simpson ... to find her filling the dolorous role of wall-flower...'. Many, if not all, of Ella Hepworth Dixon's women, I would argue, are aware of playing roles, of fulfilling social expectations in behaving, externally at least, as women should, or rather as they are expected to. Perhaps the frequent references to mirrors, glasses, and reflections emphasize the importance of appearance. One of the most poignant moments in the story is surely where Effie catches sight of herself in a '*blurred* mirror opposite' (my italics). They could also

---

[67] Quoted in *As I Knew Them* (London, 1930), p. 98.

[68] *The Story of a Modern Woman* (1894, repr. Peterborough, 2004), p. 142.

[69] *Ibid.* p. 122.

[70] *Lady's Pictorial* (May 14, 1898), p. 732.

serve to stress the double-sided nature of existence for many women, and the self-examining which exposes the discrepancies between the realities of life as it has to be lived and the world of the imagination, or between the image that society projects on women and what women in fact are, a recurrent preoccupation in other writers such as George Egerton.

Effie hints at a corollary to this when she mentions 'the whims and caprices' of her brother's wife who 'had got tired of the sister-in-law from England', and had undoubtedly hastened her return. This notion of woman's unkindness to other women, and conversely, their occasional support for each other, is a theme constantly re-worked in women's writing and in that of male writers such as Henry James, if one is to trust the heroine in Ella Hepworth Dixon's story mentioned earlier, 'A Man of Pleasure'. When prompted by a young American suitor to talk about herself, Stella Magnus declares, 'I believe in what Mr Henry James calls the "larger latitude"....', and, when asked to elucidate, continues:

> Ah - the 'larger latitude' is for women - not for men. ... It's the one thing I feel very strongly about. We ought to help, to sympathise, to care for each other. We should be more charitable to the sins, the weaknesses of women, and less so - for practically we condone everything - to those of men.

Ella Hepworth Dixon comes back to this issue at greater length in her novel, as well as in other short stories such as in 'Its Own Reward',[71] a story in which a woman, having earned her living on the stage with all the implicit immoral connotations, returns, a wealthy widow, to take care of her less fortunate sister, or in 'A Suburban Tragedy'[72] where it is the slighted woman who, in trying to overcome her own grief, concentrates on caring for her younger sister, or yet again in 'The Goddess from the Machine'[73] where a younger woman, to her own detriment, promotes the emotional affairs of her older maiden aunt.

Practical and economic concerns are obviously also important, and Ella Hepworth Dixon has a keen eye for such considerations: Effie's 'one luxury ... was a small bedroom to herself, built in the garden, at the very end of the hall passage.' One has here the ingredients of Virginia Woolf's 'A Room of One's Own', but the room without the wherewithal to support oneself is not much use: 'it was humiliating for a woman past thirty not to have a penny of her own, to be dependent on the caprices of a bad-tempered, parsimonious mother.' Ultimately, when 'she looked round the little room, with its damp-stained walls and shabby furniture, seeing a vista of drab years in which she would only be half-alive', death seems preferable. The room, thus, enables Effie not to lead a fulfilling life, but to

---

[71] Originally published in the *Christmas Number of The World* (November 26, 1896), pp. 50-53.

[72] Originally published in *Lady's Pictorial* (December 27, 1890), pp. 1104-1105. This story was not included in the 1904 collection.

[73] *The Lady's Pictorial Christmas Number* (1896), pp. 1-5. This story was not republished in the 1904 collection.

put an end to a miserable existence, woman's self-sacrificing nature, so much acclaimed throughout the Victorian era, taking on a quite different meaning.

This is the lot of other New Woman heroines, which often led to accusations of morbidity or hypochondria, but lest one should think Ella Hepworth Dixon concentrates only on women who 'by a sleep ... end/The heart-ache and the thousand natural shocks/That flesh is heir to',[74] let us consider a different type of heroine, one who, like Mary Erle in *The Story of a Modern Woman*, will stoically 'stand alone, to fight the dreary battle of life unaided'.[75]

> There are tragedies of which the world never hears. It is the women who elect to live, and not the women who elect to die, who are the most pitiful figures in the drama of human passion. Their pale monotonous lives, dragged out to the far end, are a hundred times more bitter than the sharp struggle which ends in self-destruction.[76]

Thus begins 'A Suburban Tragedy' which in many ways re-writes significant elements of 'One Doubtful Hour', particularly the conclusion. At the beginning of 'A Suburban Tragedy' we are told 'Mary Merrit had (n)ever thought of suicide as a possible end to her troubles; she had been too carefully brought up for that'.

The story again centres on a young woman who falls in love and experiences 'the one happy hour she had ever known'. Sadly for her the young man in question, Ferdinand Bartlett, rather like Rochester, is already married to, although separated from, a woman in the colonies, in this case a Boer. He confesses the truth, and returns to the Cape while the heroine not only blames herself, but also assumes the guilt and ostracism imposed on her by the suburban society in which she lives. Time passes during which they exchange letters ever less frequently and she refuses an offer of marriage from the local doctor, a means of regaining respectability if she had so wished. The story might have ended there, but one day she receives a letter from her former lover announcing the death of his wife and his imminent return to England. The final twist occurs at the end of their first evening together when he announces he is to marry a girl he met on the steamer coming home. With tremendous delicacy Ella Hepworth Dixon describes the fluctuations in the heroine's emotions from the anxious anticipation to the awful realization of a second disappointment. Initially and outwardly, 'it was taken quite calmly. ... Yet it seemed to Mary as if a century had passed before she could articulate a word.' Later, 'inside her little bedroom she threw herself, dressed on the narrow bed, and lay there, with wide, staring eyes, till morning.' When finally 'for the first and last time' she tells 'her pitiful story' to the doctor, he comments to himself 'women have all the worst troubles to bear, all the worst pain. Yet they live long, they live long', a refrain picked up again later by Ella Hepworth Dixon in 'The Sweet of the

[74] *Hamlet*, III, i, lines 61-62.
[75] *The Story of a Modern Woman* (1894, repr. Peterborough, 2004), p. 192.
[76] *Lady's Pictorial* (December 27, 1890), p. 1104.

Year',[77] exemplifying the notion that she often re-worked characters and themes from different angles.

An altogether different type of heroine appears in 'The World's Slow Stain',[78] which begins, 'I'm going to marry a man who jilted me ten years ago', at once awakening the reader's curiosity. No passive protagonist is Adela Buller. She is certainly not the 'shy, modest little woman' her husband thinks he has married. Even her name resounds with strength of a particular kind. Nor is she a Jamesian heroine on the threshold of her destiny; like many a *fin de siècle* woman she has had time and opportunity to have had a past. She is described as 'a woman of thirty - perhaps over - who was vaguely supposed to be twenty-six'.

She addresses the opening words, which in themselves raise a variety of questions about motivations for marriage, not, as one might in the past have expected, to her diary, an adoring sister or a close female friend; her interlocutor is in this instance male. In fact, as the story develops it is he, Gilbert Vincent, who 'feels it' when she decides to marry. Once again Ella Hepworth Dixon compares and contrasts male and female behaviour, this time tracing the desire for revenge, a rather different reaction to rejection. The stereotypical images of the male as active while the female is passive are invalidated here: both are equally susceptible to suffering and are shown to be equally capable of seeking and obtaining revenge. This example serves to highlight Ella Hepworth Dixon's resistance to promote essentialist feminism; she seems to suggest throughout that human nature is the same for all, and that society imposes certain artificially gendered behaviours on the sexes.

Adela Buller and Gilbert Vincent resemble each other in a variety of ways. Both are writers who have enjoyed success; she with the one novel she had written under a male pseudonym after being jilted, he as a dramatist. This could explain why he considers her in dramatic terms: 'what excellent "copy" she would make; what a capital type she would be on stage; the young lady who is forever hovering on the brink, but who has "kept straight" all the same. Really, he must make an exhaustive study of Adela.' He considers her to be 'a modern type', a 'curious girl, but only one of a new species'. When he realizes she is serious about marriage, he calls it 'inartistic', and when she 'throws him over altogether', he first ascribes it, rather stereotypically, to 'exasperated nerves'. At the same time he repeats the comment which he had earlier quoted to Adela as coming from the mouth of a 'fool' at the club, 'that your modern woman wasn't complex at all - only hysterical'. He then persuades himself that 'she was essentially a comedian, and she evidently thought it part of her role as a bride to talk in such fashion on her wedding day.' Her creator in part shared Gilbert Vincent's opinion, since much of Adela Buller's character and even some of her words would find their way into Ella Hepworth Dixon's unique play, *The Toyshop of the Heart*, produced in 1908, to which I shall return in chapter six.

---

[77] *The Yellow Book* IX (April 1896), pp. 158-163.

[78] Originally published in the *Christmas Number of The World* (November 21, 1895), pp. 59-61.

Like Effie Lauder, Mary Erle and others, Adela Buller is only too aware of playing a prescribed role, or a succession of roles as the situation demands, and she is good at this. Her first gesture in the story is described as 'taking the attitude in which she had been told, often enough, that she looked her best'. When later she prepares to meet her future husband, having 'an artistic sense of the eternal fitness of things', 'she looked her part to perfection', and Anthony Mellingham is taken in by it all, or, perhaps more accurately, merely projects the image he desires on the woman. In his eyes 'she was just the nice-looking, amiable, simple-minded little woman he wanted'. It is difficult to sympathize with such a short-sighted man who had declared earlier that he 'had waited long enough', totally oblivious of the pain and suffering he had inflicted on her. She, on the other hand, cannot forget it and for one moment even wishes that, like Effie, she had 'died then - when Tony went away ...'. This she admits only to herself; outward appearances are maintained, but the reader catches a glimpse of depth of feeling below the smooth surface.

'Time had besmirched her', nevertheless, and, like the colonel in 'One Doubtful Hour', she feels revulsion when he kisses her, revealing at the same time that there have been many men in her life since he left. She is very far from being the 'nice girl like one reads of in books', although she claims to have been one once, 'a hundred years ago', as she tells Gilbert Vincent:

> I was a good girl, with deep feelings, and ideals, and all that sort of thing ... . I - I imagined that men were ... decent, you know, and that the women who were treated unfairly were the exceptions, and that it was their own fault, generally, if they were. I did not know that women were stuffed with idiotic theories from their very childhood, and that all my life I should suffer, suffer, suffer, for what I had been taught then. We are not told what life is, what it all means, or how to play the game. We are like children to whom a pack of cards is thrown, and who are set down to play a strange game with men who are confirmed gamblers. The rules are never told us, so that we blunder helplessly along, and unless we cheat outrageously, or mark the cards, there's small chance of our winning. And what's so funny is, that most 'good' men like us to be like that, ignorant, silly, helpless - even cheats. They think it pretty.

The image of woman as 'ignorant, silly, helpless' is precisely what many *fin de siècle* writers of both sexes were trying to dispel. Ella Hepworth Dixon almost succeeds here. For much of the story the action is set in motion by a different sort of female, an active, rather than a passive, protagonist. Adela seems very much in control in the opening pages, but as the story develops, her attitude changes somewhat and she reveals a desire to cast off the intervening years and the rather dissolute life she has been leading. Nevertheless, on her wedding day both life and literature catch up with her. When she tells Gilbert Vincent, 'Listen, once for all, Gilbert. You and I say goodbye to-day for good. I'm not going to see you, I'm not going to see any of the set I've been in for the last few years. I hate, I loathe the whole worldly lot. ... For Heaven's sake, give me a chance ...', her 'friend' cannot accept that she is to be 'separated from him for good', and he in turn plans to be avenged. He consequently plants a copy of the novel she had written out of her suffering ('of course, like all amateurs, and most women-novelists, she had drawn on her own experience ...') in her husband's luggage, again thinking in theatrical terms. 'It struck him suddenly, what a dramatic effect you could get by making a young husband read his bride's version of his life .... If Vincent could only be there to see!' The reader is privileged to witness what Vincent can only project: 'Anthony Mellingham, the "Man of Pleasure"[79] of the book, had been carefully painted as an insufferable cad and egoist. And she had married him.' The last image is thus of newly-weds, but far from their ever being 'as jolly a couple as' the once happy bridegroom had hoped and as literature often led one to expect, they are faced with 'the whole odious situation', and, like the reader, are left with 'the vision of an eternal rancour'. Such an ending is more easily associated with Ella D'Arcy's portrayal of marriage, for example in 'Irremediable', or George Egerton's 'An Empty Frame', where there is little prospect of conjugal happiness. In all three stories it would be impossible to say exactly where the responsibility lies. Obviously there is no escaping one's past, but more important is the idea that marriage does not provide the panacea custom would have us believe. Expectations can so rarely be lived up to.

'The Disenchantment of Diana', Ella Hepworth Dixon's contribution to *The Lady's Pictorial Christmas Number* 1895,[80] in spite of what one might expect from the title, ends on an altogether brighter note. It again picks up and plays on literary allusions throughout, raising pertinent questions about the relationship between fiction and reality. The Diana of the title, another mother-less heroine, is presented as a typical feminine stereotype in nineteenth century fiction, letting literature permeate and influence her life, the very term 'disenchantment' surely carrying such connotations. First introduced, rather like a character from a George Egerton story, as 'a slim, nervous-looking creature, with the wide, pale eyes of those who see spiritual things', she is pictured 'sitting at a writing table' in a rather affected pose. She is, in fact, 'enamoured of the writer's craft', and suitably 'awestruck' when at a dinner-party she is placed opposite the poet Astel Verlase whose reputation was of the kind 'which imposes on the imagination'. If added emphasis were needed Diana also quotes Browning, himself referring to Shelley. She is not alone in being taken in by it all: her uncle-guardian was 'every whit as proud as his niece', and to the younger poets 'the affair was an idyll, and the existence of the poet's wife - a dipsomaniac, put away in a Home these many years past - only added piquancy to a romantic story.' Diana lives in a world of fiction within Ella Hepworth Dixon's world of fiction.

The story actually begins and ends with a written rejection of marriage as well as the suggestion of an ultimate acceptance into 'genteel poverty'. Diana Bethune

---

79 As mentioned earlier Ella Hepworth Dixon herself wrote a short story of the same title which appeared in *The Lady's Pictorial Christmas Number* (1894), pp. 17-19. When 'The World's Slow Stain' first appeared Adela Buller/Andrew Burn's novel was entitled 'The Man of Honour'.

80 *The Lady's Pictorial Christmas Number* (1895), pp. 9-12.

is not the first heroine to decline or accept an offer of marriage. What is interesting here is the way in which Ella Hepworth Dixon examines motivations and a growing awareness of illusions. Diana must choose between two men: one, the fairly famous poet whose muse she had become, and the other, a much younger, devoted lover. 'It was obviously the poet, not the man, whom she worshipped', so initially she prefers the life of the imagination, as, indeed, many a reader might. As the story progresses and the 'hero of her dreams' reveals his 'pathetic respectability', like 'a leaf torn from the pages of half a hundred hopeless, humdrum lives', Diana becomes less enchanted and returns home to 'a gayer place' to the young lover, and to write the letter of rejection she will this time send. This is not to say that she has abandoned fantasy altogether; it is almost possible to hear Diana quoting Keats' 'Oh, for a life of sensations rather than of thoughts!'[81] The very air into which she steps with her lover is described as 'intoxicating'. It is spring and 'the open air' is surely healthier than the bleak, musty alternative with the ageing poet. It is up to the reader to use his/her imagination from then on.

The story may be questioning the fairly common practice of older men marrying young girls, a situation which Ella Hepworth Dixon reverses in 'The Goddess from the Machine', where a celebrated woman novelist is wooed by an admirer fifteen years her junior. More interesting for our present purposes, however, is the influence of literature on the heroine. In the earlier-cited story 'Its Own Reward',[82] 'another grim picture out of the tangle of life,'[83] according to *The Illustrated London News* reviewer, while the elder sister, Lily, 'so strong, so determined, so resourceful', goes off to make both their fortunes, the other sister, Amy, withers away at home, writing and reading, neither adequate substitutes for life.

Again Ella Hepworth Dixon sets the tone from the very first sentence: '"Aren't men beasts!" cried Lily, ... "I'll pay them out some day, see if I don't!"' She is in fact outraged on behalf of her sister whose fiancé has just deserted her since 'his parents were reluctantly obliged to withdraw their consent to the match'. Lily in her practical way perceives the financial reasons behind the change of heart - the girls have recently become penniless orphans, and 'she longed to revenge Amy'. 'But Amy, *womanlike*, found excuses for her lover. Indeed, she talked of him and their marriage continually,' (my italics) so much so that she becomes obsessed by the whole idea. As on the last page of *My Flirtations*, 'womanlike' should give us pause for thought, This was surely the passive, acquiescent reaction women were supposed to have. At the beginning of the story Ella Hepworth Dixon had already underlined society's projected image of womanhood: 'So obvious was the rôle for which Nature had intended the two Waltons, that the sight of either of them evoked a vision of a young mother caressing a little child.'

---

[81] John Keats, letter to Benjamin Bailey, November 22, 1817, *Letters*. ed. Hyder Edward Rollins, (Cambridge, 1958).
[82] *Christmas Number of The World*, (November 26, 1896), p. 52.
[83] (Unsigned), 'A Reviewer's Miscellany', *The Illustrated London News* (August 20, 1904), p. 260.

Lily doggedly defies society's and, I would suggest, the reader's expectations, making a success of her life as an actress, coming back, not a fallen woman as might have been predicted, but a rich young widow. While she acts in every sense of the word, Amy, the more stereotypical girl, 'who had not "disgraced"' the maiden aunt with whom she lives, re-acts and becomes neurasthenic. 'Starved in body and soul ... (she) clung to the memory of her one happiness.' She even goes so far as to hound the young man with letters until, exasperated, he threatens her with a summons. By this time 'she hardly left the sofa' so, although she continues 'scribbling letters', her aunt no longer posts them. The problem is that 'in all the hundreds of novels she had read, it was always argued that - for a woman, at least - one love was sufficient for a life-time. She brooded on this', and 'when she went to bed she sat, escaping from the sordid monotony of real life, devouring penny novelettes far into the night.'

This was obviously the silly sort of literature that George Eliot had criticized earlier and which came under increasing attack. In her chapter on New Woman fiction, Kate Flint claims 'what counted was the development of writers' perceptions about the relationship between fictional texts and the society of their readers, and the ways in which readers could be invited to use similar techniques when approaching both novels and their lives.'[84] She concludes 'when fiction, such as that by New Woman novelists, suggests that reading may be a route to gaining knowledge rather than escaping from social realities, it encourages the interpretation of society in quite a different light.'[85]

One cannot help feeling that is exactly what Ella Hepworth Dixon was trying to do through her own fiction. At the end of this story, it is the outgoing, independent sister who triumphs, rather than the model 'good girl' who had remained at home, waiting for her prince to return. When she learns that her former fiancé is now a widower, his wife having died significantly in childbirth, and Lily who 'is capable of anything' says, 'with the air of a princess', 'if she has any fancy for him still, why it can be arranged', Amy's reaction is 'Oh Lily! No, no. Let me go away with you, dear. ... Let me go away with you.' Sisterhood is preferable to the traditional story-book ending - marriage. Again Ella Hepworth Dixon challenges the idea of wedlock being the sole option available to, or desired by, women.

'A Political Comedy'[86] deals with very different aspects of women and writing, since the female protagonist is herself a writer who uses a male pseudonym. Interestingly, this is, in fact, the story which Ella Hepworth Dixon changed most, revealing changes perhaps in her own interests as well as those of her reading public. The 'New' and the 'Woman Question' had given way to more directly political concerns. In the original 'John Bathurst' wrote a collection of short stories entitled 'Yearnings' which dealt with the 'New Revolt', and the editor, Wentworth Johnson, in turn suggested giving her a column on the Woman Question. In the re-

---

[84] Kate Flint, *The Woman Reader* (London, 1993), p. 315.

[85] *Ibid.* p. 316.

[86] Originally entitled 'A Scribbler's Comedy' and published in *Pall Mall Magazine* V (1895), pp. 286-294.

published version she writes not fictional texts, but political essays on Free Trade and in the end her motivations are discovered to be the forwarding of the political career of her husband, a contingency the editor had never considered.

The title and first sentence display traces of Ella Hepworth Dixon's humour which set the tone of the whole story: 'though an editor, he was human' and, above all, I would be tempted to add, a man. His incomprehension of women is evident, and reminiscent of Freud, when he declares, 'Hang it all, ... what do the women want?'[87] 'John Bathurst' knows only too well how to play on the editor's masculine weaknesses, indulging for example in flattery, and on his predictable reactions to an attractive woman, which she exploits mercilessly. To him, she appears so different from the stereo-typical 'lady journalists in pince-nez and navy serge'[88] whom he automatically associates with 'meddling women' and 'women with grievances'. For 'an unimaginative Briton' he is remarkably observant of the 'radiant vision' and sensitive enough to be receptive to the sound of 'her rustling silk skirts' as well as 'the delicate, yet intoxicating odour of iris'. In spite of, or could it be because of, his 'somewhat antique collection of British prejudices', Mr Wentworth Johnson becomes totally charmed by 'John Bathurst'. 'And he wondered ... why such a pretty woman should want to write political pamphlets. Pretty women, he imagined, in his *brutal masculine way*, had generally something better to do' (my italics simply because this seems an unusual comment for Ella Hepworth Dixon, and more worthy of George Egerton).

'John Bathurst' is thus rather different from the other women hitherto encountered in Ella Hepworth Dixon's short stories: she is already married, a grown up heroine for whom marriage is merely the beginning of new developments. Wentworth Johnson describes 'his radiant vision' as '*the legal property* of a tall, middle-aged, military man, who looked as if he meant to take care of her' (my italics), again revealing his own clichés with regard to marriage. 'John Bathurst' and her husband, Colonel Bloodgood, seem to share a rare, enviable complicity. This is manifest in their eye-contact: 'more than once during the dinner those smiling eyes (of 'John Bathurst') shot a look of intelligence at her husband across the table', and the Colonel is described as 'gazing at his young wife' 'admiringly'. When she later lights 'her cigarette at the end of her husband's cigar', and 'the two smiled at each other with an air of comradeship', the undertones are as erotic, if not more so, than many of George Egerton's tremulations or Olive Schreiner's intensities. Ella Hepworth Dixon had displayed similar conjugal camaraderie in an earlier story, 'A Dear Little Girl',[89] where the heroine describes her husband as 'my greatest friend on earth' and he in turn considers her 'the best fellow going'. Likewise at the end of 'His Sweet Disaster',

[87] *Ibid*. p. 287.

[88] 'Waterproofs' in the original, p. 286.

[89] *The Lady's Pictorial Christmas Number* (1889) pp. 21-24. This story was not included in the 1904 collection.

the final comment on a happy couple is 'what friends they were, those two – as well as lovers!'[90] Clearly, the marital state could lead to contentment.

In contrast, the last image of 'A Political Comedy' reveals the editor, once his lapse into the world of the imagination is over and he has returned home on foot to rather squalid domestic circumstances, united with his wife bending over a child's cot. Obviously, home did not always meet men's expectations, either, and they, too, had to adjust to situations they might not have chosen. For the most part, however, they did have their clubs and their work, so it was easier for them from time to time to escape from the stifling hearth and home.

One theme which is touched upon in 'A Dear Little Girl' and 'The Fortune of Flora' is that of conjugal jealousy. Ella Hepworth Dixon treats this topic in greater depth and with more gravity in 'Mlle Mankovich'.[91] Lady St. Ambrose has more obvious cause for anxiety over her husband's fidelity and, like Adela Buller, confides not in a close female friend, but in a very different sort of male friend. Ella Hepworth Dixon here suggests that true complicity between the sexes can exist outside of marriage as well: 'The two looked at each other as people look who have a genuine friendship for each other'. This particular confidante is worthy of the name, his advice is followed and proves sound. What is also revealed is that 'the other woman', Mlle. Mankovich, is a fortune-hunter with a difference: she is engaged in collecting funds for a political cause to which she has dedicated herself, maintaining purely platonic relationships with the opposite sex. In each of the stories where jealousy might have caused a rift, the relationship survives because it is shown to be founded on trust and goodwill in the first place.

'When Purfleet Went to the War'[92] is more concerned with a wife's infidelities which may have shocked some readers. While it was more or less accepted that men would not always maintain high moral standards, it went without saying that a woman's conduct would be irreproachable, as indeed the author assures readers Lady Purfleet's was. 'One may as well say at once that Lady Purfleet ... favoured none of these swains beyond bounds.' Her problem is that she 'lived in the vapidest set in town' which might explain why she was so taken in by 'the literary poseur' and 'his grave eloquence, his rather deliberate manner, his searched-for phrases'. The wife's honour is saved *in extremis* when, about to succumb to his entreaties, she learns of her husband's bravery and determines to go and join him, as a dutiful wife should.

In 'The Kidnapping of Phil Altamore'[93] the protagonists are similar: a young writer, 'a boy of genius. Another Shelley!' and a mature older woman, a widow this time. On this occasion, however, it is she who saves him from a dangerous liaison;

---

[90] *Lady's Pictorial* (November 26, 1898), p. 9.

[91] Originally published as 'Mademoiselle Mankovich' in *The Ladies' Field* (November 29, 1902), pp. 457-459.

[92] Originally published as 'When Purfleet *Came Back* From the War' in *The Ladies' Field* (December 1, 1900), pp. 484-486.

[93] Originally published in the *Lady's Pictorial* (November 25, 1899), pp. 805-807, and entitled 'The Kidnapping of Phil Kynaston'.

he is about to be the victim of a marriage plot. Interestingly, the story is narrated by a male persona, an employee of the British Embassy, who in spite of making scathing remarks about marriage being ridiculous or preposterous, also has designs on the widow. The end is again inconclusive, but the two have the makings of a fine friendship. One of the most interesting aspects of this story for present-day readers is that it provides the plot and most of the characters for Ella Hepworth Dixon's play, but with significant changes. In the play, which will be discussed at greater length in chapter six, much more sympathy is shown for Rosie Rosalba, who rejects the idea of being bought off, whilst the young poet remains rather a weak, easily-influenced individual.

The last story in the collection, 'The Sweet o' the Year', originally appeared in Volume IX of *The Yellow Book*,[94] and was apparently translated into Czech.[95] It is a rather poignant tale about an old woman, an unusual choice of protagonist, but a fitting ending to 'sidelights on the feminine temperament' and to any discussion of Ella Hepworth Dixon's short stories. Not only does it encapsulate some of her dominant themes and exemplify her style, but it also demonstrates her expertise in the genre.

M. Georges, the hero of the story, 'was sorry for women, especially for old women. Being a Frenchman, he had an innately tender regard for the sex.' In other stories Ella Hepworth Dixon occasionally makes scathing remarks about British men. For example, Wentworth Johnson is 'an unimaginative Briton' and Gilbert Vincent calls Adela Buller's husband 'a blundering, idiotic, British Philistine'. It is significant, therefore, that M. Georges who expresses such sympathy and understanding is French. More important still, he is a young painter. This allows Ella Hepworth Dixon to comment not so much upon the relative merits of French Schools of Art as opposed to the British which she does elsewhere, especially in *The Story of a Modern Woman*, but rather to demonstrate the role of art in general.

M. Georges therefore listens as Virginie, his maid, tells her story, or to be more exact, she listens as he reads aloud, and is deeply moved by, the love letters she had received from Victor Gérault, 'whom the younger generation called the Master'. For the reader both inside and outside the story art can thus be seen as a revelation and as a means of coming to terms with life's experiences. What remains when youth and beauty have gone is precisely art: in this case Virginie's portrait as 'Psyche' and her collection of letters. Although by no means a substitute for life, art can, when kept in proportion, help make life livable and, to re-state ideas expressed by George Eliot, extend our sympathies.[96]

Mayne, the principal narrator in Ella D'Arcy's 'The Pleasure-Pilgrim' rightly declares at one point, 'The looker-on generally gets the best view of the game', but

---

94 *The Yellow Book* IX (April, 1896), pp. 158-163.

95 The Grant Richards archives at Urbana, Illinois contain a letter dated July 14, 1904 addressed to a certain M. Victor Hladik granting permission to do so.

96 'The greatest benefit we owe to the artist, whether painter, poet or novelist, is the extension of our sympathies,' George Eliot, 'The Natural History of German Life', *Westminster Review* 174 (July, 1856), pp. 51-79.

not every looker-on has the powers of observation of M. Georges or Ella Hepworth Dixon. Thanks to her artistic eye yet realistic vision aspects which are so often omitted or not considered worthy of mention are described in fine detail. Virginie is portrayed quite bluntly as 'old and shrivelled and unsightly'. In her youth, however, like Diana Bethune, she had inspired great art, only to be abandoned by her artist-lover when fame and fortune came his way. Yet, she betrays no bitterness: 'when one is a woman, and one has been very, very happy, and – and – it is all over – one has to learn to forget. ... Life is like that. ... It is hard for women.' Re-iterating the words of Dr Bloxam in 'A Suburban Tragedy', she concludes, 'And women live long, M. Georges. In spite of their sorrows, they live long ... .'

This might serve as Ella Hepworth Dixon's conclusion. The lot of women, to echo Mona Caird,[97] is not easy, but nor is it presented as impossible. As Patricia Stubbs amongst others has suggested, 'it is through literature ... that dominant images of women and their experience ... have been most easily and, until recently, most widely elaborated',[98] but literature can also propose alternative images, and such is what I would claim Ella Hepworth Dixon's fiction does. She offers her readers not one representation of women, but many, presenting women from various backgrounds, with different characters and at varying stages in their development.

One might be surprised that Ella Hepworth Dixon thus assumes more the role of an observer than an active participant in contemporary debates such as 'The Woman Question'. She was clearly not writing in a vacuum and there is ample evidence in her work that she was not ignoring the burning questions of day. I would suggest that she made a determined effort not to be constricted in the exercise of her own art. In this she was greatly aided by her use of humour. Without being corrosive, her satirical pen went a long way in allowing her to defuse rather than exacerbate tensions, and perhaps even open up discussions. In her short fiction she certainly raises many questions about women's changing roles and challenges some stereotypical notions such as the idea that marriage would resolve all problems and that single women are to be pitied or ridiculed, or conversely that marriage is the cause of most evil. Diversity and experimentation are all important. The reader is thus left with a strong sense of 'this varying, this unknown and uncircumscribed spirit'[99] that constitutes life in its myriad forms.

The Times Literary Supplement of June 24, 1904, aptly described Ella Hepworth Dixon's collection of short stories as 'clever modern tales'. After the success of *The Story of a Modern Woman* (1894), the subject of my next chapter, for her contemporaries Ella Hepworth Dixon's name was clearly synonymous with 'Modern'.

---

[97] Mona Caird, 'The Lot of Women', *Westminster Review* (July, 1910), pp. 52-59.
[98] Patricia Stubbs, 'Introduction', *Women and Fiction: Feminism and the Novel, 1880-1920* (Sussex, 1979), p. ix.
[99] Virginia Woolf, 'Modern Fiction' (1925, repr. London, 1984), p. 150.

Chapter 5

The Story of a Modern Woman[1]

When Ella Hepworth Dixon published *The Story of a Modern Woman* she was 36 years old. Like the majority of the New Woman authors cited by W.T. Stead in his 'Book of the Month' article 'The Novel of the Modern Woman',[2] she was, therefore, no *artiste en herbe*, making her debut in the literary world; she was already a mature writer who had been earning her living by her pen for many years. As discussed in the preceding chapters, before producing a full-length novel, mirroring to some extent the career patterns of many eminent men and women writers, including George Eliot, Ella Hepworth Dixon had contributed innumerable articles and short stories to a variety of periodicals, including *The World*, edited by Edmund Yates and *The Woman's World*, edited by Oscar Wilde.

Her own career in fact exemplified one of the major changes taking place in the literary world in the last years of the nineteenth century: many writers, male and female, who had hitherto remained anonymous, as she had done for some of her periodical articles and short stories, or used pseudonyms, as she had done for *My Flirtations*, were now openly acknowledging authorship, as she did for her novel. Another look at W.T. Stead's list of New Woman works reveals different stages in the shift from anonymity to the use of one's own name: the authors of *The Superfluous Woman* and *A Sunless Heart* remained unknown at that time, whilst 'George Egerton' and 'Iota' are obviously *noms de plume*, and although *The Story of an African Farm* had originally appeared under the name of 'Ralph Iron', by 1894 everyone knew 'he' was Olive Schreiner. Women were thus gradually abandoning the use of pseudonyms, no longer hiding their identities, adopting a male persona or remaining silent, and were beginning to speak out in their own voices. Such was the hope, or the fear. On the other hand, some male writers such

---

[1] For the purposes of my discussion I shall generally refer to the more readily available edition of the novel recently republished by Broadview (Peterborough, 2004). This follows the 1894 version published by Cassell's in New York, and is, on the whole, closer to the original serial publication, which appeared in the *Lady's Pictorial* from January 6 - March 24, 1894, than the version published by Heinemann in London in May 1894, which was republished in 1990 by Merlin. I shall indicate the nature and significance of any differences in the course of the chapter.

[2] (W.T. Stead), 'The Book of the Month: The Novel of the Modern Woman', *The Review of Reviews* 10 (July, 1894), pp. 64-74. Olive Schreiner is the main exception because, although she was born within a few years of Ella Hepworth Dixon, Sarah Grand, Iota, Mona Caird and George Egerton, her novel had been published eleven years earlier than the others on Stead's list. For the complete list see chapter 2, footnote 3.

as Grant Allen, author of the notorious *The Woman Who Did* (1895), and Arnold Bennett again took to adopting female pen-names, perhaps reflecting, or taking advantage of, what was considered an increasing feminization of the literary world.[3] In Grant Allen's case *The Type-Writer Girl* appeared in 1897 and was ascribed to Olive Pratt Rayner. Arnold Bennett, especially whilst he was editor of *Woman*, regularly signed articles with women's names. The adoption of female pseudonyms by male writers had apparently already been rather common in the 1860s in the heyday of 'Sensation fiction'. Gaye Tuchmann also suggests that many an eighteenth century novel ascribed to 'a lady' had been written by a man.

Critics such as Laurel Brake, N.N. Feltes, and Rita S. Kranidis[4] have pointed out that the development of 'new' journalism towards the end of the nineteenth century, exemplified by the likes of W.T. Stead[5] and so finely depicted in *The Story of a Modern Woman*, encouraged the trend away from anonymity towards a more personal, identifiable type of writing. As mentioned in chapter three such tendencies were not always welcomed. Whilst more conservative writers such as Matthew Arnold upheld principles of objectivity and greater reserve, others for very divergent reasons likewise preferred anonymity since it allowed them the freedom, for example, to contribute to several journals simultaneously without injury to their reputations.

Already in the opening pages of the novel Ella Hepworth Dixon adroitly contrasts the newer and older types of journalism: 'the brisk, smartly-dressed young gentleman who came to do a leader for a daily paper, ... proceeded to make a number of notes in shorthand, asking innumerable questions as his omnivorous glance travelled rapidly round the study',[6] whilst 'another press-man - a small, apologetic man with greyish hair and a timid cough asked to see the house for the *Evening Planet*'.[7] It might be argued that here the author was simply drawing a distinction between journalists working on daily papers and those engaged on weeklies, and in the Heinemann version changed the title to the *Weekly Planet*, as if to emphasize the difference. Even so, the production and the consumption of the two forms of publication were, and remain, quite different. The most striking representative of the 'new idea in journalism' in *The Story of a Modern Woman* is Bosanquet-Barry, the editor of the *Comet*, 'pluck(ed) nice and hot from Oxford ... who has none of the old hackneyed Fleet Street ideas'.[8]

---

[3] For a more detailed discussion, see Gaye Tuchmann, *Edging Women Out: Victorian Novelists, Publishers and Social Change* (London, 1989).

[4] See especially Laurel Brake, *Subjugated Knowledges* (Basingstoke, 1994), N.N. Feltes, *Modes of Production of Victorian Novels* (Chicago, 1986), and Rita S. Kranidis, *Subversive Discourses* (New York, 1995).

[5] See for example W.T. Stead's essay 'The Future of Journalism', *The Contemporary Review* 50 (1886), pp. 663-679.

[6] *The Story of a Modern Woman*, p. 44. 'This is not quite the way things are done,' argues the critic in the *St. James's Gazette,* quoting the same extract, but without further explanation. (Unsigned) 'A Modern Woman', *St. James's Gazette* (June 30, 1894), p. 5.

[7] *Ibid.*

[8] *Ibid.* p. 93.

Rather like George Gissing, to whose *New Grub Street* (1891) she makes allusion by entitling one of the chapters of the novel 'In Grub Street', Ella Hepworth Dixon was writing about the publishing world from first-hand experience. Moreover, as mentioned in chapter one, having studied in Paris and, like her heroine, initially having contemplated making her living by her brush rather than by her pen, she was almost equally equipped by personal experience to describe the Art world, which forms an essential back-drop to the novel.

Many other short stories and novels by New Woman writers also centre on a heroine who attempts to reconcile quotidian constraints with her desire to create, whether in the domain of music, literature or the fine arts. For example, both Sarah Grand's *The Beth Book* (1897) and Mary Cholmondeley's *Red Pottage* (1899) have a writer heroine, while in Mona Caird's *The Daughters of Danaus* (1894) the main female protagonist, defying all conventions, foresakes husband, home and children to develop her musical talents. It is important at this stage to stress the seriousness or professionalism of these pursuits which had long been considered simply acceptable pastimes or even required accomplishments for young ladies. In Ella Hepworth Dixon's novel the contrasting attitudes of Vincent Hemming and Mary Erle to her artistic ambitions are revelatory:

> He was relieved, distinctly relieved, when Mary announced her intention of adopting art as a profession. Painting, especially in water-colours, he considered an eminently lady-like occupation; it was, indeed, associated in his imagination with certain drawings of Welsh mountains and torrents, executed by his mother with the prim technique of the forties … .[9]

She, however, 'wished to make her way in the world and compete with men'.[10] For him such an 'occupation' means merely a domestic hobby for ladies using techniques fifty years out of date, whereas for her it is a 'profession' which ultimately signifies a career and independence acquired through paid employment. This he in turn dismisses as 'the modern craze for work', at best to be abandoned on marriage.

I shall return to the topic of marriage a little later, but lest one should think Vincent Hemming's opinions were merely a reflection of his gender, equally telling, albeit for different reasons, are the comments of Alison Ives when Mary Erle announces her plans 'to try her luck at art':[11] 'No woman ever made a great artist yet ... but, if you don't mind being third-rate, of course go in and try. I suppose it'll mean South Kensington, the Royal Academy, and then - portraits of babies in pastel or cottage gardens for the rest of your life.'[12]

Both Vincent Hemming and Alison Ives reflect varying contemporary conceptions of woman and art. For him, as for many a lay person, watercolours were considered the domain of the lady amateur. Nevertheless, some women artists

---

[9] *Ibid.* p. 79.
[10] *Ibid.* p. 98.
[11] *Ibid.* p. 72.
[12] *Ibid.*

such as Kate Greenaway and Helen Allingham thereby attained a certain fame, particularly in illustrating children's books. Others like Mildred Anne Butler and Rose Barton went so far as to exhibit their paintings at the Royal Academy. It should also be remembered that the Pre-Raphaelites, mostly male, produced some of their finest works using watercolours. Alison Ives's comments, on the other hand, reveal a greater awareness of the difficulties facing women artists. Some did 'try their luck' at subjects other than landscapes, gardens and children's portraits, but very few made a significant mark on the male-dominated Art world.[13]

Alison Ives may, therefore, have a point, but more encouragement might have been expected from a close woman friend, especially one described as an 'eminently modern young woman'.[14] Besides, she herself is regularly referred to in artistic terms, although this could simply highlight the commonplace that women are more often the objects or subjects, rather than the creators, of Art. She is described, for example, as wearing a Gainsborough hat or, as in her first appearance in the novel, looking:

> Like a Reynolds, with her handsome, clever face, her superb air, and her huge hats tied under the chin. With that grave sweetness which endears to us the Siddons in the National Gallery she yet had the look of a thinker, modernized by a slightly bored expression, and a little distinguished way which at once made other women in her vicinity look dowdy or vulgar.[15]

Alison Ives is thus immediately associated with more traditional artistic representations;[16] the rational dress of the contemporary New Woman is not for them. She may be attributed 'a caustic tongue', she may swear, albeit in French, and it may be 'whispered that she had serious views', but she defies any stereotyping. 'She never smoked, was ignorant of billiard cues and guns, and hated playing the man.' She is, moreover, no philistine. She could 'interpret Chopin like an artist',[17] had apparently worked in a sculptor's studio in Paris, and even takes poor girls to visit the National Gallery to explain Mantegna to them.

Why, therefore, should she be so scathing of her friend's artistic plans? The answer to this may in part lie simply in her own disposition for practical work. At a time when the Aesthetes were defending 'Art for Art's Sake' and proclaiming the importance of being over doing, Alison Ives is very much a 'doer'. *The Sketch* critic aptly describes her as 'the woman who hides the light of good works under

---

[13] For further insight into the world of Victorian women artists, see in particular the works of Deborah Cherry and Pamela Gerrish Nunn.

[14] *The Story of a Modern Woman*, p. 70.

[15] *Ibid.* pp. 69-70.

[16] Similarly, in a later short story, 'The Wooing of Lord Warminster', in *Lady's Pictorial* (November 25, 1905), p. 860, the main protagonist, Cecilia, is also compared to portraits by Van Dyck, Reynolds and Lawrence.

[17] *The Story of a Modern Woman*, p. 70.

the bushel of nonchalance', and comments on her 'eminently practical bent'.[18] In some ways she could be categorized as the 'angel out of the house' since she 'devote(s) herself to the task of helping young girls', but rarely draws attention to it: 'I couldn't bear any one to say that I had "taken up slumming".[19] You know how I detest the whole attitude of the upper and middle classes towards the poor.'[20] 'It would look like a pose,' she adds, and I suspect herein reside some of her misgivings about her friend's artistic pretensions. One can sympathize with her to a certain extent when she comes to release Mary Erle, already 'somewhat desponding and disheartened', from the agony of drawing and stippling the Laocoon prescribed for the next competition for admittance to the Royal Academy and exclaims '*Nom de Dieu.*! ... am I to stand by and see you become a British female artist? .... the whole thing is a farce. ... Schools of cooking, and not schools of art, are what we want.'[21] With her emphasis on useful occupations, Alison Ives is here reflecting ideas expressed by a certain number of New Woman writers. Ella Hepworth Dixon may to some extent be prefiguring Olive Schreiner's *Woman and Labour* which appeared in 1911 and in which there is much discussion about the 'parasitism' of inactive women. As it happens, when, after dreary months, Mary Erle is not accepted at the Royal Academy and abandons her aspirations to be an artist, she herself describes it as 'a foolish pretence at work',[22] reminding the reader of Alison Ives' earlier unfavourable comparison between The Central London School of Art[23] and 'a serious French studio, where they *work*' (her italics).

Significantly, apart from the somewhat uncomplimentary sketches of Mary Erle's fellow students, the only other image of a woman engaged in artistic activities in the novel is that of Mary Erle's governess 'laboriously *copying* in water-colours a lithographed bunch of roses'[24] (my italics). This merely accentuates the gulf between life and art which is so distasteful to Alison Ives, and which Mary Erle learns to recognize. Both her reading, which in the beginning had served as 'a revelation in the possibilities of life'[25] and had subsequently required continual reconsideration, and her writing, which also necessitated revision, this time to please her editor and his particular public, highlight her avid concern with seeing 'life as it is'. In this, she and Alison Ives are worlds apart from the admirers of the galleries of the Society of United Artists on press day depicted in chapter XIV or the playgoers described in chapter XVI on the first-night at a fashionable theatre

[18] L.F.A. (perhaps Austin who also wrote reviews in *The Illustrated London News*) 'The Book and Its Story', subtitled 'A Novel with Brains', *The Sketch* (June 27, 1894), p. 476.
[19] Terry Eagleton discusses the growing interest in 'slumming' in 'The Flight to the Real', chapter 1 in *Cultural Politics at the Fin de Siècle* ed. Sally Ledger and Scott McCracken (Cambridge, 1995).
[20] *The Story of a Modern Woman*, p. 76.
[21] *Ibid*. p. 88. The expletive was toned down to '*Nom d'un chien*!' in Heinemann's version.
[22] *The Story of a Modern Woman*, p. 88.
[23] 'Very cleverly' described, according to the *Sunday Times* critic.
[24] *The Story of a Modern Woman*, p. 56. A detail not in the original serialized version.
[25] *Ibid*. p. 53.

who are only too happy to see what is 'so adorably *untrue to life*' (my italics). Even at art school painting from life is considered a 'kind of frivolous extra'.[26]

Mary Erle's failure, therefore, might be a reflection not so much on her own abilities as on the short-comings of the Academy, and Ella Hepworth Dixon may at this point be raising questions about the Art world in general as well as woman's place therein, highlighting the differences of opinion and ensuing polemics surrounding the Art world of London. In 1893 a new art magazine, *The Studio*, to which, incidentally, Marion Hepworth Dixon later contributed,[27] met with immediate success. The editor, Joseph Gleeson White, regularly castigated the Royal Academy, describing the Academicians as 'toothless old women mumbling sentimentalities',[28] the kind of comment Ella Hepworth Dixon might well have attributed to Alison Ives. On the other hand, the influence of French art was much in vogue and British avant-garde artists such as Aubrey Beardsley were encouraged. It is perhaps significant that Mantegna was a particular favourite of his which may indicate Ella Hepworth Dixon's desire to reveal Alison Ives as specially knowledgeable about the contemporary art world and thereby justified in her comments.

The most successful artist represented in the novel, Perry Jackson, certainly reflects Ella Hepworth Dixon's own insights into the London Art world and the contemporary debates about the commodification of Art. 'Life in a School of Art is happily described; but what will the Academicians say to Mr Jackson...?'[29] asks *The Sketch* critic. Perry Jackson did indeed progress from Hampstead Road to South Kensington, even buying a house with its entire contents from one of the Royal Academicians who had fallen from public favour, but 'it's all for show'. He is first acclaimed for a picture, perhaps reminiscent of Rossetti's *Rosa Triplex* (*circa* 1874), entitled *The Time of Roses* which had sold for two thousand pounds. 'That was what *did the trick,* the girls and the roses. Agnew bought it, sold thousands of engravings ... . I'm told that in America they give away an autogravure of that picture with every pound of Scourer's soap and every bottle of Parkins' Pain-killer',[30] (my italics) admits the artist, who intends to paint, alongside young girls and cemeteries, 'nothing but roses', perhaps the very ones which will later be copied by numerous governesses.

The association of women with flowers and death or inanimate states was extremely common in Victorian art, both in Britain and America. One has only to think of some of the works of the Pre-Rapaelites, and later John Collier's *The Death of Albine* (*circa* 1895) and Charles Courtney Curran's *The Spirit of Roses* (*circa* 1899) are typical illustrations of this trend. Throughout the novel, however, the contrast between life and death, real and copy, firmly situates Mary Erle with

---

[26] *Ibid*. p. 85.

[27] See Appendix 4 for further details.

[28] Quoted in *Studio International: Special Centenary Number*, Volume 201, 1022/3, *High Art and Low Life: 'The Studio' and the fin de siècle* (London, 1993), p. 7.

[29] L.F.A., *The Sketch* (June 27, 1894), p. 476.

[30] *The Story of a Modern Woman*, p. 128.

the former and suggests, as Alison Ives would agree, that Art, or imitation, is no substitute for life. Mary Erle is thus repeatedly associated with real flowers deliberately chosen to suit each occasion: 'wax-like exotic flowers ... with their sensuous odour' in the opening chapter announce the demise of Professor Erle; roses, peonies and tiger lilies are purchased with hard-earned money when she expects a visit from her lover, whilst lilacs and hawthorns accompany her in the last pages set in the cemetery at her father's graveside. Ella Hepworth Dixon's pen in fact awakens the senses far more acutely than any silver point drawing or lithographed copy could, and lush descriptions, reading at times rather like set pieces, permeate the prose. For example, at the funeral, contrary to pathetic fallacy, 'in a neighbouring laburnum-bush, a thrush was swelling its brown throat with a joyous morning song. Athwart the pale sky dappled with fleecy clouds, the lilac bushes were burgeoning with waxen, pinkish blossoms. The very air throbbed with coming life.'[31] Or, later when Mary Erle, impatiently waiting for her lover's return, sits in Regent's Park 'it was high midsummer now; there was a velvety smoothness on the trim lawns, the green light filtered through a canopy of broad chestnut leaves, and the beds were odorous with heliotrope, purple with pansies, and aglow with geraniums'.[32]

In contrast, when she goes to interview Perry Jackson he is at work on a picture, *The Hour of Lilies*, destined for the following year's Academy, which again stereotypically assimilates flowers and lifeless women:

> The pale, pensive faces of the young nuns, faces of unnatural loveliness, with haunting eyes and flower-like mouths, shadowed by wide blue headdresses, were seen bending over beds of white lilies, while here and there a transparent hand was stretched to gather the passionless, immaculate flowers.[33]

When Mary Erle asks if he has 'a Message' and suggests, as surely some of the defenders of Art for Art's sake might have, 'the cult of beauty, the pagan love of form, the delight, so to speak, in a physically perfect existence',[34] his reply is, 'All I want to do is make the thing pay.'[35]

His obvious ambition and frank admission of pandering to the taste of a certain public may merit respect, and *The Sketch* critic even suggests he is 'the only man in the book you can respect'. Undoubtedly, they emphasize some of the current controversies in the domain of the Arts. Just as amongst writers and critics there was a growing concern to distinguish between literature as an art or Art and literature as a business or a trade, so in the Art world itself mercantile and aesthetic interests were being hotly disputed. L.F. Austin in *The Illustrated London News* drew attention to some of these issues by entitling his review of Ella Hepworth

---

31 *Ibid*. p. 46.
32 *Ibid*. p. 115.
33 *Ibid*. p. 134.
34 *Ibid*. p. 135.
35 *Ibid*.

Dixon's novel 'Art in One Volume',[36] and beginning, 'It is characteristic of British haphazardness that in the controversy about the three volume novel little is said of fiction as an art.' He goes on to complain that 'it rarely occurs to any disputant that publication in this form is a direct encouragement to every possible vice of style', basically to appease 'Mudie Moloch'. Mary Erle's impression of the press day of the Society of United Artists where Perry Jackson's painting, *Two Sisters*, 'hung in the place of honour', displays an innate reticence to compromize for commercial interests: 'Everywhere was the obvious, the threadbare, *the banal*; everywhere there was a frank appeal to the Philistinism of the picture-buying public'[37] (her italics). Even if she does ultimately have to adjust her writing to please her editor, it is difficult to imagine that, had she managed to gain access to the Royal Academy, she would have had a less arduous existence as an artist than as a writer.

In her memoirs, with a certain amount of self-deprecation, Ella Hepworth Dixon recounts her own early 'journalistic activities', incidentally rather more amusing than those she accords to her writer heroine. 'In the 'nineties, I "commenced author" - first with a book under a pseudonym ... and, in 1894, with *The Story of a Modern Woman.*'[38] By 'commenced author', she would appear to be signalling an important distinction between publishing in journals and publishing in book form. Elsewhere in her memoirs, however, she writes that Oscar Wilde's friend, Robert Ross, '"commenced author", as the phrase goes, by writing in the *Saturday Review*'.[39] 'Author' thus seems to have connotations of a more serious *attitude* to writing and to the recognition of a certain professionalism, rather than to the actual content or form. It could also simply be a case of a woman treating her own early work with less seriousness than she accords to the writing of a man. In the novel, however, there is a distinct shift from Mary Erle's 'first attempts at fiction', produced with 'the easy facility of an amateur' and on a par with 'hundreds of third-rate authors', the *cacoëthes scribendi* which 'the supercilious editor' of *The Fan* ascribes to his contributors, and later references to 'her new *profession* of journalist'[40] (my italics). In 'My Faith and My Work', Ella Hepworth Dixon speaks of being asked what led her to 'adopt the *author's craft as a profession*'[41] and then goes on to refer to '*scribblers*' (my italics) into which category, with 'a becoming sense of modesty', she apparently placed herself.

In the same article, she also asserts:

> Before the fate of this booklet (My Flirtations) was settled, I found myself at work on something more serious. *The Story of a Modern Woman* (which was written by-the-bye in 1892-3, before the rush of 'woman-books' began)[42]

---

[36] L.F. Austin, *The Illustrated London News* (August 11, 1894), p. 174.
[37] *The Story of a Modern Woman*, p. 126.
[38] *As I Knew Them* (London, 1930), p. 136.
[39] *Ibid.* p. 35.
[40] *The Story of a Modern Woman*, p. 126.
[41] *Woman* (September 23, 1896), p. 8.
[42] The *Lady's Pictorial* article about Ella Hepworth Dixon in the 'Lady Journalists' Series which appeared on February 10, 1894 (p. 176), when the novel was being serialized, states

> was an effort to show how unequal is the struggle between the sexes - a struggle which has never been so bitter in the history of the world before - for the things that are most worth having.

Ella Hepworth Dixon, therefore, was not merely participating in, and writing about, changes in the publishing world, and joining in the debate about the functions of Art or the relationships between High and Low culture. *The Story of a Modern Woman* also reveals a profound preoccupation with the wider social and economic issues then so much under scrutiny, and, more especially, the role of women. Nevertheless, there is little mention of political activities, and several critics commented positively on the relative absence of what William Sharp in *The Academy* called 'the views without which no novel now seems complete'. It would, for example, be difficult to identify one single representation of the New Woman, and, in fact, in the novel Ella Hepworth Dixon never employs the expression, referring, as in the title, only to the *modern* woman. As discussed in chapter two, naming the New Woman was in many ways demeaning and reductive, so Ella Hepworth Dixon may deliberately have wished to avoid the term, and, wisely perhaps, may have simply preferred to diversify, rather than restrict, the image of the modern woman.

For some critics, however, both in her own day and now, including the compilers of the recent *Edwardian Fiction: An Oxford Companion*,[43] Ella Hepworth Dixon's life and work, particularly *The Story of a Modern Woman*, epitomize the *fin de siècle* New Woman writer. Certainly, the novel prominently features New Woman topics such as moral double standards and a re-examination of marriage. Moreover, the theme of purposeful paid employment as a means to independence for women, in contrast to 'the trivial round of civilized feminine existence' or the 'monotonous toil'[44] of women such as seamstresses, further broadens the scope of the text. In her essay 'The End of the Century and Conflicting Fantasies of Femininity' Susan P. Casteras points out that in the world of art:

---

it 'has been written expressly for these pages' which might suggest that it had been commissioned by the journal.

[43] *Edwardian Fiction: An Oxford Companion*. Sandra Kemp, Charlotte Mitchell and David Trotter (eds) (Oxford, 1997).

[44] The last sentence of chapter one in the London book version describes Mary Erle's 'immense pity ... for the patient figure bending ... over her foolish strips of flounces, the figure of the woman at her monotonous toil', seemingly referring to Mary Erle's seamstress. In the original and the Amercan version 'an immense pity ... for the patient figure bending ... over her foolish strips of flounces' is separated from the last sentence, and 'It was not so much a woman, but The Woman at her monotonous toil' is written as a distinct paragraph, thereby making a rather more forceful, general statement. The French translation, 'une profonde pitié pour cette pauvre créature penchée sur un vain morceau d'étoffe, ... la femme fléchissant sous sa tâche monotone', is, as usual, closer to Heinemann's version.

> In the realm of the working woman, the sempstress and the governess were viewed as objects of sympathy and also victims of unjust conditions, but their picturesque appeal centred on their lost beauty or stature, not on the real causes of their misery. Redgrave[45] was a particular innovator in this category, and his depictions of the oppressed teacher and needlewoman popularized the format of a suffering single figure in abject penury.[46]

The history of Ella Hepworth Dixon's own publications in book form reveals much about the practical problems encountered by writers, male or female, and serves as illuminating background both for the novel and the period as a whole. She may well have benefited, as does her heroine, from family connections in the publication of her first book, although by that time her father had been dead for twelve years, but then, again like her heroine, experienced a certain amount of difficulty in pleasing her publishers with her subsequent work. The correspondence from Chatto and Windus concerning *The Story of a Modern Woman* has much in common with Mary Erle's publisher's comments in the novel.

Chatto and Windus write:

> It would have afforded us much pleasure to have been able to have offered you a higher price than we paid for *My Flirtations* but we are sorry to say that *in view of the somewhat pessimistic tone of the story*, and also of the limited success of *My Flirtations* we find we are unable to make you a better offer for the present work than £35 for the remaining British Book rights, and to divide with you any sum received from the American market.[47] (my italics)

In the story itself, Mary Erle tells Perry Jackson, the barometer of public taste, 'I've even thought of writing a realistic novel', but 'my idea was too sad - too painful, all the publishers said. It wouldn't have pleased the British public.'[48] Ironically, perhaps, throughout the novel Ella Hepworth Dixon reveals a keen understanding of the enormous diversity of the reading public, from Mary Erle's own background of literary classics to the office boy's inexpensive comics to the nurses' penny novelettes as well as the various specialized periodicals, from Vincent Hemming's political tracts to Dunlop Strange's medical journals, not forgetting the smart gossipy glossies, sensational dailies and more refined weeklies, often produced by the same publishing company. In short, the novel seems to question assumptions made by publishers, both real and fictional, as well as their understanding of the literary market. While Mary Erle's editor insists on 'a three-volume novel on the old lines - 'a dying man in a hospital and a forged will in the first volume; a ball and a picnic in the second; and an elopement, which must, of course, be prevented at the last moment by the opportune death of the wife, or the husband - I forget

---

[45] Richard Redgrave (1804-1888) notably painted *The Governess* (1843), *Poor Teacher* (1845) and *The Sempstress* (1846).
[46] Susan P. Casteras, *Writing About Art* (New Jersey, 1994), p. 190.
[47] Chatto and Windus archives (Reading University). Letter dated June 4, 1893.
[48] *The Story of a Modern Woman*, p. 130.

which it is to be - in the last',[49] to be published in serial form, W.T. Stead's list of New Woman writers testifies that a range of genres from traditional three-volume novels to short stories or mere sketches, was not only possible, but could even be successful. Nevertheless, Mary Erle's editor, perhaps reflecting Chatto and Windus, tells her, 'The fact is novels are - er - well - novels. The British Public doesn't expect them to be like life ... . There must be a thoroughly breezy book.'[50]

Curiously enough, this is a more fitting description of Ella Hepworth Dixon's memoirs where there is rarely a hint of a suggestion of a problem in her own publishing career. Echoing the critics in *The Sketch* and *The Graphic* who commented on 'the sombre note of the book' and found 'the theme ... somewhat sombre, as, perhaps, the story of a woman's singlehanded combat with the world is bound to be', she describes her novel as 'a somewhat gloomy study of the struggles of a girl alone in the world and earning her own living', and adds, 'To my great surprise, it caught on at once'.[51] Bearing in mind Chatto and Windus' cool reaction, Ella Hepworth Dixon's declared surprise was perhaps not feigned. In one of her 'Pensées de Femme' when discussing 'the things which THRILL', she suggests 'perhaps the best means of experiencing it is to write a book ... and wake up one morning to find it reviewed at length in *The Times.*'[52] According to the *Lady's Pictorial* overview of her career written whilst the novel was being published, 'its striking originality and power (had) already caused considerable sensation and elicited much admiring comment'.[53] Certainly, once *The Story of a Modern Woman* had been accepted and published in the *Lady's Pictorial* and then by Heinemann, it was, like much of the New Woman fiction, an astounding success, thus disproving in actual fact the claims of her fictional editor as well as her own earlier publishers.

In her memoirs in the chapter devoted to William Heinemann,[54] Ella Hepworth Dixon describes him as 'a lifelong friend', and declares, 'when he accepted my first (and only) novel, *The Story of a Modern Woman*, I felt proud.'[55] Perhaps it was the 'lifelong friend' or the experienced publisher who persuaded her to make changes

---

[49] *Ibid*. The original indicated 'a forged will in the first volume; a ball and a picnic in the second; a dying man in a hospital, and an elopement, which must, of course, be prevented at the last moment by the opportune death of the wife, or the husband - I forget which it is to be - in the last', whilst in Heinemann's version there was to be 'a ball in the first volume; a picnic and a parting in the second' before the elopement.

[50] *Ibid*. p. 182.

[51] *As I Knew Them* (London, 1930), p. 136. I am reminded here of the comments Netta Syrett makes in her autobiography, published a few years after Ella Hepworth Dixon's, concerning her first novel, *Nobody's Fault* (London, 1896): 'It is years since I read or even saw the book, ... I have long since lost my copy. That its disappearance is no great tragedy a vague memory no doubt rightly suggests, ... and I recall long and enthusiastic reviews which at the time filled me with delight and, much more important, my mother and father with pride and satisfaction.' *The Sheltering Tree* (London, 1939), p. 85.

[52] 'Pensées de Femme', *Lady's Pictorial* (May 23, 1896), p. 774.

[53] 'Lady Journalists. (Fifth Series)', *Lady's Pictorial* (February 10, 1894), p. 176.

[54] *As I Knew Them* (London, 1930), pp. 187-190.

[55] *Ibid*. 187.

in the text for book publication in Britain, Cassell's in New York republishing almost exactly the original. Unfortunately no correspondence concerning either Ella Hepworth Dixon's novel or her memoirs is to be found in The Random House Archive and Library, where both the Heinemann and Hutchinson files are kept, but in an article entitled 'The Literary World'[56] in the *St. James's Gazette* announcing the issue of the novel 'on the Continent in the Tauchnitz Collection, and by Mr Heinemann in his Colonial Library', mention is made that 'the American Rights were purchased by Messrs. Cassell and Company, of New York, before the novel appeared in serial form in England.' The primary difference is the deletion of the whole of the original third chapter, entitled 'Wonderings', which describes the heroine's education in Germany. This was in fact highly autobiographical, as the author reveals in her memoirs decades later,[57] and her motivations for suppressing this section may have been an attempt to distance herself from the literary text. As a consequence chapter numbers are slightly altered. Each version, however, still contains twenty-four chapters since, in the Heinemann edition, Ella Hepworth Dixon divided the original final chapter into two and reversed the titles, ending thus not with 'The Woman in the Glass', but 'In Which Civilization Triumphs'. Not only is the unity of time maintained with the novel beginning and ending in spring, but also the added artifice of the chapters reflecting the number of hours in a day gives the text a rigid structure.

The novel was reviewed in prestigious journals such as *The Times* and *The Athenaeum*, where the name may still have carried some weight since her father had been editor of the magazine from 1853 to 1869,[58] as well as many others including *The Academy*, the *British Weekly*, the *Daily Chronicle*, the *Daily Telegraph*, *The Graphic*, *The Illustrated London News*, *Pall Mall Gazette*, *The Review of Reviews*, *The Sketch*, *St. James's Gazette* and *The Weekly Sun*.

> Mr T.P. O'Connor, ever generous to young authors devoted the whole front page of his Sunday weekly[59] to it; Mr W.T. Stead made much of it in the *Review of Reviews*; it was translated into French[60] and appeared in

[56] Unsigned (November 12, 1894), p. 12.

[57] *As I Knew Them* (London, 1930), pp. 22-25 and 50.

[58] So far, however, I have found few references to paternal influence: in the *Sunday Times* (June 3, 1894), p. 2, Ella Hepworth Dixon is described as 'the talented daughter of an eminent father', and advertisements for the second edition of the novel published in, for example, *St. James's Budget* (November 9), p. 27, and *The World* (November 14, 1894), p. 31, quote from *The Graphic* claiming 'Miss Dixon has inherited no small share of her father's literary gifts'.

[59] Signed simply T.P., as was the editor's wont. 'A Book of the Week: The Story of a Common Crime' *The Weekly Sun* (July 29, 1894), pp. 1-2.

[60] Entitled '*Une Femme Moderne*', translated by G. Labouchère, it was published by la bibliothèque de La Vie Moderne, 83, bvd Soult, Paris. A copy is to be found at the Bibliothèque Nationale in Paris and there is now a microfiche copy in the Bibliothèque Publique et Universitaire, Geneva. The French translation not surprisingly follows Heinemann's edition rather than the serial version. Mary is alternately 'Mary' and 'Marie' whilst Alison is always 'Alice'.

> Tauchnitz, in the Colonies and in America, and was advertised by Messrs. Heinemann as one of 'the books of the year'. This led to many literary friendships.[61]

Elsewhere, Ella Hepworth Dixon recounts how she was invited by 'The Vagabonds' dining club along with five other ladies, whose names, unfortunately, she does not mention, 'as the author of one of the six "most successful novels of the year", after the publication of my first novel, *The Story of a Modern Woman*'.[62] In retrospect, one can wonder what it was about the novel that made it so appealing to its contemporaries and even question whether it was in fact so representative of New Woman writing. A closer examination of contemporary reviews might thus prove invaluable for a general appreciation of the reception of Ella Hepworth Dixon's work and an evaluation of its innovatory nature.

As mentioned in chapter two, W.T. Stead took his cue from her title for his overview of New Woman fiction in general[63] and is, perhaps predictably, along with T.P. O'Connor, the most sympathetic critic, describing both Mary Erle and Alison Ives as women 'of the modern variety', and using the term 'heroical' to describe their behaviour. Ella Hepworth Dixon's title, simple as it is, solicited comment in both *The Sketch* and *The Atheneaum*. 'The title of this book may be a little alarming to the nervous man who has read many novels lately in which life is represented as a flaming pathway of woman's vengeance for centuries of subjection,'[64] states the former, although:

> The modern woman in Miss Dixon's story is not the aggressive champion of her sex, chanting the battle-cry of freedom, but the patient toiler in a world which is apt to be hard on women who work for their living, a world which expects them to cultivate the artificial delicacies of conventional ignorance, and to bruise themselves against the rough edges of the social system with 'an acquiescent feminine smile'.[65]

The reviewer in *The Athenaeum* takes a similar view: 'the title of Miss Hepworth Dixon's story is unnecessarily forbidding for her heroine has little in common with the self-assertive, heartless, sexless thing whom various writers have brought into fashion and almost tempted the public to regard as the typical modern woman.'[66] He continues, 'Mary Erle is a gentle and essentially feminine creature ...' with 'little "modernity"' and 'a quiet charm'. Her friend, Alison Ives, in comparison, is

---

[61] *As I Knew Them* (London, 1930), p. 136.
[62] *Ibid.* p. 107.
[63] 'The Book of the Month: The Novel of the Modern Woman', *The Review of Reviews* 10 (July, 1894), pp. 64-74.
[64] L.F.A., *The Sketch* (June 27, 1894), p. 476.
[65] *Ibid.*
[66] (Unsigned), *The Athenaeum* (June 16, 1894), p. 770.

judged 'decidedly more "up-to-date"'. This opinion is shared by Kate Flint in her introduction to the 1990 re-issue of the work:[67]

> The radicalism of this novel, unlike the 'new woman' genre as a whole, does not lie in the details of its treatment of sex and marriage, nor in its representation of an outspoken heroine. Rather, it is a novel which lays bare the relationship between social expectations and women's capacity to achieve self-fulfilment.

I would agree that on the surface Ella Hepworth Dixon does not deal as openly with sex and marriage, or the lack of either or both as, for example, Mona Caird, George Egerton, and Sarah Grand so forcefully do. In many ways she seems to be giving the reading public what they expect, but on closer inspection she is also seriously subverting these expectations. She takes many of the Victorian icons, such as the home, marriage, maternity, and then reveals their shortcomings. Such ideals I would suggest were, according to Victorian thought at least, and perhaps continue to be, very closely, if not inextricably, linked to 'social expectations' and 'self-fulfilment', both in fiction and life at large. Since marriage still represented the mainstay of society, a glance at Ella Hepworth Dixon's treatment of this theme will illustrate the extent of her modernity and her radicalism.

The Story of a Modern Woman certainly contains much discussion about marriage, offers of marriage, refusals of marriage, arranged marriages, extra-marital sex and even divorce. The older generation in particular, represented by Alison Ives' mother and Mary Erle's doctor, still view marriage as the ultimate achievement in a young woman's life. At the end of the novel, Lady Jane Ives, having overcome her own daughter's death rather rapidly, makes almost a profession out of arranging marriages for young girls, as unmarried women of even advanced years are called throughout:

> All that had happened five years ago. This was the second niece that she had successfully launched in society; the first had made an excellent match, and Lady Jane only hoped ... that Victoria would not think of marrying quite so soon, for it was charming ... to have a girl to take out.[68]

In turn, Dr Danby tells Mary Erle 'I should like to have all you young ladies living a healthy out-of-door life, happily married, and with no mental worries.'[69] Doubts about the probability of reconciling all three criteria were regularly aired by New Woman writers.

The doctor's comments, however well-meant they may be, actually highlight the impossibility for Mary Erle to meet such social expectations, and herein lies 'the moral of the whole story', according to T.P. O'Connor, '- the tragic disadvantages of the middle-class girl born in the transition period between early and universal

---

[67] Kate Flint, Introduction to *The Story of a Modern Woman* (London, 1990), p. xiv.
[68] *The Story of a Modern Woman*, p. 175.
[69] *Ibid*. p. 144.

marriage and our own time of the growing independence of women.'[70] Ironically, following months of emotional strain and work-induced fatigue, it is only after she has learnt that the man for whom she has been waiting is to marry a rich heiress that Mary Erle finally consults a doctor. Interestingly, she turns not to Dr Dunlop Strange whose 'speciality was nervous diseases', but to Dr Danby, the family physician, indicating that she was suffering from no specifically feminine malady. He could warn her of hereditary weaknesses, very different from 'this disgusting talk about heredity' mentioned later by the theatre-going public and perhaps also much in the minds of Ella Hepworth Dixon's own readers, and remind her that even her father had not been 'able to stand the strain'.

Unlike some New Woman heroines, for instance Mona Caird's Hadria in *The Daughters of Danaus*, or Menie Muriel Dowie's Gallia in the eponymous novel, or Angelica in Sarah Grand's *The Heavenly Twins*, Mary Erle, as is her wont, remains silent when confronted with the doctor's explanation. Consequently, the reader is spared long theoretical discussions so common in other writers, which in part might account for *The Athenaeum* reviewer's comment on her gentleness. It certainly highlights the terseness of Ella Hepworth Dixon's work and the difficulty of situating her precisely in relation to her more propagandist contemporaries. The doctor's words, however, are recalled a little later in the novel when, faced with her editor's disapproval at her daring to give a realistic twist to her fiction including 'a young man making love to his friend's wife',[71] Mary Erle's capacity to achieve professional self-fulfilment is likewise questioned. In fact, here she seems to have the makings of a New Woman novelist herself, now speaking up about infidelities and moral double standards, again at odds with the image of a timid, old-fashioned girl some have taken her to be. The 'Two Ultimatums' of the title of this chapter therefore exemplify how, to repeat the author's own words quoted in the Stead interview, 'social laws press upon women'. At this point in the story, Ella Hepworth Dixon also speaks of cares 'pressing' upon Mary Erle and notes her 'obstinate courage' as she determines to take the doctor's practical advice to enable her to get better and to fulfil both professional and private obligations.

Such courage has been present from the opening pages of the novel when Mary Erle is first shown coping with the practicalities of her father's death. A little later, on his first visit after the funeral, Vincent Hemming notes 'her mouth had got those little obstinate tucks at the corners now, which he knew so well'.[72] Nevertheless, he compliments her on her decision to stay in London and paint, saying, 'That's so brave - and so like you', to which she replies, 'It isn't brave at all. ... I should go mad if I sat down to think.'[73] One is reminded here of the plight of the nameless narrator in Charlotte Perkins Gilman's 'The Yellow Wallpaper' (1892) who is driven mad by confinement and enforced inactivity. Later Mary Erle finds, as does Perry Jackson when she declines his offer of marriage, 'in work there was at least

[70] T.P. (O'Connor), *The Weekly Sun* (Sunday, July 29, 1894), p. 1.
[71] *The Story of a Modern Woman*, p. 146.
[72] *Ibid*. pp. 78-79.
[73] *Ibid*.

forgetfulness'.[74] Activity may save her from the madhouse to which, as is only too well known, many Victorian women found themselves condemned, but at a cost: even if 'she had never stopped working', 'her nerves were completely unstrung'.[75] Such quiet resistance in the heroine is indeed worthy of the reader's admiration, as is the author's own tactful insistence not so much on the theories of women's claims for more independence, or even on the application of such theories, but on the painstaking daily efforts required 'of a girl alone in the world and earning her own living'.[76]

Dr Danby's lamentation that 'there is something wrong somewhere ... with our boasted civilisation. It's unnatural. Not fit, not fit for girls',[77] as well as the title of the penultimate chapter which then became the last, 'In Which Civilisation Triumphs', and the description of Dr Dunlop Strange's abandoned mistress as 'a martyr of civilisation' consequently acquire varying layers of interpretation. Moreover, the above-mentioned discussion with the editor about appropriate topics for literature is skilfully bracketed between the newsboys' cries about the Blaythewaite scandal, including 'revoltin' details', and punctuated by the editor's comments over the telephone to a journalist/illustrator working on the affair advising him to get pictures and 'see that they're touched up'.[78] The reader is thus implicitly encouraged to question the role of literature and newspapers in helping, as Mary Erle's editor, along with many a critic, would wish, to perpetuate civilization's false expectations. One is then again lead to reflect further upon glaring contradictions between life and art, supposed fact and fiction, not forgetting that this in itself is a fictional representation. As Elizabeth Robins claimed in her autobiography, 'It is the business ... of men and women writers to correct false ideas about women which many writers of the past have fostered.'[79] This is precisely what New Woman writers in general and Ella Hepworth Dixon in particular were attempting to do.

The chapter entitled 'A Comedy in Real Life' is a fine example of Ella Hepworth Dixon's art in subtly yet subversively dramatizing such contradictions. The scene is set in a fashionable theatre, an ideal site in which to unite all the protagonists, and it is precisely here that Mary Erle learns of her lover's betrayal. Her pain is even exacerbated because the object of her affections becomes an object of ridicule under the caustic scrutiny of others. Just as Mary Erle comments, albeit to herself, on 'the hideous comedy going on in the box' and 'the foolish, inane, unreal comedy on stage',[80] so some in the audience, including Lady Jane Ives, Mr Bosanquet-Barry and Mr Beaufort Flower, self-appointed arbiters of social *mores*, also pass judgement on others present, especially Lady Blaythewaite,

---

[74] *Ibid.* p. 144.
[75] *Ibid.*
[76] *As I Knew Them* (London, 1930), p. 136.
[77] *The Story of a Modern Woman*, p. 144.
[78] *Ibid.* p. 147.
[79] Elizabeth Robins, *Way Stations* (London, 1913), p. 110.
[80] *The Story of a Modern Woman*, p. 142.

the 'coming heroine of the divorce court', whose divorce case has become a *cause célèbre.* In the theatre, just as in the paper, falsifying fiction and scandalous reality are juxtaposed. The play, a new comedy about two sets of lovers, is described as 'a charming, pretty piece ... . Quite an idyll, and so wholesome, ... a thoroughly English piece with a happy ending',[81] prefiguring the editor's later advice to Mary Erle about novel-writing. From the snippets of detail filtered through the dialogues, however, it sounds more like a 'Sensation Novel' of the 1860s centering on a bigamist adventuress. Even if she comes to no good and the sentimental lovers are rewarded, the reader is, nonetheless, called upon to examine the divergences between the opinions and the behaviour of the audience, between their theories about art and life, and the artistic representations of them, and the underlying hypocritical double-standards of so-called 'civilized mankind'.

Such themes were common in much of the New Woman fiction, but Ella Hepworth Dixon typically complicates the issues. Lady Blaythewaite is acclaimed, for example, for her *crâne* in daring to appear so publicly three days before the court hearing, while at the same time the outcome of the case is being bet upon in the clubs. The question of heredity is also broached as she is unfavourably compared with her mother who sounds like a New Woman forerunner, having smoked in public, and who is referred to as 'a sort of Mrs Norton'.[82] In this case, the daughter is declared as not having inherited her mother's wits since she 'committed the fatal error of being found out'.[83] Surely this accentuates the lack of moral discernment in the speakers and raises doubts about the moral standards of all concerned. In the next chapter what has become 'The Great Divorce Case' 'hung like a pestilence over England',[84] and yet two months later Lady Blaythewaite is back in society, 'in her favourite swaggering attitude'.[85] No verdict has been obtained, but 'Sir Horace was old, ugly, and vicious; she was young, pretty, and in a notably tolerant set', so all ends in her favour and the scandal subsides. It is not only 'the common, soulless little Cockney'[86] who does it 'all for show'. Significantly, Lady Blaythewaite is one of the few women in the novel who is not presented in a sympathetic light. She is, not surprisingly however, still there at the end, now appropriately entangled with Dr Dunlop Strange, another survivor, who is said to be devoted to her. With finesse Ella Hepworth Dixon implies an unwholesome furtiveness as 'he slipped his nervous, sinewy fingers round her (Lady Blaythewaite's) wrist in the shadow of the curtain'.[87] One cannot help feeling the two deserve each other.

---

[81] *Ibid.* p. 143.

[82] Caroline Norton, after a particularly unpleasant marriage, a divorce scandal, and subsequent haggling over custody of the children, had been a prominent campaigner for divorce-law reform.

[83] *The Story of a Modern Woman*, p. 139.

[84] *Ibid.* p. 145.

[85] *Ibid.* p. 154.

[86] *The Sketch* critic L.F.A.'s epithet for Perry Jackson.

[87] *The Story of a Modern Woman*, p. 176.

A parallel must be drawn between the scene in the theatre and the one in the hospital where Alison Ives in turn begins to learn about the questionable behaviour of Dr Dunlop Strange, then her suitor. As mentioned in chapter three, Ella Hepworth Dixon drew upon an earlier short story, 'Murder – or Mercy?',[88] for some elements of the novel as a whole, but much of this chapter in particular had appeared as 'Number Twenty-nine', one of the weekly 'Town and Country Tales' published in *The World*.[89] The story is unsigned, as was customary, and there are a few minor changes, for example the doctor is called Sir Kenneth Brandon and 'number twenty-nine' had been his lawful wife, whilst the lady, here called Lady Sibthorpe, a wealthy widow, embodies the later roles of both Alison Ives and Mary Erle since, as well as engaging in philathropic work, she also writes articles for reviews. Whole sentences, however, have been transposed from the short story to the novel, leaving room for little doubt about the identity of its author.

With astounding economy and impressive restraint Ella Hepworth Dixon depicts both the confrontation in 'Charlotte Ward' and the next and final meeting between Alison Ives and Dr Dunlop Strange at a society dinner. His referring to 'the girl he had taken such a fancy to, ... the girl who had been so fond of him', who was now 'a shapeless lump', 'a horrible wreck', as 'the unsightly corpse ... of his dead pleasure'[90] is particularly evocative. Later, the doctor even has the brutality to refer to her as symptomatic of 'cankerous evils, eating away the very life of our social system'. Number Twenty-seven, as she has become, may euphemistically be referred to as a 'morally deficient person', but as far as Alison Ives is concerned she 'has urgent claims on all men's honour, on all women's pity'.[91] Ella Hepworth Dixon, like many a New Woman writer, perhaps most notably Sarah Grand in *The Heavenly Twins*, again implies that the real moral inadequacies are not where they appear to be. Dr Dunlop Strange's cast-off mistress, the Number Twenty-seven of the title of the chapter, obviously does not benefit from the social advantages of Lady Blaythewaite, implying that class as much as, if not more than, gender led to discrimination. Alison Ives, like Mary Erle, having to come to terms with the truth about her private life in a public arena, reacts in much the same calm, yet serious, way. She has an advantage, however, in that it is she who can put an end to their relationship. She may express herself softly and quietly as was expected of women, but she points out in no uncertain terms the deficiencies in her lover's pretence at morality, and her 'royal scorn' makes it perfectly clear to the doctor that all is over between them.

Nevertheless, in the course of the novel, three weddings do take place. They would not, however, meet the requirements of the matriarchal Lady Jane, the paternalistic family doctor, or the fictional editor who claimed to know what the British public would accept: there are not many love-scenes, nor is there a

[88] *The Woman's World* (October, 1888), pp. 466-469.
[89] *The World* (April 15, 1891), pp. 29-32.
[90] *The Story of a Modern Woman*, p. 152.
[91] *Ibid*. p. 160.

traditional wedding at the end, nor is there even a happy ending in marital terms since not one of the marriages that does take place fulfils romantic expectations.

Earlier romances, and many a later work, might have concluded 'with the pretty-pretty, the obvious'[92] so acclaimed by her editor, and which Mary Erle herself had long hoped for, had her lover returned after many trials and tribulations to reclaim the best part of himself, as he calls her at the beginning of the novel, and to take care of her. He had, however, in the meantime, married a woman he neither admired nor loved in order to further his career, so when he does have the gall to come back, bemoaning his lot and suggesting a liaison thus making a *dis*honest woman of Mary Erle, claiming, predictably, that she 'would inspire (him) to noble things',[93] no such happy end is possible. When Vincent Hemming tells her he is going to catch the mail train to Paris and begs her to come with him, suggesting, 'We - we could live somewhere in France ... in some little place where English people don't go',[94] he reminds readers of Rochester who, after Jane Eyre has learnt of the existence of his wife, says, 'You shall go to a place I have in the south of France ... .'[95] At this stage, Vincent Hemming may also be blinded or maimed emotionally and professionally, but Ella Hepworth Dixon allows him no convenient consolation.

While one might be willing to show a certain amount of understanding for a man who could no longer love his wife, or for a gifted young man who, lacking the financial wherewithal to achieve his aims, had made compromises he later regretted, throughout the novel Vincent Hemming has been a model of egocentricity, and one's sympathies go out to his wife and daughter, as indeed do Mary Erle's, even if she had initially commented on 'the triumphant expression of the underbred young woman who had secured a desirable husband'.[96] Ultimately, one can also sympathize with Miss Violet Higgins who, like many a young woman, may have been 'sold' into a loveless marriage, and could be the heroine of another New Woman novel. Who knows, for example, what diseases Vincent Hemming, like the husbands in *The Heavenly Twins*, might have brought home with him? How appropriate and satisfying, therefore, that just as Mary Erle has to 'do another happy ending, the rapturous *finale* which the public demanded',[97] the divide between life and fiction should again be emphasized as she burns Vincent Hemming's picture fuelling the blaze with his love-letters, thus marking the conclusion of what she terms 'a mere episode'.

In turn, Mary Erle's brother, having got to Oxford thanks to her sweat and toil, 'did little more ... than entangle himself with, and finally marry, a scout's

92 *Ibid.* p. 148.
93 *Ibid.* p. 183.
94 *Ibid.* This was changed to Cattaro on the Dalmatian coast for American readers.
95 Charlotte Bronte, *Jane Eyre* (1847, repr. Harmondsworth, 1964), chapter 27, p. 331.
96 *The Story of a Modern Woman*, p. 143.
97 *Ibid.* p. 190.

daughter'.[98] At least he does 'the decent thing', unlike Dr Dunlop Strange who seduces and then abandons his mistress. As the *The Times* reviewer remarked, man generally cuts 'a very poor figure'[99] indeed. The *Lady's Pictorial* 'Emancipated Fiction' reviewer goes even further in saying 'the troubles of both (Alison Ives and Mary Erle) arise from the faults and feeblenesses of men'.[100] Nevertheless, Ella Hepworth Dixon does not belabour the point. She leaves it to the reader to see the ironic significance in the fact that both Vincent Hemming and Dr Dunlop Strange consider themselves, and are considered, experts on women, the former writing a book on the Woman Question, and the latter specializing in nervous diseases, long thought to be female maladies. Marriage with either of these men would hardly be desirable and, although spinsterhood is by no means glorified, Mary Erle and Alison Ives can ultimately be seen as having had narrow escapes. This opinion is in part shared by the *Lady's Pictorial* reviewer who declares:

> No decent woman, whether emancipated or no, would marry a man who had treated a girl as cruelly and callously as Dunlop Strange treated 'Number Twenty-seven', or one who had been so ready to jilt her for mere monetary considerations as Vincent Hemming jilted Mary Erle.[101]

Surely much of the New Woman writing was concerned with drawing attention to precisely such occurrences.

The wedding which is described in most detail and with all the trimmings, including a veil and orange blossoms, is that of Evelina, the 'fallen' woman befriended by Alison Ives. There must again be an element of irony in Ella Hepworth Dixon's careful descriptions of Evelina in her second-hand white silk dress and a gold locket containing a curl of her baby's hair being conveyed to 'matrimonial respectability'. Earlier in the novel Mary Erle's childish vision of a wife as 'a person who began by wearing a beautiful white satin train, with white flowers and a veil'[102] is closely associated with her dead mother who had supposedly become an angel. 'The child was not sure whether she would best like to be a bride or an angel' and 'thought, probably, that matters might be compromised, and that she could be a wife and have a halo, too'.[103] Making a link between Mary Erle's dead mother, who sounds like the archetypal 'angel in the house', and the fallen woman, thus her exact reverse, might seem to some readers almost sacrilegious. It might also highlight the hypocrisy of social conventions and raise questions about accepted moral standards, as do the earlier mentioned differing attitudes towards infidelity and divorce. With her customary skill, Ella Hepworth Dixon does not pontificate; it is enough that Evelina's baby is said to

---

98 Deleted from the American version, but at the end of the chapter entitled 'The World Wags On' in both the serialized version and Heinemann's edition.

99 *The Times* (June 30, 1894), p. 19.

100 (Unsigned), 'Emancipated Fiction III', *Lady's Pictorial* (October 13, 1894), p. 534.

101 *Ibid.*

102 *The Story of a Modern Woman*, p. 53.

103 *Ibid.*

belong to the anti-marriage movement since he screamed through the whole ceremony.[104]

I would be reluctant, however, to place either Mary Erle or Alison Ives, or even Ella Hepworth Dixon, in Mrs Oliphant's anti-marriage league.[105] Significantly, Evelina's wedding takes place after both Mary Erle and Alison Ives have given up all ideas of marriage for themselves. It might seem odd, therefore, that Alison Ives should encourage her *protégée* to marry. It should not be forgotten that she is her mother's daughter and has obviously inherited or acquired a propensity for match-making. When, for example, she learns that Vincent Hemming is back in England, she declares, 'I think I shall insist on the marriage coming off at once', 'I'm in the vein for weddings',[106] and when she discusses Evelina's wedding with Mary Erle, it is the latter who says 'poor little Evelina' and who finds the whole affair 'pathetic'. Such comments reveal a change in Mary Erle: she has always shown an awareness of the practical concerns involved, but, having spent a great deal of time awaiting to no avail her lover's return, here she appears, justifiably, somewhat disillusioned.

Alison Ives, as well as encouraging others to marry, admits 'in her world, one had to marry some day or other',[107] even if she adds 'the later the better'.[108] Her reasoning is purely pragmatic: 'it was absurd to think that old maids had any influence on people's lives; and Power, to put it plainly, was what the modern woman craved'.[109] This might explain why *The Athenaeum* and the *Lady's Pictorial* 'Emancipated Fiction' reviewers considered her and not Mary Erle the more up to date. On the other hand, I think it is precisely here that the latter is an example of a 'modern woman'. Not only does she not possess Alison Ives' financial advantages, she also has a dependent brother and yet does not view marriage as a panacea. When Vincent Hemming first proposes, her response is not what was usually expected of a young heroine: she 'tasted for the first time, in all its intensity, the helplessness of woman, the inborn feeling of subjection to a stronger will, inherited through generations of submissive feminine intelligences'.[110] Later, her ambition to be accepted in the Academy is motivated by a desire for 'independence, a profession, a happy union', in that order. Rather than seeing herself as a kept woman, she now has more active incentives to be a helpmate on an equal standing with her husband. If ultimately she may be said to choose to be an old maid since she rejects a marriage proposal from a man who 'would like to have saved her from the struggle of the woman who works, the fret and fever, the dreary fight for existence',[111] it is partly because at this point she is

---

[104] A detail added to the book version on both sides of the Atlantic.

[105] (M.O.W.O.) Mrs Oliphant, 'The Anti-marriage League', *Blackwood's Magazine* 159 (1896), pp. 135-149.

[106] *The Story of a Modern Woman*, p. 113.

[107] *Ibid*. p. 92.

[108] *Ibid*.

[109] *Ibid*.

[110] *Ibid*. p. 82.

[111] *Ibid*. p. 136.

still expecting, albeit with foreboding, to marry Vincent Hemming. Her 'strange misgiving' suggests that her hopes are slim, but nonetheless she prefers to keep her independence even if it means that, needing to earn a living and competing in the world of men, she has 'to walk alone, to fight the battle of life unaided'.[112] Alison Ives had earlier commented, 'One couldn't permit one's self the *luxury* of being an old maid, unless one had an income of over five thousand pounds a year'[113] (my italics), and yet Mary Erle, financially much less secure than her friend, does choose that option. Her life is far from what one would normally consider 'luxurious', but the suggestion is that her independence and self-reliance are priceless, a sentiment other New Woman writers, especially Olive Schreiner and Mona Caird, would share.

In Ella Hepworth Dixon's fiction, therefore, marriage is rarely, if ever, motivated by traditional romantic notions or even contemporary eugenic ideals. Nonetheless, it is not that marriage itself is rejected, as Mary Erle's occasional dreams of suburbia testify, or that divorce is endorsed, or that any alternative is offered. Part of Ella Hepworth Dixon's merit lies in her refusal to simplify or to impose ideological restrictions on her characters, or her readers. Very often she presents the reader with images, ideas, suggestions, rather for the arousal of compassion than for moral judgements. As *The Sketch* reviewer remarked, 'Miss Dixon is too true an artist to preach cut-and-dried plans of social regeneration.'[114]

One can thus begin to see the wider concerns of the novel; it is not merely about the domestic affairs of women, but also about their finding a place outside the home that was acceptable. This was obviously a challenge to social expectations. The very idea that a woman might seek self-fulfilment beyond the confines of the private sphere, although by then a recurrent theme in fiction, was still troubling from many points of view. Unlike some of the New Woman writers Ella Hepworth Dixon demonstrates that such preoccupations were not limited to one social milieu only and suggests that a variety of different solutions might be available, though none of them easy or without certain risks. Her 'plea for a kind of moral and social trades-unionism among women'[115] thus takes on deeper significance. Several reviewers commented on what the critic in the *Lady's Pictorial* series on 'Emancipated Fiction By One who has the Misfortune to be a Man' calls the 'new sisterhood'.[116] *The Sketch* critic refers to 'the ideal of sisterly ties' which are 'to bind women together in a league more promising than the franchise'. *The Times* reviewer, on the other hand, concludes, 'Miss Dixon is a smart and clever writer, who will do better when she dissociates herself from the sisterhood who are rending heaven with laments about the "torture of women's lives - the helplessness, the impotence, the emptiness!"' The references to a 'sisterhood' are obviously a clear

---

[112] *Ibid.* p. 170.
[113] *Ibid.* p. 149.
[114] *The Sketch* (June 27, 1894), p. 476.
[115] Ella Hepworth Dixon quoted by W.T. Stead, p. 71.
[116] (Unsigned), 'Emancipated Fiction III', *Lady's Pictorial* (October 13, 1894), p. 534.

identification of Ella Hepworth Dixon with a number of other women novelists described by W.T. Stead as the 'school' of the Modern Woman.

In fact, throughout the novel many women do help others of their sex, the most obvious example being Alison Ives, although even her mother in her own way, albeit within a much narrower domain, does what she thinks is best for young women. By choosing to go out to help the poor and often 'fallen' women who had surely sought a better life away from their own homes, Alison Ives could typify a certain number of upper middle-class women, doing good amongst the less fortunate. Such pursuits were not considered unwomanly. Nevertheless, Alison Ives does rather more than simply engage in what might be deemed mere charity work. Her 'real desire to be in sympathy with her sex'[117] and her lack of snobbishness, or what *The Athenaeum* reviewer deprecatingly calls her 'taste for violent social contrasts', are distinctive, and, as it turns out, through her benevolent work she contracts a chest infection from which she rather quickly dies.

This could in turn have led to a mawkish deathbed scene, so common in Victorian fiction, but it is in no way sentimentalized. As her friend lies dying Mary Erle:

> Remembered that Death, the great destroyer, had an irony which is all his own. Beautiful, noble, helpful lives were crushed, destroyed, annihilated. Death made no more account of them than a schoolboy does of a beetle, on whom, in passing by, he tramps wantonly[118] in a ditch. A minute ago they breathed, and hoped, and loved; another minute in the aeons of time, and the insect was a mere blotch of slime, one's passionately loved idol lay rotting under the sod.[119]

Just as Perry Jackson had no message for Mary Erle's public, so Alison Ives has 'nothing literary, with a meaning' for Ella Hepworth Dixon's readers. Significantly, the writer provides no dying words of wisdom for either Alison Ives, who worries about whether her feet will get slim again, or Professor Erle who, much to a journalist's disappointment, says nothing: 'he just died in his sleep'. It is, in fact, the fallen woman, Number Twenty-seven, who speaks out 'at the last' revealing the unpleasant truth about Dr Dunlop Strange although 'she never mentioned his name'. Even in death her sense of honour is far greater than her seducer's.

On many levels, therefore, Ella Hepworth Dixon is refusing to cater to popular taste. It may be argued that Alison Ives sacrifices herself and Mary Erle may wait for her lover's return and accept his choice of another bride seemingly 'with no touch of wounded vanity or bitterness in her sorrow'.[120] *The Athenaeum* reviewer

---

[117] *The Story of a Modern Woman*, p. 70.

[118] Surely reminiscent of Gloucester's 'As flies to wanton boys, are we to the gods;/ They kill us for their sport.' *King Lear*, IV, i, lines 36-37. Ella Hepworth Dixon may distance herself from some contemporary literary modes, but would appear to be aligning herself with a longer, greater tradition.

[119] *The Story of a Modern Woman*, p. 172.

[120] *The Athenaeum* (June 16, 1894), p. 770.

may consider 'there is little "modernity" in such resignation', but Mary Erle does speak of 'the intolerable burden which society has laid on her sex'.[121] In the chapter entitled 'The Woman Waits' she describes in a kind of interior monologue 'how dreadful it is to be woman, and to have to sit down, and fold your hands, and wait',[122] and again in the next chapter, entitled 'The Man Returns', she voices to herself 'the horror of waiting, waiting, and waiting'.[123] Moreover, on several occasions, for example when her best friend is dying, she reveals a latent resistance, rather different from the meekness attributed to her: 'The injustice of life revolted her. ... When she was a little child she used to stiffen herself with silent rage when any one accused or struck her unjustly.'[124] Again, fittingly, much as Alison Ives had earlier shown quiet force in bringing to an end the relationship with Dr Dunlop Strange, so, after her last meeting with Vincent Hemming, it is Mary Erle who finally leaves him waiting. As consolation it may be minimal, but as a sign of potential strength, it is highly significant.

In her work on twentieth century women writers, Rachel Blau DuPlessis explores at length the ways in which at the end of the nineteenth century New Woman writers were searching to find 'a way of thinking about narratives with women that was not synonymous with thinking about romance for women'.[125] In writing against stereotypical representations of women and the whole construct of the feminine ideal, part of which includes self-sacrifice and pretty young girls waiting for a charming prince to appear or reappear 'with a wedding at the end',[126] Ella Hepworth Dixon obliges the reader to re-think the implications of such stereotypes. Such unwillingness to falsify reality and provide a happy end can be seen as a deliberate refusal to conform to tradition. A generation later, in her essay on 'Modern Fiction' Virginia Woolf was to encourage similar resistance: 'The writer seems constrained, not by his (sic) own free will but by some powerful and unscrupulous tyrant who has him in thrall, to provide a plot, to provide comedy, tragedy, love interest ... . But ... is life like this? Must novels be like this?'[127]

Kate Flint rightly points out that Mary Erle 'defines herself and her life against forms of story-telling', and describes the novel as 'like much women's fiction of the time, self-conscious about its own textual status'.[128] The difficulties inherent in writing, reading and interpreting infiltrate the text from beginning to end. The novel opens with Professor Erle laid out in a darkened upper-floor room whilst downstairs in a little study Mary Erle is seen at her desk writing what she recognizes to be 'worn-out, foolish sentences, ... all the stock phrases of

---

[121] *The Story of a Modern Woman*, p. 65.
[122] *Ibid.* p. 119.
[123] *Ibid.* p. 121.
[124] *Ibid.* p. 171.
[125] Rachel Blau DuPlessis, *Writing Beyond the Ending: Narrative Strategies of Twentieth Century Women Writers* (Bloomington, 1985), p. 56.
[126] *The Story of a Modern Woman*, p. 147.
[127] 'Modern Fiction' (1925, repr. London, 1984), p. 149.
[128] Introduction to *The Story of a Modern Woman* (London, 1990), p. vii.

condolence'. At the end, when she arranges for another well-known phrase, the last line of Tennyson's 'Ulysses', 'To strive, to seek, to find, and not to yield',[129] to be re-engraved this time over her dead father's body on his tomb, one cannot help questioning the significance and sincerity of the expression. Is it merely a re-affirmation? Is it then the triumph of patriarchy? Or does it rather signify that the motto has been tried, tested and adopted by the daughter? Or yet again, since there is a certain ambiguity in Tennyson's poem, does it suggest a re-reading of the original? Just as the image of the aged, proud Ulysses may not be as complimentary as it first seems, so Professor Erle, although he may have been a similarly great public figure, 'the best-known man of science of the day', in private on closer inspection was not the best of fathers. As mentioned earlier, T.P. O'Connor in *The Weekly Sun* considered this the central theme of the text, and based the whole of his long review on his interpretation of the novel as 'an indictment of the manner in which our daughters are brought up – especially the daughters of our professional men'.[130]

In a similar vein, Garrett Stewart has suggested that much New Woman fiction 'involves not the companionable reading of a story but the resistant, if tacit, re-reading of inherited stories en masse, a re-reading through the now corrective lenses of an adjusted feminist vision',[131] thus implying that both reader and character are obliged to revise their readings. To my mind, Ella Hepworth Dixon continually appeals to a well-read reader and deliberately provokes the above-mentioned re-appraisal of accepted narratives. In reference to *David Copperfield*,[132] for example, Mary Erle's apparently childish question about whether Mr Steerforth was a lost man since he goes to Italy with little Em'ly who is definitely considered 'a lost woman' should raise questions about double moral standards. Likewise, Ella Hepworth Dixon's description of the notoriously misogynist Jean-Jacques Rousseau's *Le Contrat Social* as 'a work which it behoved a person of fourteen, a person who wished to understand the scheme of civilisation, to know'[133] would

---

129 The phrase is still often quoted in memory of great men, for example on Scott's Antarctic Memorial.

130 *The Weekly Sun* (July 29, 1894), p. 1.

131 Garrett Stewart, *Dear Reader: The Conscripted Audience in Nineteenth Century British Fiction* (Baltimore, 1996), p. 154.

132 A detail added to both book versions. In the serialized version at sixteen Mary Erle takes Browning's 'Men and Women' with her to Germany, and when she returns a year later 'from the virile optimism of Browning she could not now afford to part.' This is closer to the author's own experience since twice in her memoirs Ella Hepworth Dixon mentions taking Browning's work with her to Germany: in the chapter on Professor Ihne of Heidelberg she writes, 'I arrived ... with a volume of Browning's poems under my arm', and in the chapter on Robert Browning, Algernon Charles Swinburne and Sir William Watson, she describes in greater detail having been '"brought" up on Browning' by her elder sister, Edith, and arriving 'with a much-thumbed and underlined copy of Browning's verse ... at the house of Professor Ihne, at Heidelberg.' *As I Knew Them* (London, 1930), pp. 23 and 50 respectively.

133 *The Story of a Modern Woman*, p. 56.

surely suggest not only re-evaluating 'the Swiss philosopher's diatribes', but also remedying inadequacies in the education of women. The title of the novel itself might be a passing reference to Olive Schreiner's *The Story of an African Farm,* often considered the proto-type of New Woman fiction and a work much admired by Ella Hepworth Dixon,[134] suggesting perhaps that one need not go to exotic places to find women like Lyndall. Such women were not so 'far removed from the round of English daily life'[135] and could be seen 'in the twilight of the suburban road'.[136] This would further highlight the inadequacies of Vincent Hemming's research on the Woman Question for which he has to travel the world. Vincent Hemming's journeys might even be an ironic reflection on some of the adventure stories by writers such as Rider Haggard, Bram Stoker and Robert Louis Stevenson about male protagonists going off to faraway places and facing all sorts of dangers. Ella Hepworth Dixon would certainly be turning the tables on that narrative since here the would-be hero comes back practically betrothed, and later bemoans 'the dreariness, the vulgarity, the commonplace'[137]of his life.

Although Ella Hepworth Dixon displays none of Olive Schreiner's religious fervour, rarely mentioning religion at all, or concern with motherhood, and I would hesitate to draw too many parallels between the two works, there are certain similarities shared by Lyndall and Mary Erle: they are both orphans, acquiring from books much of their sadly inadequate education and, realizing that 'books do not tell everything',[138] they subsequently become desirous of 'seeing things as they are'.[139] This description could superficially fit most heroines of female *bildungsroman*, but a distinctive feature of New Woman writing, and the works of Olive Schreiner and Ella Hepworth Dixon are no exceptions, would seem to be an attempt to show that 'nothing happened as it does in tales and romances'.[140] That literature is not life even Mary Erle's editor would agree, nor can it allow one to make up one's mind once and for all, as the young Mary Erle had thought, but it can awaken pity and extend the readers' sympathies, as George Eliot had earlier claimed and as Ella Hepworth Dixon suggests both in Mary Erle's reading in the novel and in the Stead interview. As a child Mary Erle often expressed sympathy for those who suffered, whether she read about them in the Bible, in newspapers or in Literature, making no distinction between fact and fiction. Even as an adult she continued to empathize with others, for example, watching her seamstress 'an immense pity seized her for the patient figure',[141] or the woman in the park, later referred to as 'Number Twenty-seven', who, 'keeping a rendezvous with a lover

[134] For example in her 'Pensées de Femme', *Lady's Pictorial* (August 17, 1895), p. 231, Ella Hepworth Dixon refers to Olive Schreiner's 'masterpiece'.
[135] 'R. Iron', Author's Preface to *The Story of an African Farm* (1883, repr. London, 1924), p. v.
[136] *The Story of a Modern Woman*, p. 192.
[137] *Ibid.* p. 181.
[138] *The Story of an African Farm* (1883, repr. London, 1924), p. 16.
[139] *The Story of a Modern Woman*, p. 147.
[140] *Ibid.* p. 45.
[141] *Ibid.* p. 49.

who had not yet appeared', 'seized her imagination'. 'Mary felt drawn towards her; she would have liked to have gone up and said something kind.'[142]

Like many a Victorian heroine, including Lyndall, Mary Erle has been motherless for years. The book begins with her father's death, leaving her practically alone in the world. Her only sibling, a younger brother, is a source of little comfort, but he does provide an opportunity to show that she was neither the 'heartless, sexless thing' *The Athenaeum* reviewer, probably along with much of the reading public, took the New Woman to be, nor was she quite the 'gentle and essentially feminine creature' *The Times* reviewer suggests. Even if at the birth of her brother, she had shown a strong dislike for babies, just as she had 'held the whole race of dolls in high scorn',[143] decidedly not what would be expected of a feminine stereotype, and after her father's death 'a demon of unrest possessed her', she would not automatically 'forsake home ties and duties' and could still be an 'angel in the house', if necessary. Nevertheless, instead of languishing and feeling sorry for herself, she displays none of the usual neurasthenic heroine's symptoms of female frailty such as lack of appetite. Whereas 'in innumerable novels she had read how the heroine, in a house of mourning, lies on the bed for days and steadily refuses to eat', she was hungry, and 'it was as if she could not eat nourishing food enough'.[144] She also takes action, including rejecting the offer of a home from a High Church Aunt living in Bournemouth, thus declaring her desire for independence from the beginning.

Her determination and resourcefulness are likewise present from the start and disprove *The Athenaeum* reviewer's idea of her accepting her role 'meekly'. Self-help and solidarity with others replace self-pity and self-denial. Alison Ives comments on how 'we women are so incredibly dependent on other people',[145] but Mary Erle insists, 'we've got, … fortunately or unfortunately, to depend upon ourselves in all the crises of life',[146] which is precisely what she sets out to do and succeeds in doing. That there is a price to be paid, however, for such a valiant struggle, the author never denies, as Alison Ives' premature death and Mary Erle's poor health testify.

W.T. Stead seems perfectly justified in employing the term 'heroical' to describe both women, just as his use of 'optimistic' to describe Ella Hepworth Dixon is surprisingly appropriate, even if she herself thought the novel 'rather gloomy', and indeed it would hardly qualify as a 'thoroughly breezy book'. As mentioned earlier, there is no wedding at the end, but nor does it end with death. Ella Hepworth Dixon chooses not to conclude with the termination of the relationship with Vincent Hemming or even with Alison Ives' death, as another writer might well have done. Nor, like the notorious *The Woman Who Did*, does the

---

142 *Ibid.* A detail deleted from the American version, but in the original and Heinemann, pp. 121-122.
143 *Ibid.* p. 51.
144 *Ibid.* p. 45.
145 *Ibid.* p. 71.
146 *Ibid.* p. 73.

novel terminate with the heroine's suicide. In the chapter appropriately entitled 'The Woman in the Glass', with admirable honesty, Ella Hepworth Dixon explores Mary Erle's confrontation with her own image of herself and that reflected in the mirror, such as society might hold up to her. She contemplates 'the eternal question of sex' describing how easy it would have been to succumb to Vincent Hemmings' overtures and to her own desires, and how painful it was for a woman to live 'in a world of artificial laws; of laws made for man's convenience and pleasure'.[147] After a dark night of the soul, however, in which she fights the temptation[148] to become his mistress and thus a social outcast, and suicide, death of another kind, Mary Erle makes a fitting return to her father's grave, echoing the first chapter of the novel, aptly entitled 'An End and a Beginning'.

Here again Ella Hepworth Dixon would seem to be drawing on the well-read reader's familiarity with earlier works. T.P. O'Connor notes the resemblance, for example, between this scene and:

> That awful passage at the close of *Père Goriot* in which Lucien de Rubempré[149] looks down from Père la Chaise on Paris. ... Doubtless, too, the resemblance is intentional, for the two passages mark the everlasting difference between man and woman. Lucien de Rubempré shakes his clenched hand in fierce and brave defiance; but the woman's hand 'ended in a vain gesture'. Defiance and conflict and victory are the hopes, and often the portion of the man; but tranquil endurance and blind obedience is the highest to which woman can reach.[150]

I would argue, however, that Mary Erle also has her portion of 'defiance and conflict and victory' and hopes. The last scene may take place in a cemetery, but ultimately the heroine turns her back on the grave-yard, not on the city, surely emphasizing the triumph of life over death. There may be disillusion, but there is little lamentation and even less of a sense of defeat. Mary Erle may not have achieved all she set out to do, and she may be even more alone than she was at the beginning, with her best friend dead and both her brother and her lover married, but she is no Ruth, 'sick for home'. She has survived and can 'plod homewards'. The final note, therefore, however tenuous, remains positive. It is even possible to see similarities with the opening of Wordsworth's *Prelude*, 'from yon City's walls set free, ... The earth is all before me',[151] itself a reflection of the end of Milton's *Paradise Lost*[152] - 'The world was all before them.' If, unlike Adam and Eve, 'hand

---

[147] *Ibid*. p. 189.

[148] The *Lady's Pictorial* reviewer notes, 'The temptation was terrific, but not triumphant.' *Lady's Pictorial* (October 13, 1894), p. 534.

[149] Eugène de Rastignac in the original.

[150] T.P. (O'Connor), *The Weekly Sun* (July 29, 1894), p. 2. In fact, at the end of the original French version Rastignac merely surveys Paris and says, 'A nous deux maintenant!' (The Penguin Modern Classics edition translates this as 'It's war between us now'.) His first 'act of defiance' is then to go and dine with Mme de Nucingen, Père Goriot's daughter.

[151] *The Prelude*, Book First, lines 7-15.

[152] *Paradise Lost*, Book XII, line 646.

in hand', Mary Erle was to stand alone, and 'in all this gaiety of a new-born world only she was to have no part',[153] she does, however, face the city. Earlier when she had stood on the self same spot with her brother after their father's funeral, she had shown surprising enthusiasm for the metropolis: 'Jim, there's London! We're going to make it listen to us, you and I. We're not going to be afraid of it - just because it's big, and brutal and strong.'[154] At the end as she once more surveys London, she again describes it not in typically Victorian hostile terms, but as 'majestic, awe-inspiring, inexorable, triumphant.'[155]

Such changing attitudes to public spaces and the city in general are a significant feature of *fin de siècle* fiction, as Sally Ledger[156] amongst others has pointed out, and similarities between the New Woman and the pleasure-seeking *flaneur* have been drawn. Walter Benjamin in particular has written about the *flaneur* in Paris 'as much at home among the façades of houses as a citizen in his four walls. To him the shiny, enamelled signs of businesses are at least as good a wall ornament as an oil painting is to a bourgeois in his salon.'[157] Art, too, was thus being put on public display, as the tremendous boom in advertising hoardings and posters of the time testify, even meriting exhibitions in Paris and New York. Public space was thus being taken over by a more consumer-oriented society, but as Elizabeth Wilson[158] has rightly pointed out this was primarily the domain of masculine gaze, so I would be reluctant to class Mary Erle as a *flaneur*. Neither she nor Alison Ives strolls through the streets in search of sensation; both go about their business, the latter to help girls in the East End of London and the former en route to her publishers or interviews. Certainly it is significant that Mary Erle feels no sense of threat:

> The well-dressed loafers who find their pleasure in accosting ladies in the street ... were perhaps more easily disposed of than some of the men who took her in to dinner, men who had tired eyes and a dubious smile, and who were fond of starting doubtful topics with a side-long, tentative glance.[159]

Ella Hepworth Dixon's insistence on the street-walking of both Mary Erle and Alison Ives marks a decided change in a woman's claiming of public space.

Ella Hepworth Dixon may not cater to some readers' expectations, whether of the old or the new school; the good do not necessarily prosper nor are the wicked punished, but a certain sense of satisfaction is provided and, more important, the

---

153 *The Story of a Modern Woman*, p. 270. This phrase was not in the original version.
154 *Ibid.* p. 48.
155 *Ibid.* p. 192.
156 See in particular *The New Woman: Fiction and Feminism at the Fin de Siècle* (Manchester, 1997), chapter six 'The New Woman in the Modern City' in which Sally Ledger discusses the *flaneuse* or the woman of the streets.
157 Walter Benjamin, *Charles Baudelaire: a Lyric Poet in the Era of High Capitalism* (London, 1973).
158 Elizabeth Wilson, 'The invisible *flaneur*', *New Left Review* (January/February, 1992), pp. 90-110.
159 *The Story of a Modern Woman*, p. 67.

reader is left with a heightened awareness of possibilities, of untapped alternatives. Self-fulfilment is by definition a continuous process so the openendedness of the last page is appropriate and precisely one of the novel's most interesting aspects. In this lies much of Ella Hepworth Dixon's innovatory skill, and justifies a reappraisal of her work. Just as she was drawing on past and contemporary fictional models, at the same time she was also prefiguring writers such as D.H. Lawrence[160] and Virginia Woolf, even I would argue incorporating elements of William James' 'stream of consciousness', mentioned in his *Principles of Psychology* which had been published a few years earlier.[161] For example, as Mary plods through London she surely has some of the makings of a Mrs Dalloway, though the latter would no doubt have a more elegant gait.

Present-day readers can appreciate for themselves the modernity of Ella Hepworth Dixon's writing thanks to the 2004 re-edition of the *The Story of a Modern Woman.* John Sutherland in the Preface to *The Longman Companion to Victorian Fiction* describes it as 'one of the finest New Woman novels'.[162] Contemporary critics also passed comment on what they considered the literary merits of the novel as well as its content. *The Sketch* reviewer, for example, enthuses, 'Miss Dixon's style excels in delicate vignettes, full of suggestion, and marked, above all, by that artistic restraint which is such an agreeable contrast to the fluency of the average woman-novel.'[163] William Sharp in *The Academy*[164] was even more complimentary. Athough he found the story 'in no way remarkable', the work in his opinion showed 'altogether exceptional promise'. He further praised 'the excellence of the writing and the genuine talent shown by Miss Ella Hepworth Dixon', and concluded '*A* (sic) *Story of a Modern Woman* seems to me one of the best written books which have appeared of late, whether by writers of "the larger latitude" or otherwise.'

One cannot help wondering why, therefore, like all the other works listed by W.T. Stead, it disappeared from circulation for so long, only recently to re-surface. I would argue that much of the New Woman writing dealt with difficult topics, challenged accepted beliefs and posed questions to which there were no immediate answers. Many contemporaries considered such subjects unsuitable material for literature, especially that written for and by women, and would have preferred such issues to remain unmentioned. They have, however, not gone away, and indeed many are as topical and polemical as they ever were. It is interesting to note that when Ella Hepworth Dixon's novel was first re-published in 1990 by Merlin, it was

---

160 Lyn Pykett drew my attention to the similarities with the ending of D.H. Lawrence's *Sons and Lovers,* where Paul Morel 'walked towards the faintly humming, glowing town, quickly'. See Lyn Pykett, *The 'Improper' Feminine* (London, 1992) for further discussion.

161 'Consciousness, then, does not appear to itself chopped up in bits. ... It is nothing jointed; it flows. ... *Let us call it the stream of thought, of consciousness, or of subjective life.*' William James, *Principles of Psychology* (New York, 1890), p. 239 (his italics).

162 John Sutherland, Preface to *The Longman Companion to Victorian Fiction*, (Harlow, 1988), p. 2.

163 Signed F.L.A. 'The Book and Its Story', *The Sketch* (June 27, 1894), p. 476.

164 *The Academy* (June 16, 1894), p. 494.

not in the context of re-awakened interest in *fin de siècle* writing, nor even by a feminist press, but in a wider ranging spectrum of 'time, style, (and) authors'.[165] Unlike some of the New Woman writers, Ella Hepworth Dixon manages to prevent propaganda getting the upperhand to the detriment of fiction, and strikes a happy balance between the socio-political and the literary.

Over thirty years after the *annus mirabilis* of New Woman writing, Virginia Woolf claimed that women are:

> Less interested, it would seem, in themselves; on the other hand, they are more interested in other women. ... One of the motives that led them to write was the desire to expose their own suffering, to plead their own cause. Now that this desire is no longer so urgent, women are beginning to explore their own sex, to write of women as women have never been written before; ... .[166]

She concluded, 'From this it is a short step to the practice of the sophisticated arts, hitherto so little practised by women - to the writing of essays and criticism, of history and biography.'[167] It is almost as if she is describing in retrospect the New Woman writers for, like several others, after the success of her novel, Ella Hepworth Dixon did indeed channel her energies elsewhere and, as far as I know, never attempted to produce another long work of fiction. Some of the writers engaged in political action, such as the suffrage movement, some continued their careers in other fields. Ella Hepworth Dixon was offered the editorship of a new magazine, *The Englishwoman*, which she undertook enthusiastically. At the same time she continued to write both short fiction and non-fiction, and later tried her hand at drama, the topic of my next chapter.

---

165 John Lucas, 'General Introduction' to *The Story of a Modern Woman* (London, 1990).
166 Virginia Woolf, 'Women and Fiction', (1929, repr. London, 1958), p. 82.
167 *Ibid*. p. 84.

Chapter 6

'The World of the Theatre'

> The world of the Theatre was an amusing one in the 'nineties and nineteen hundreds. Every actor of note had his own theatre, and entertained lavishly. The playhouse was not then commercialized, and 'run' from Bradford and Huddersfield. Actors and actresses were made much of in Society; many great ladies demanded a return by soliciting boxes for famous 'first-nights', and Royalty came to these festivities.[1]

Whilst Ella Hepworth Dixon's retrospective description, like much in her memoirs, may sound rather flippant and predictably partial, it encapsulates many essential elements of the late Victorian and early Edwardian theatre world. She was, moreover, again speaking from first hand experience from both sides of the curtain since, besides mixing professionally and socially with a vast range of theatre society, in 1908 she also had a play of her own, *The Toyshop of the Heart*, produced on a West End stage at The Playhouse Theatre with celebrated actors of their day, Liliane Braithwaite and Harcourt Williams, in lead roles.

One cannot help wondering what motivated Ella Hepworth Dixon at a relatively advanced point in her career to try her hand at a new genre altogether. As her play formed part of a 'fashionable matinée'[2] in aid of The Infants' Hospital, Vincent Square, London, her immediate aims were ostensibly philanthropic. If, however, one considers the general social and political climate of the Edwardian era as well as the narrower context within which the play was performed, what might at first sight appear as mere dabbling in amateur dramatics could conceal less superficial, more important motivations.

As I Knew Them abounds with portraits of illustrious actors, critics, managers, writers and so on, reading rather like a contemporary roll-call of fame. Ella Hepworth Dixon recounts meeting the legendary Sarah Bernhardt, seeing Isadora Duncan and Eleonora Duse perform, and gives sympathetic descriptions of both Ellen Terry and Henry Irving, whom she admits to not knowing well though she 'went to his parties on the stage'. More time and space is understandably allocated to writers, including notables such as Arnold Bennett, George Bernard Shaw and Oscar Wilde whom she had met early in her own career in the world of journalism and before they, too, had turned to the theatre.

---

[1] *As I Knew Them* (London, 1930), p. 230.
[2] H. Hamilton Fyfe, *The World* (December 1, 1908), p. 1027.

Other celebrities of the day with whom she was obviously on intimate terms are less familiar to twenty-first century audiences. 'Sir James Barrie once did me the honour to read a one-act play of mine and sent me, through his wife, a most kindly judgement on it',[3] she writes, and I presume she is referring to *The Toyshop of the Heart* as I have found no evidence of other plays by her pen. J.M. Barrie (1860-1937) remains well-known today largely thanks to *Peter Pan* (1904) rather than, as then, for *The Admirable Crichton* (1902) or *What Every Woman Knows* (1908), although Ella Hepworth Dixon claims 'no-one is more popular - in the best sense of the word - than Sir James Barrie'. In the same section she also speaks of 'Henry Arthur Jones (1851-1929), who was so prominent a dramatist in the nineties, when many of his plays had phenomenal successes'.[4] Ella Hepworth Dixon suggests that *The Liars* (1897) would 'probably survive' and, indeed, it is perhaps the best-remembered, but between 1900 and 1914 '"Henry Arthur" as he was always known' had eleven plays acted on London stages and three in New York. Arthur Wing Pinero (1855-1934), 'universally known as "Pin"', according to Ella Hepworth Dixon, 'was then his only rival', 'besides being the best dramatist of the nineteen-hundreds'.[5] Sir Arthur Wing Pinero, is usually remembered for *Trelawny of the 'Wells'*, first performed in 1893 and often revived on several occasions in the Edwardian era, and *The Second Mrs Tanqueray* (1893).

Ella Hepworth Dixon's greatest praise is reserved, not surprisingly perhaps, for Ibsen. 'Indeed, Ibsen played a more revolutionary and far-reaching effect on the drama of his day than Shakespeare, with all his incomparable genius, ever did. ... (H)is plays have transformed the drama of the civilized world',[6] she declares and then, with her customary self-deprecation, recounts *not* meeting him. The first occasion, she describes 'as if one had the intrepidity to write, "Oh, yes, Shakespeare paid me an afternoon visit - I was out, but he left his card"'. On a trip to Oslo, she had left 'a much too flattering letter of introduction' from William Heinemann with the dramatist who then called in her absence. On the second opportunity two years later, not daring to approach the 'Immortal' as he sat drinking beer in the Grand Hotel where she was lunching, she admits she 'funked the whole situation', thus revealing 'of what cowardly stuff, speaking journalistically, (she) was made'.

In her portrait of Ibsen, however, Ella Hepworth Dixon also hints at more serious implications behind both amateur dramatics and the theatre in general. She mentions participating along with William Archer, 'the distinguished dramatic

---

[3] *As I Knew Them* (London, 1930), p. 177.

[4] *Ibid.* p. 175.

[5] *Ibid.* p. 176.

[6] *Ibid.* p. 77. Ella Hepworth Dixon wrote of the same missed encounters in one of her *Sketch* articles, 'Woman's Ways', *The Sketch* (December 4, 1912), p. xxii. See also her letter to Max Beerbohm, dated November 27/8, to be found in Merton College Library. In the letter she compliments Beerbohm on his *Christmas Garland* (London, 1912), which describes the imaginary meeting between Robert Browning and Henrik Ibsen in Venice, and adds 'I am not allowed now to write much about books in *The Sketch*, but I have managed to bring it in (next week) by describing my only meeting with Ibsen.'

critic and translator of Ibsen', William Heinemann and Elizabeth Robins in a play-reading 'in what passed for Norsk' of *John Gabriel Borkman* (1896) for copyright purposes. It would seem that this was by no means an uncommon activity amongst a certain intellectual elite. J.C. Trewin in his overview of the Edwardian theatre[7] describes a similar 'formal morning walk-through for copyright purposes' of Harley Granville-Barker's play, *Waste*, as well as an earlier private production of the play by the Stage Society in November 1907. Because the topic of abortion[8] was raised, the play was nevertheless banned until 1920. Indeed as the Edwardian era advanced, tension grew between dramatists of what is often called the 'Theatre of Ideas', including dramatists such as Shaw, and the Lord Chamberlain's office which granted licences for public performances. In 1909 a Joint Select Committee met to discuss the whole question of censorship, but little was resolved. One way of keeping within the law was simply to give special free, officially private, performances. J.C. Trewin gives the example of Eden Phillpotts' *The Secret Woman* (1912) which had displeased the censor because of its explicit dialogues. More familiar to today's public is perhaps George Bernard Shaw's *Mrs Warren's Profession* which, although written in 1893, was performed by the Stage Society only in 1902, and refused a licence until 1926, largely because of its treatment of what was considered unsavoury subject matter.

Below the surface glamour of the Edwardian theatre there were, therefore, subversive undercurrents. Yet Ella Hepworth Dixon's image of the theatre as primarily a place of entertainment and amusement would seem to be borne out by J.C. Trewin's list of the fifty Edwardian stage productions which were most successful, running as they did for over 350 performances. Only seven are called simply 'plays'; the rest are described variously as 'comedy', 'farce', 'musical play', 'musical comedy', 'comic opera', 'melodrama', 'revue', 'musical entertainment', 'farcical comedy', 'romantic comedy', much more in keeping with the 'Theatre Theatrical'. Several recent studies, however, have drawn attention to what lay beyond the 'round of commercial at-homes', to use Michael R. Booth and Joel H. Kaplan's expression,[9] which constituted the main-stream of Edwardian theatre, and more attention has been focussed on women in the theatre other than actresses. Critics and scholars such as Jean Chothia, Viv Gardner, Fidelis Morgan, Kerry Powell, Sheila Stowell, Dale Spender, and Lisa Tickner[10] have demonstrated that,

---

[7] J.C. Trewin, *The Edwardian Theatre* (Oxford, 1976).

[8] Surprisingly, Elizabeth Robins' *Votes for Women!* (1907), which also has mention of an abortion, did receive a licence. Jean Chothia, in her Introduction to *The New Woman and Other Emancipated Plays* (Oxford, 1998) mentions Ian Clarke's idea expressed in *Edwardian Drama* (London, 1989) that the Examiner of Plays was more concerned about Harley Granville-Barker's comments on political life. She herself suggests that it might be because the abortion had taken place in the distant past, or simply that the censor missed the reference altogether.

[9] Michael R. Booth and Joel H. Kaplan (eds), *The Edwardian Theatre: Essays on Performance and the Stage* (Cambridge, 1996).

[10] See in particular Lisa Tickner, *The Spectacle of Women: Imagery of the Suffrage Campaign 1907-1914* (London, 1987), Viv Gardner and Susan Rutherford (eds), *The New*

contrary to popular opinion, although the theatre in the pre-suffrage period was still essentially a male-dominated sphere, more women, continuing in the wake of the New Woman, were not only performing in plays, but were also writing and even producing them. In the same year her play was performed Ella Hepworth Dixon herself commented on the fact that 'so many women are taking up theatrical management'.[11] With her usual humour she then expressed the hope that consequently 'a settlement may be hoped for on the great matinée-hat question', a topic to which she regularly made allusion in her weekly column in the *Lady's Pictorial.* For example, a month before the performance of her play she wrote, 'Only the other day the actors at an afternoon performance played second fiddle while a brief and burning drama was enacted in the stalls, the principal *rôles* being filled by an irate gentleman and two ladies with monster hats.'[12] More seriously, Susan Torrey Barstow[13] has recently drawn attention to the importance of the matinée itself where invariably the audience was predominantly female. Matinées, which had been popular since the 1870s, became even more in vogue in the Edwardian era. It is within this context of women participating more actively on both sides of the curtain that I would situate Ella Hepworth Dixon's theatrical venture.

Before the turn of the century some male dramatists such as Ibsen and Shaw had shown a certain sympathy towards the difficulties inherent in women's lives and had consequently given actresses a few fine roles, but they were very much in the minority. Nor were even these staunch supporters of women entirely unambiguous as Shaw's Vivie in *Mrs Warren's Profession* testifies, displaying as she does some rather unsympathetic traits. It became, therefore, incumbent on women to portray the realities of life as they lived it, or would prefer to live it. Not that this was by any means an easy undertaking. In spite of advances made in the last years of the nineteenth century and W.T. Stead's claim in his famous 1894 article[14] suggesting that women were finally writing 'from a woman's standpoint', in a Women's Social

---

Woman and Her Sisters: Feminism and Theatre 1850-1914 (New York, 1992), Sheila Stowell, *A Stage of Their Own: Feminist Playwrights of the Suffrage Era* (Michigan, 1992), and the Introductions to the following: Dale Spender, *How the Vote was Won and Other Suffragette Plays* (London, 1985), Fidelis Morgan, *The Years Between: Plays by Women on the London Stage 1900-1950* (London, 1994), Kerry Powell, *Women and Victorian Theatre* (Cambridge, 1997), and Jean Chothia, *The New Woman and Other Emancipated Plays* (Oxford, 1998).

[11] 'Soufflés', *Lady's Pictorial* (May 16, 1908), p. 778.

[12] *Lady's Pictorial* (October 17, 1908), p. 686. For more details about the theatre-going public in general, see Dennis Kennedy's essay 'The New Drama and the new audience' in *The Edwardian Theatre: Essays on Performance and the Stage* edited by Michael R. Booth and Joel H. Kaplan (Cambridge, 1996), pp. 130-147.

[13] See in particular '"Hedda is all of us": Late-Victorian Women at the Matinée', *Victorian Studies* Volume 43, Number 3 (2003), pp. 387-412.

[14] 'The Book of the Month: The Novel of the Modern Woman', *Review of Reviews* 10 (July 2, 1894), pp. 64-74. For more details, see chapter 2.

and Political Union pamphlet of 1907, *Woman's Secret*, Elizabeth Robins, celebrated actress and active dramatist, notes:

> Let us remember it is only yesterday that women in any number began to write for the public prints. But in taking up the pen, what did this new recruit conceive to be her task? To proclaim her own or other women's actual thoughts and feelings? Far from it. Her task, as she naturally and inevitably conceived it, was to imitate as nearly as possible the method, but above all the point of view, of men. ... What she is really doing is her level best to play the man's game, and seeing how nearly like him she can do it. So conscious is she it is *his* game she is trying her hand at, that she is prone to borrow his very name to set upon her title page.[15] (her italics)

It is difficult to know exactly what she means by 'yesterday'. In the *fin de siècle* period more women did begin to use their own names rather than pseudonyms, but in her autobiography Cicely Hamilton maintains that when her first play, *The Sixth Commandment*, had been staged in 1906 she had been advised by the producer Otto Stuart 'to conceal the sex of its author until after the notices were out, as plays which were known to be written by women were apt to get a bad press. My name, therefore, appeared on the programme in the indeterminate abbreviated form, C. Hamilton.'[16] She adds, 'It is certain that the one or two critics who had discovered that C. Hamilton stood for a woman were the one or two critics who dealt out harsh measure to her playlet.' Such biased criticism was not limited to the stage; in *Woman's Secret* Elizabeth Robins also comments:

> Contrary to the popular impression, to say in print what she thinks is the last thing the woman-novelist or journalist is so rash as to attempt. Here even more than elsewhere (unless she is reckless) she must wear the aspect that shall have the best chance of pleasing her brothers. Her publishers are not women.

Nevertheless, as women continued exploring the expectations and limitations of their changing roles and took control of representing them on stage as well as demonstrating for civic rights more publicly in the streets and popular press, an atmosphere of great excitement must at times have been prevalent.[17] In Dale Spender's words, 'Drama and political agitation were soon proceeding hand in hand',[18] and one can begin to see what might have attracted Ella Hepworth Dixon to participate actively in such dynamic times.

A closer examination of her own background reveals more substantial long-standing commitments than she overtly admits. Again in her memoirs, in the same paragraph as she mentions that her mother 'went to all Ibsen's plays (by herself)

[15] Elizabeth Robins, quoted in *Way Stations* (London, 1913), pp. 5-6.

[16] Cicely Hamilton, *Life Errant* (London, 1935), p. 60.

[17] The recently opened Women's Library contains fascinating material on the subject.

[18] Dale Spender, Introduction to *'How the Vote was Won' and Other Suffragette Plays* (Oxford, 1985), p. 4.

when they were first produced',[19] daring enough in itself, she adds, 'it was she who presented me, on my return from school-days in Germany, with a petition to sign for women's suffrage.' Ella Hepworth Dixon was thus early made aware of the struggle for women's political representation and the more serious possibilities and repercussions of dramatic art which were later to be exploited with variable success by fellow-women writers in the period leading up to the First World War. Indeed, if *The Times'* obituary[20] could declare that through her father she was 'born to journalism', I would argue that through her mother she was weaned on drama and suffrage, two elements which became inextricably linked in women's writing, especially for the theatre, in the first decade of the twentieth century.

Certainly, as mentioned in earlier chapters, Ella Hepworth Dixon was by no means the only eminent woman writer of the New Woman era to diversify her talents after the polemics had died down and the *fin de siècle* had come and gone without, as some had predicted, western civilization entirely disintegrating. Many of her contemporaries concentrated on more strictly political activities; Sarah Grand, for example, became increasingly active in the National Union of Suffrage Societies, whilst Olive Schreiner developed her views in *Women and Labour*, published in 1911. George Egerton also experimented at the same time with the theatre, notably producing *His Wife's Family* in 1908 and *The Backsliders* in 1910. Nor was it uncommon amongst writers of both sexes to adapt works from one genre to another, which generally involved rewriting a novel or a short story for the stage, as Ella Hepworth Dixon did, or, conversely, re-writing a popular play as a piece of fiction. Throughout the Victorian era numerous adaptations of novels were made for the stage, often without the author's permission, perhaps one of the most famous cases being that of Mrs Henry Wood's *East Lynne* (1861). Such practices continued well into this century, for as late as 1925 George Bernard Shaw in his Preface to *The Admirable Bashville; or, Constancy Unrewarded* commented that the only guaranteed protection for authors was to write their own play version. For instance, Elizabeth Robins' highly acclaimed play *Votes for Women!* (1907), 'the most influential piece of literary propaganda to come out of the suffrage movement' according to Elaine Showalter,[21] was republished as a novel entitled *The Convert* in the same year, Cicely Hamilton's *Diana of Dobson's* (1908) and *Just to get Married* (1910) both appeared as plays and as novels, whilst *How The Vote Was Won* (1909) had begun as a pamphlet and had proved so successful that with the help of Christopher St. John (Christabel Marshall) it was adapted for the stage where it became a box-office triumph.

The titles of these works at once reveal their authors' engagement in women's suffrage movements. Significantly, in her memoirs Ella Hepworth Dixon describes Elizabeth Robins as an:

---

[19] *As I Knew Them* (London, 1930), p. 14.

[20] (Unsigned), *The Times* (January 13, 1932), p. 14. Interestingly, her father's obituary in *The Times* mentions that he, too, had written a play that was never published. *The Times* (December 29, 1879), p. 4.

[21] *A Literature of Their Own* (London, 1991), p. 218.

> Amazing mixture of actress, novelist and centre of a literary clique. As *Hedda Gabber* (sic) and the rather sinister heroine of *The Master-Builder*, Elizabeth Robins could not have been bettered; it was the time of Revolt and the Feminists and Miss Robins seemed to embody the whole movement.[22]

However, unlike Elizabeth Robins and Cicely Hamilton and, for example, Sarah Grand, George Paston, Olive Schreiner, Evelyn Sharp and May Sinclair, and in spite of claiming 'I have always been in favour of Women's Franchise',[23] Ella Hepworth Dixon is noticeably absent from the registers of the Women Writers Suffrage League founded in June 1908. Nor does she appear to have had anything to do with the Artists Suffrage League, also founded in 1908, or the Actresses Franchise League with prominent figures such as Ellen Terry and Evelyn Sharp. Nor does her name even figure in *The Suffrage Annual and Woman's Who's Who* of 1913. This seems all the more difficult to understand because, as discussed in earlier chapters, both in her fiction and non-fiction, in the interview she accorded to W.T. Stead in *The Review of Reviews* and in her running of *The Englishwoman* she had always promoted women's interests. Alison Ives in *The Story of a Modern Woman* calls for solidarity amongst women and Mary Erle predicts that 'all we modern women are going to help each other'.[24] In the Stead interview Ella Hepworth Dixon is quoted as describing her novel as 'a plea for a kind of moral and social trades-unionism among women'.[25] Why, then, is there no obvious evidence of her professed support for her own sex in suffrage organizations? Was Ella Hepworth Dixon deliberately distancing herself from her more radical contemporaries?

It has to be said that the names of Mona Caird and Menie Muriel Dowie, equally, if not more, famously associated with the New Woman, were also absent. It is perhaps worth noting that earlier eminent women writers such as George Eliot and Florence Nightingale had likewise retained a distance from public alignment with the suffragette movement since neither of them signed the petition presented to parliament by John Stuart Mill in 1866. Mona Caird's *Times*' obituary noted 'she was prominent and effective among the pioneer champions of the "woman's movement" but declined to join the militants'.[26] Likewise, Ella Hepworth Dixon clearly reveals her distaste for militancy when, in writing of Prime Ministers she has known, she describes 'one of the big Suffrage meetings at the Albert Hall with Lloyd George, then Chancellor of the Exchequer, in the chair':

---

[22] *As I Knew Them* (London, 1930), p. 221.

[23] *Ibid.* p. 41.

[24] *The Story of a Modern Woman* (1894, repr. Peterborough, 2004), pp. 213-214.

[25] 'The Book of the Month: The Novel of the Modern Woman', *Review of Reviews* 10 (July 2, 1894), p. 71.

[26] Quoted by John Sutherland in *The Longman Companion to Victorian Fiction* (Harlow, 1988), p. 100.

> Mrs Lloyd George had kindly invited me to sit with them on the platform. Although Lloyd George was far more in sympathy with the Suffragettes than were Asquith, McKenna and others in the Liberal Government, the militant ladies distrusted him, probably because he could not promise them anything definite just then. For once, with the incessant heckling, and noisy interruptions, he seemed non-plussed. His speech was necessarily indefinite. It was *a horrible, unforgettable scene of disorder and unnecessary brutality.* Lloyd George never finished his oration.[27] (my italics)

On another occasion in her portrayal of Gertrude Kinnell, 'always a Constitutional Suffragist, (who) was associated with the late Dame Millicent Fawcett in the London Society for Women's Suffrage', Ella Hepworth Dixon writes:

> When the Suffragette movement was at its wildest, and old women and young girls were being hustled off to prison, and gilded banners were borne high through the streets of London, we used to remind each other, smiling, and a little shamefaced, that we had neither of us 'burned for our faith'.[28]

Lest latter-day feminists should consequently condemn such apparent cowardice, even Cicely Hamilton, whose feminist leanings could not be doubted, writes in her autobiography, 'I came into the "movement" because it gave me a chance to advocate what I did believe in - voluntary marriage and voluntary motherhood.'[29] On several occasions she returns to the topic, perhaps to justify what might seem inexplicable:

> I never attempted to disguise the fact that I wasn't wildly interested in votes for anyone, and ... if I worked for women's enfranchisement (and I did work quite hard) it wasn't because I hoped great things from counting female noses at general elections, but because the agitation for women's enfranchisement must inevitably shake and weaken the tradition of the 'normal woman'. The 'normal woman' with her 'destiny' of marriage and motherhood and housekeeping, no interest outside her home - especially no interest in the man's preserve of politics! [30]

She continues, and perhaps here echoes Ella Hepworth Dixon's views:

> My personal revolt was feminist rather than suffragist; what I rebelled at chiefly was the dependence implied in the idea of 'destined' marriage, 'destined' motherhood - the identification of success with marriage, of failure with spinsterhood, the artificial concentration of the hopes of girlhood on sexual attraction and maternity ... .

[27] *As I Knew Them* (London, 1930), pp. 200-201.
[28] *Ibid.* pp. 216-217.
[29] Cicely Hamilton, *Life Errant* (London, 1935), p. 251.
[30] *Ibid.* p. 65.

Although some critics claim that after the *fin de siècle* the primary concern of women writers had changed from marriage to maternity, the latter had already figured prominently in the writings of Mona Caird and Menie Muriel Dowie, whilst the former still preoccupied many in the Edwardian period. Just as in his 1894 play Sydney Grundy had insinuated that the New Woman only required a husband, so even in *Votes for Women!* more than a decade later the suggestion is that all the play's main protagonist, Vida Levering, needs is 'some "nice" fella to marry her'.[31] That this opinion was again voiced by a man should by no means allow one to believe that only men held this view. In Cicely Hamilton's aptly named play *Just to get Married*[32] the protagonist, Georgiana Vicary, describes herself as:

> A perfectly useless woman. And what is a perfectly useless woman to do but marry? ... Even when she does not care for the man who asks her. ... Every woman is expected to get herself a husband, somehow or another, and is looked on as a miserable failure if she doesn't. ... I've nothing to look forward to if I don't marry ... .[33]

In fact, the population distribution being what it was, there were still not enough eligible men for the number of women of a marriageable age, an argument which ultimately persuades the husband in *How the Vote was Won* to support women's franchise and thus allow a measure of autonomy to the female members of his family, who would otherwise be dependent on him.

The problems of such 'odd women' were no doubt exacerbated by class, a subject treated in several plays of the time. It might even be argued that whereas the New Woman period had concentrated primarily on the lives of middle-class women, after the turn of the century more attention was paid to women of lower classes, which consequently led to more extensive discussions about women's work. In *The Story of a Modern Woman* Ella Hepworth Dixon had already finely portrayed the difficulties of 'the woman who works, the fret and fever, the dreary fight for existence',[34] a theme that was to prevail throughout the pre-suffrage period. Elizabeth Baker's *Chains* and Cicely Hamilton's *Diana of Dobson's*, one of the most popular plays of the time, running as it did for 143 performances, and withdrawn only because Lena Ashwell who played the lead required a rest before going on tour with her company, depict the problems of working women and the relative merits of marriage, still often considered the preferable alternative. Originally planned as a single matinée performance on April 18, 1909 at the Court Theatre, *Chains* was revived the following year at the Duke of York, under Harley Granville-Barker's direction, and might have run for longer than it did but for the theatre's financial difficulties. J.C. Trewin, who accords little space to women in

---

[31] *Votes for Women!* (Oxford, 1998), Act 1, lines 264-265.

[32] First performed at the Little Theatre on November 8, 1910, produced by Gertrude Kingston, a member of the Actresses Franchise League, and later published as a novel under the same title by Chapman and Hall (London, 1911).

[33] *Just to get Married* (London, 1914), Act II, pp. 55-57.

[34] *The Story of a Modern Woman* (1894, repr. Peterborough, 2004), p. 136.

his appraisal of the Edwardian theatre, refers to it rather scantily and ascribes it merely to 'a woman dramatist'.[35]

Evidently, many of the concerns associated with the New Woman such as marriage, moral double-standards, women's oppression, problems linked to meaningful employment and so on remained unresolved. In some ways, therefore, although Ella Hepworth Dixon was not writing overtly suffrage drama and did not align herself publicly with the militants, I would suggest that in reworking and rewriting themes she had treated in earlier fiction she continued to be in the forefront of both literary and social movements.

The actual context of the production of *The Toyshop of the Heart* was typical of its time when there were many one-act plays, many short runs, many matinees, and many charity performances. The play was performed at The Playhouse, a theatre run by Actor/Manager Cyril Maude who had previously been manager of The Haymarket from 1896 to 1905, and of whom Ella Hepworth Dixon writes enthusiastically in her memoirs: 'A comedian quite apart is Mr Cyril Maude ... an entirely charming personage, with all the manners of the world, but with a gaiety and good-humour quite his own.'[36] Cyril Maude had had leading roles in plays by Pinero, notably in *The Second Mrs Tanqueray* (1893), and had starred as Colonel Cazenove in the first performance of Sydney Grundy's *The New Woman* (1894). For the charity matinée in question he took the major role in the opening play, *French as He is Spoke*, whilst his first wife, Winifred Emery, who had played the lead in Wilde's *Lady Windemere's Fan* (1892) as well as Margery in *The New Woman*, had a major role in the second, *Soldiers' Daughters*. Lest one should suspect that this was due to manager's privilege,[37] it should be noted that Winifred Emery was an eminent actress in her own right who became a very active member of the Actresses Franchise League and would presumably have welcomed the chance to further the cause of women.

The afternoon's entertainment consisted of four playlets punctuated with varied musical recitals. In *The Story of a Modern Woman*, the site of the protagonist's all-too-painful moment of awakening is 'a modish theatre', where Ella Hepworth Dixon alludes to 'the foolish, inane, unreal comedy on the stage'.[38] Such comments might almost be applied to two of the plays in the programme. The afternoon began with *French as He is Spoke*,[39] which had received a licence in 1907 and was revived for the occasion. Briefly, it is about a French father catching up with a runaway daughter, the eldest of five, in a London hotel with a relatively impecunious English suitor. It is basically a farce with the humour generally provided by an inadequate translator standing in for the usual interpreter who is significantly absent celebrating his divorce. More troubling undertones, however,

---

[35] J.C. Trewin, *The Edwardian Theatre* (Oxford, 1976), p. 95.

[36] *As I Knew Them* (London, 1830), p. 230.

[37] In her autobiography, Cicely Hamilton recounts being thrown out of work twice to make room for a manager's mistress. *Life Errant* (London, 1935), p. 47.

[38] *The Story of a Modern Woman* (1894, repr. Peterborough, 2004), p. 142.

[39] *French as He is Spoke*, adapted by Gaston Mayer from the French of Tristan Bernard.

can be detected as the father, having initially refused his consent, willingly allows his daughter to marry the man of her choice once it is discovered that the young man in question has after all been promoted. Marriage as a trade indeed!

Likewise the third sketch, the third act of *Still Waters Run Deep*, an 1850 play by Tom Taylor,[40] again based on a French novel, *Le Gendre* by Christian de Bernard, is somewhat sinister in its implications. J.C. Trewin draws attention to the number of works translated from French, suggesting this gave a certain seal of approval. This could indicate a significant change from earlier attitudes to French literature, so regularly associated with the scabrous and licentious at the end of the Victorian era, for example in *The Heavenly Twins* (1893) the husband of Evadne, one of the heroines, gives his wife books by French authors in the hopes that this will weaken her resolve not to consummate their marriage. It should be noted, however, that the works translated for the stage were of a rather different nature, usually farces, upholding traditional moral values, as the present examples testify. *Still Waters Run Deep* is essentially a sort of who-dunnit, recounting the intrigues of a shameless adventurer, the son-in-law of the French title, who juggles, by means of letters and blackmail, with the reputations of apparently respectable women. Ultimately, however, it is about the reassertion of a manly husband and is severely misogynist in tone. The dowager aunt, appropriately named Mrs Sternhold, is seen to be the one who holds sway over her elder brother's household as well as over her niece and her young husband who exasperatedly declares, 'You think a man ought to let a wife lead him by the nose; that a woman should control everything; in fact, you're the head of the family.' He, on the other hand, is 'nobody'. At the end, after various tribulations by which he has shown himself perfectly able to turn situations to his advantage, he tells his wife:

> Your father's doting fondness and your aunt's mischievous example have made you what you are. Trust to me, henceforth, to make you what a wife should be - I should prefer to win you by a lover's tenderness, but if I cannot do that, I know how to make a husband's rights respected.

It is difficult to share in any amusement from such ominous threats. The play does touch on a few salient points, however, such as when the father has settled money on his daughter, she has no control over it yet her husband can dispose of it as he wishes. Thanks to legal changes, such a situation would be less likely in 1908, but this is small consolation for the overall unpleasant stereotypical representation of humanity of whichever gender.

The other two plays of the afternoon, on the other hand, are altogether more interesting. *Soldiers' Daughters*, or *A Soldier's Daughters* as the play was sometimes called, the second play on the programme, had received a licence in

---

[40] Although practically unknown to present-day audiences, Tom Taylor's plays were typical of their time and enjoyed prolonged popularity. David Daiches in his *Critical History of English Literature* (London, 1969) Volume IV, p. 1102, mentions the 'domestic melodramas' of Tom Taylor, and gives a later date, 1855, for *Still Waters Run Deep*.

May 1908 and had first been performed at Lena Ashwell's Kingsway Theatre where *Diana of Dobson's* had opened on February 12, 1908. The play consists almost entirely of a dialogue between two sisters living in constrained circumstances. In 'Its Own Reward',[41] a much earlier short story, Ella Hepworth Dixon also treats the theme of an actress who, having made her fortune, returns to take care of her younger sister. Everyone had expected the worst of the actress and her so-called benefactor, but she had been 'capable of anything; even becoming a rich young widow'. In *Soldiers' Daughters* the situation is rather different. The elder sister, Helen, is an independent typist, finding it difficult to keep up with the competition from cheaper typing pools, whilst Pamela, the younger sister, is an actress who, to remedy the situation, is ready to sell herself. This, however, is where the censor intervened. The British Library typescript copy of the play contains a letter from Lena Ashwell, lessee and manager, indicating that the lines marked by the censor, which I have placed in parenthesis, were not spoken. Naturally, on the day of Ella Hepworth Dixon's play, the expurgated version must have been employed, but the censored version provides much food for thought. Pamela declares she has:

> Something which a rich benefactor will buy. (Something that every woman has to sell these days if she wishes to compete with her sisters who work). The only marketable commodity that we superfluous women are given. (Virtue, - that's what it's called in the dictionary. And it can only be kept by the women who loll at home at ease. I am selling mine to the highest bidder. The offer has been made, - I take it eagerly, greedily!) What's the good of it to me. It's merely a boast, a drawback. I have worked and slaved, and eaten out my heart. I have seen others go over my head who haven't an eight (sic) part of my ability and experience. They have paid their premium (with their virtue). Everyone pays a premium to get his foot on the ladder, men and women pay hard cash to become barristers, doctors, solicitors. Women pay to go into shops, typewriting offices, and the stage - if they've got the money. (If they haven't they have got their bodies, and these they sell) I have kept mine and remained an understudy, 'a capable actress', 'adequate'- in her character a woman who can wear dresses like a gentlewoman, speak correctly, move correctly, do everything correctly, and remain merely useful. I am sick of this - sick of it. I can act and I *must* act. (her italics)

Helen admits she had been expecting this for some time, and significantly begins to clean their father's tarnished sword which they will be required to dispose of if they move from their present lodgings, as Pamela's changed circumstances would necessitate. In the last lines of the play Pamela revokes her decision; she remembers she is a soldier's daughter and would not like to leave a stain on their father's reputation. This might seem rather tame to present-day readers, but even with the censor's cuts, Pamela's discourse remains outspoken and daring for its

---

[41] Originally published in the *Christmas Number of The World* (November 26, 1896), pp. 50-53, and republished in Ella Hepworth Dixon's collection of short stories, *One Doubtful Hour* (London, 1904).

time. The reviewer in the *Lady's Pictorial* comments that the actresses, 'Miss Winifred Emery and Miss Beryl Faber, as the two sisters, typist and actress respectively, brought tears to many eyes.'[42]

Ella Hepworth Dixon's play in comparison may initially seem less forceful. I would argue, however, that in her usual understated way, without launching into polemics, as with her New Woman novel, Ella Hepworth Dixon again takes popular issues such as art and life, love and marriage, women and work, and gives them a slightly different slant. The title, adapted from Pope's 'The Rape of the Lock', 'With varying vanities, from every part,/ They shift the moving toy-shop of the heart',[43] which appears both on the original typescript and the theatre programme, suggests elements of a trifling nature. The audience could thus expect a light-hearted divertissement, which is indeed how the play opens. Closer analysis of the context of the quotation beginning 'Oft, when the world imagine women stray'[44] could, nevertheless, indicate greater gravity. A woman's straying, whatever the circumstances, could never be taken lightly, as the heroine of the play discovers to her cost. Likewise, with the unfolding of the action, what begins as domestic melodrama ends on a note of social pathos as the overall tone of the play shifts to a more sombre mood, and finally one is left rather more moved than one might have expected.

This was the last entertainment of the afternoon, which would imply that it was given prominence and, indeed, several reviewers do single it out for particular praise, laying emphasis, as in *The Stage*[45] review, on its originality. *The Times* critic notes, 'The only novelty was *The Toyshop of the Heart* by Miss Ella Hepworth Dixon, a promising little play',[46] whilst *The Era* critic echoes, 'The novelty of the afternoon was *The Toyshop of the Heart*. ... Miss Hepworth Dixon has a pretty command of language, and writes nicely.'[47] Due credit was also given to the cast. 'Miss Liliane Braithwaite, as the dancer, did the monologuing with eloquent intensity, and Mr Leslie Faber and Mr Harcourt Williams looked their parts admirably as the First Secretary and the poet respectively,' writes *The Times* critic. According to *The Era*:

> Liliane Braithwaite furnished a pathetic portraiture of Rose Rosalba, and the tragic note of it struck deeply into the hearts of the audience. The role of the dreaming Philip with the artistic temperament proved an interesting study in the hands of Mr Harcourt Williams, and Mr Leslie Faber was a dignified and matter-of-fact personage as Poyning.

---

[42] (Unsigned), 'At the Play', *Lady's Pictorial* (December 5, 1908), p. 1027.
[43] 'The Rape of the Lock', lines 99-100.
[44] *Ibid.* line 91.
[45] (Unsigned), *The Stage* (December 3, 1908), p. 17.
[46] (Unsigned), 'The Playhouse', *The Times* (November 27, 1908), p. 9.
[47] (Unsigned), 'The Playhouse Matinée in Aid of Infants' Hospital', *The Era* (November 1908), p. 19.

Ella Hepworth Dixon was obviously well-served by the actors. In her memoirs she describes Liliane Braithwaite as 'so competent and so lovely; she has worked hard, and deserved her success'.[48] Liliane Braithwaite, incidentally, had also played the lead role in the single matinée performance of Netta Syrett's controversial first full-length play, *The Finding of Nancy* (1902).[49] Interestingly, the rich collection of William Hepworth Dixon's papers held at the University of California Library contains a few letters to Ella Hepworth Dixon, one of which is from Leslie Faber dated the day after the performance, telling her what a great pleasure it had been to play Edward Poyning.

The basic plot of *The Toyshop of the Heart* centres on what would generally be considered a *mésalliance*, a common enough theme both in the Edwardian era and earlier, between a professional dancer, Rose Rosalba, without doubt the central and most interesting character lending her 'surname' to the subtitle 'The Rosalba', which appears on page two of the typescript, and an aristocratic poet, Philip Altamore, whose heart does seem to resemble the toyshop of the title. 'We all know the "adventuress" who captivates the young man of good family, but is foiled by the polished middle-aged attaché who has met her passing under other names in other capitals of Europe,' writes Max Beerbohm[50] in *The Saturday Review.*[51] 'Miss Hepworth Dixon, however, breathes life and novelty into these familiar figures.' These figures were all the more familiar to regular readers of Ella Hepworth Dixon as one of her earlier short stories, entitled 'The Kidnapping of Phil Altamore',[52] recounts a similar tale, but from the attaché's point of view, thus considerably altering the overall tone. The narrator, simply called Kenneth, is far more interested in the kidnapp*er* of Phil Altamore, a mature older woman, Mrs Jack, who has saved the young man *in extremis* from 'an insane, ridiculous marriage' with Rosie Rosalba. The hero, therefore, although described as 'a boy of genius. Another Shelley!', remains relatively insignificant, as does the jilted young woman, and herein lie the greatest differences between the prose fiction and the play.

On stage, from his opening lines Philip, as he is now known, still appears rather stereotyped, unworldly, disconsolate, fatigued, more in love with the idea of love than with a flesh and blood woman. Indeed, when he speaks of his fiancée it is first as 'the most exquisite *thing*' (my italics), and then as 'the Innocent, Instinctive, Primordial Woman'. Rather like Gerald Casenove in Sydney Grundy's *The New Woman*, already a pastiche of *fin de siècle* aesthetes, Philip Altamore is extremely sensitive to his environment. For example, he is very keen on surrounding himself

---

[48] *As I Knew Them* (London, 1930), p. 157.

[49] For more details, see Kerry Powell, *Women and Victorian Theatre* (Cambridge, 1997).

[50] In her memoirs, writing of Max Beerbohm, Ella Hepworth Dixon declares, 'I shall not forget that he not only came to a Charity Matinée, but wrote in praise of my one-act play, *The Toy-shop of the Heart.*' *As I Knew Them* (London, 1930), p. 252. She omits to mention that he referred to it as 'Love's Toyshop'.

[51] *The Saturday Review* (December 5, 1908), p. 697.

[52] Originally published in the *Lady's Pictorial* (November 25, 1899), pp. 805-807, and entitled 'The Kidnapping of Phil Kynaston', the protagonist's name was changed to 'Altamore' when the story was republished in *One Doubtful Hour* (London, 1904).

and others with flowers, azaleas and lilacs on this occasion, both eye-catching and sweet-smelling. It is surely not fortuitous that the woman of his dreams is 'fond of fanciful, flower-like names', calling herself now 'Rose Rosalba' and, although unknown to him, 'Hyacinth Grey' in earlier days. The audience never learns her true name, either. His strongest criticism of his mother, otherwise described as 'quite exquisite', is that 'she lives an unlovely life':

> In the winter, she is out in the bleak fields, hunting foxes, or else she invites dreadful men in check clothes to come and shoot pheasants - the pheasants with their exquisite shining golden plumage. She has the most adorable gardens in England, and she uses them to give odious fêtes - garden parties for the Primrose League! Then, they never look at home, at the wonderful Rembrandt in the hall, nor at the Tintoretto in the drawing-room. It is in the drawing-room that they chiefly play a dreadful game called Bridge. There is noise, hurry, and coming and going - but they do not know how to live!

His fiancée later gives a rather different evaluation of such society, castigating what she terms 'the point of view of the Philistines', and showing how issues of gender could be accentuated or exacerbated by differences of class. Philip Altamore is also shown to be kind to birds, but otherwise has few saving graces. That he seems upset at the idea of having to do without Danvers, his faithful valet, after his marriage may indicate a genuine liking for the man, but it is more probably further evidence of his self-interest. Until Danvers raises the question Philip Altamore has not given the slightest thought to what would become of his man-servant if his own financial circumstances changed, as they threaten to do were he to marry against his family's wishes. On the whole he remains rather a weak caricature and arouses no sympathy whatsoever when the woman he professes to love casts him off. If further proof were needed, the speed with which he organizes his departure to join a friend on a Mediterranean cruise shows that his powers of survival are never in doubt. Likewise in the short story, Phil Altamore had transferred his affections from one woman to another with astounding ease.

Rose Rosalba, on the other hand, is altogether a more complicated character, and on stage gains remarkably in interest and stature. Like Vida Levering in *Votes for Women!*, first produced the previous year and surely still very much in the public's mind, the heroine, also a woman with a past, is discussed at some length before appearing in person and allowing the audience to judge for themselves. Even then she resists neat categorization, which was not to everyone's taste. For example, Hamilton Fyfe in *The World* declares:

> The fault of it as a play is that the author does not make her intentions sufficiently clear. For a long time we are left in doubt whether Rosalie the dancer is a really bad lot or a woman more sinned against than sinning; whether she is devoted to her art or anxious to find a more stable prop for her declining years.[53]

[53] *The World* (December 1, 1908), p. 1027.

It might, however, be argued that this rather testifies to Ella Hepworth Dixon's fine sense of dramatic tension and her skill in maintaining suspense until almost the very last speech. On her entrance, Rose Rosalba does seem rather superficial, very concerned about her appearance, trying to look younger than she is, and yet, I would argue, she outgrows her stereotype as we learn about her past, witness her behaviour in the present and evaluate her future. Max Beerbohm rightly points out that Rose Rosalba 'is an "adventuress" seen from within; a thoroughly convincing human being, in the exposition of whose character there is pathos of a not at all mawkish kind.'[54]

Rose Rosalba is first presented through the gaze of a variety of men: her biased lover, the family friend and diplomat, here called Edward Poyning, whose professed ambition is to separate the pair, and the former's valet who, although of a different class and for different reasons, shares the latter's aim. In practically his first words, Edward Poyning points out that it is 'a bit unconventional' to take a dancer as bride. One is tempted to add 'or as a protagonist'. A dancer is in a sort of moral hinterland; she is both an independent working woman, and at the same time a public woman participating in the artistic world with all the underlying connotations of moral laxity. Ella Hepworth Dixon may have been drawing on similarities with Loïe Fuller (1862-1928), well-known for her spectacular appearances at the Folies-Bergères where she wore flowing, diaphanous veils of varied colours as she swirled about the stage, much as Rosie does when she demonstrates her latest dance to her lover, and elements of a slightly later American dancer, Isadora Duncan (1878-1927), whose fame for similar expressive dances was at its height in 1908. In her memoirs Ella Hepworth Dixon writes, 'Isadora went to Paris, to Berlin, to Moscow, to America, and became one of the most talked about persons of the time',[55] which to some degree echoes Rose Rosalba's career. At the same time her dancing also seems to anticipate creations of the Russian ballet in Paris such as *L'Après-midi d'un Faun*[56] or *Le Sacre du Printemps*.[57] Comparisons may also be made between her dancing and Nora's famous Tarantella in Ibsen's *A Doll's House*, both sensual demonstrations in front of admiring male gazes. It should be noted, however, that although Rose Rosalba designs both the clothes and the dance and seems less under men's control than Nora, at the end it is not she who shuts the door on leaving. In *The Toyshop of the Heart* the man escapes; the woman stays and still has to pay retribution.

Rose Rosalba is obviously successful, earning enough not only to keep herself, but also to run a motor car, the height of extravagance. She is also the archetypal woman with a past, and that past will pursue her inexorably. Exceptionally, as in Pinero's *The Second Mrs Tanqueray* or Elizabeth Robins' *Votes for Women!*, a woman could survive her past, but generally in the Edwardian era a woman's past

[54] Max Beerbohm, *The Saturday Review* (December 5, 1908), p. 697.
[55] *As I Knew Them* (London, 1930), p. 169.
[56] First performed in 1912 although the music had been composed in 1894.
[57] First performed in 1913.

caught up with her as no man's ever did, just as it had done in Victorian times. Towards the end of the play Rose Rosalba recognizes, 'You've closed round me, pressed me to the wall, marked me with an infamous brand till I die! The hem of my robe will always be soiled, though it comes fresh from the Rue de la Paix ! - the envy of honest women!' Nevertheless, she also has many admirable qualities; even Poyning has to admit at the end that she has 'behaved like a heroine' and 'been more magnanimous than (he) thought a woman could be'.

Hamilton Fyfe writes:

> I thought at one moment Miss Hepworth Dixon meant to cross swords with conventional morality. Rosalie was a governess in a French family. The son of the house induced her to elope with him, she thinking in her ignorance he meant marriage. When she found he did not, she eloped with someone else. Problem: ought a man who knows her story to denounce her to the young man she is engaged to marry? Miss Hepworth Dixon says 'Yes'. I wish – if only for the sake of the interest of her plot - she had taken the other view. Miss Braithewaite (the actress playing the role of Rose) could have given us some thrilling tirades on man's injustice ... .[58]

I would suggest that Ella Hepworth Dixon, even if she does not provide 'thrilling tirades', does indeed expose not only 'man's injustice', but the whole of society's injustices to women. It is not because a character in the play, in this case a diplomat who, knowing the details of the heroine's past, entreats her, with success, to withdraw from her engagement that the dramatist herself necessarily subscribes to such standards of behaviour in the world at large. In fact, Ella Hepworth Dixon could be echoing sentiments expressed earlier in the W.T. Stead interview: 'I wished to show how hardly our social laws press on women, how, in fact, it is too often the woman who is made, as it were, the moral scapegoat, and who is sent out into the wilderness to expiate the sins of man.'[59] One could argue that Ella Hepworth Dixon was merely repeating herself or stating the obvious, but a few years later, in 1911, Margaret Nevinson, a member of the Women Writers Suffrage League, was to reiterate very similar ideas:

> I have attempted to illustrate from life some of the hardships of the law to an unrepresented sex, the cruel punishment meted out to women, and to women only, for any breach of traditional morality, the ruin of the girl, the absolute immunity of the male ... .[60]

In an earlier short story, Ella Hepworth Dixon had commented on such discrepancies: 'For him, indeed, there might still be what Life has to offer to erring man; but instinctively she felt that for her, the woman, there could only be work and

---

[58] *The World* (December 1, 1908), p. 1027.

[59] (W.T. Stead) 'The Book of the Month: The Novel of the Modern Woman', *The Review of Reviews* 10 (July, 1894), p. 71.

[60] From *The Workhouse*, originally a sketch called 'Detained by Marital Authority', first performed on May 8, 1911 at the Kingsway Theatre.

self-effacement.'[61] For Rose Rosalba, therefore, the situation is even more critical because of the very nature of her work.

Rose Rosalba is consequently not merely pouring out what *The Era* critic calls 'the *illogical* excuses of her class' (my italics); she is rather accentuating the dual standards of sex and class and their inherent hypocrisies, largely embodied by Edward Poyning. On one hand he idealizes womankind, maintaining that Lady Altamore was his first love and that he has 'never worshipped any woman since, quite like that ...'. That he was thirteen at the time surely says much about the man's attitude to women, suggesting an immature fantasy which he has not outgrown. He also declares, 'I never could be "down" on women', and yet he asks Rose Rosalba to give up the man she loves and, to make matters worse, even offers her 'compensation'! This is all the more insulting as she earns large sums of money, 'forty pounds a night', by her dancing. Poyning may to some extent represent the voice of reason or conventional conduct. Here, however, one's sympathies lie with Rose Rosalba, who represents the emotions, untrammelled by convention. That she bends to circumstances, but remains heroic in front of the men on stage, only breaking down when her lover has left, serves to highlight her own strength of character. Unlike her namesake in 'The Kidnapping of Phil Altamore', she rejects a financial settlement, a cheque for £500, and unlike Effie Lauder in 'One Doubtful Hour',[62] another of Ella Hepworth Dixon's short stories which bears certain similarities to the play, she will not commit suicide, but, as for Effie and many others, 'Times winged Charriot' is at her back and the future is bleak.

Moreover, when we learn that she has rejected the advances of another aristocratic suitor, the Duc de St Galmier, our admiration for her increases. If she had wanted marriage at all costs, she would have immediately encouraged a possible replacement for Philip Altamore. One cannot help thinking, nevertheless, that theirs would not have been an ideal match. Perhaps Edward Poyning's picture of 'disillusioned middle-aged couples' was nearer the truth than either Philip Altamore or Rose Rosalba could imagine. He had clearly not given much thought to the implications of matrimony, but automatically assumed that, as was customary, she would give up the stage and he would have to keep her, while she had imagined more 'a marriage of true minds' in which they would both continue to work. For her, marriage was not an end in itself; nor was it, as for many women, a means of financial security. In one version of Ella Hepworth Dixon's script, Rose Rosalba calls it her 'rehabilitation' which suggests a desire to regain her respectability. This was later changed to 'my chance in life', a more general, but seemingly equally impossible quest.

As in *The Story of a Modern Woman*, the male characters in *The Toyshop of the Heart* come out rather badly, but I would argue women are not let off gently either. Again women are revealed as not always being generous to their own sex. Rose Rosalba's diatribe against the women of England is far from flattering. In the first

---

[61] 'A London Episode', *Christmas Number of The World* (November 25, 1897), p. 52.

[62] Originally published in *The Christmas Number of Lady's Pictorial* (1897), pp. 16-21, and later lending its name to Ella Hepworth Dixon's collection of short stories (London, 1904).

scene with Edward Poyning, Philip Altamore has indicated that his mother 'won't see Rosie - she won't hear of the wedding'. When he and his fiancée later discuss her, Rose Rosalba declares:

> I wonder if a woman like your mother could realize ... the difficulties, the temptations of a career like mine. ... O, the women of her class are very hard! ... What do they know of life - your 'guarded women' of England? They are 'presented' at eighteen. They are only permitted to see, to associate with young men with money - of their own set. Soon there is a wedding at St. Paul's, Knightsbridge; five hundred wedding presents, and then they settle down to rule their county - and - incidentally to have as many admirers as they please - until they are found out. ... Everything has been smoothed, oiled, made easy for the guarded women who judge *us*, and who fight for their men like tigresses if one of them strays our way (her italics).

Philip Altamore's response is blithely that 'when the new social order reigns, there will be great change. The women who work will also be honoured ... '. This in the meantime is of small comfort to the likes of Rose Rosalba. The various changes in the typescript suggest that it was not easy for Ella Hepworth Dixon to find exactly the right words to express the injustices and hypocrisies of a class which must have made up the majority of her public. I am reminded of George Bernard Shaw's warning in his 1898 Preface to *Plays Unpleasant* that his attacks were directed against his readers, not his stage figures, and David Daiches' later commentary that:

> Often the real villain is not a character in the play, but the audience. For the audience, the average playgoer, represents that thoughtless, complacent, sentimental society which, for Shaw, was responsible for so much distortion of vision and so much evil and suffering.[63]

This might be putting it more vehemently than Ella Hepworth Dixon herself would, but it seems a fitting appraisal of *The Toyshop of the Heart*.

Critics generally recognized that the play bore obvious traces of the pen of a prose writer rather than a playwright: 'clearly the work of a novelist rather than a practised dramatist,' asserts *The Times'* reviewer, 'I can imagine ... (it) ... making a capital short story,' writes Hamilton Fyfe, and 'We think ... that *The Toyshop of the Heart* would be better as a magazine story than a play,' concludes *The Era* critic. Perhaps reviewers remembered that in 1904 Ella Hepworth Dixon had published a collection of short stories under the title of *One Doubtful Hour and Other Side-lights on the Feminine Temperament*. In fact, as mentioned above, she was drawing on elements from earlier short stories, especially from 'The Kidnapping of Phil Altamore', 'One Doubtful Hour' and 'The World's Slow Stain', at times using almost identical dialogue from the latter:

---

[63] *A Critical History of English Literature* (London, 1969), p. 1106.

> I was a good girl, with deep feelings, and ideals, and all that sort of thing. ... I-I imagined that men were ... decent, you know, and that the women who were treated unfairly were the exceptions, and that it was their own fault, generally, if they were. I did not know that women were stuffed with idiotic theories from their very childhood, and that all my life I should suffer, suffer, suffer, for what I had been taught then. We are not told,' she went on with rising excitement, 'what life is, what it all means, or how to play the game. We are like children to whom a pack of cards is thrown, and who are set down to play a strange game with men who are confirmed gamblers. The rules are never told us, so that we blunder helplessly along, and unless we cheat outrageously, or mark the cards, there's small chance of our winning.[64]

In the short story Adela Buller adds, 'And what's so funny, is that most "good" men like us to be like that, ignorant, silly, helpless - even cheats. They think it pretty', whilst in the play Rose Rosalba claims she '*had* to mark the cards' (her italics). Whatever the motivation or the cause, a woman rarely manages to come out a winner. At the end of 'The Kidnapping of Phil Altamore' she is bought off, at the end of 'One Doubtful Hour' she gases herself, at the end of 'The World's Slow Stain' she is locked into a loveless marriage, with no possibility of mutual respect within the couple, and in *The Toyshop of the Heart* she remains alone. No ideal solution seems possible. It should be remembered, however, that in some of her stories Ella Hepworth Dixon does offer more positive alternatives.

Although her skills may be more finely tuned to short narrative fiction, I would nonetheless agree with Max Beerbohm that 'she seems to have been not at all incommoded by her new medium'.[65] Her play may be somewhat dated, but I would argue that she has rather an admirable command of dramatic suspense and one is still gripped by the story. As far as I can discover, however, this was her only completed play and its only production. In *As I Knew Them* commenting on what to her mind was 'a striking one-act play' by Lady Cromartie called *The Finding of the Sword* which had also been produced on a charitable occasion, and wondering why it had not been revived, Ella Hepworth Dixon adds, 'except that plays produced in such a manner, however well-revived, are doomed to extinction, as I know to my cost'.[66] This could suggest that she, too, had tried to have her play produced on a later occasion, but so far I have found no evidence to justify the idea. That she herself did not consider it a bad experience, however, is testified by her willingness in the summer of 1911 to work on a play with H.G. Wells:

> 'Why not,' I said, enthusiastically, 'have a real stage set like a toy theatre, push on conventional characters on slides, and make the first part a modern comedy, with a serio-comic butler, a lady who wants to elope, but doesn't, a strong silent husband, a modern flapper, and so on. At a given moment they would all shed their theatrical clothes (in the case of the women, always

[64] 'The World's Slow Stain', *Christmas Number of the* World (November 21, 1895), pp. 59-61 and republished in *One Doubtful Hour* (London, 1904), pp. 233-234.
[65] *The Saturday Review* (December 5, 1908), p. 697.
[66] *As I Knew Them* (London, 1930), p. 74.

> overdone) and appear, as their own souls, in straight white garments. Here, "H.G." is where your part of the play comes in. You can now put in all your theories of life, and end the play in whatever way you like.' It would, I ventured to assert, 'be original, and great fun.'
>
> 'H.G.' thought so, too, and asked if I would write the first part while he would do the drama of the souls.[67]

Apparently the Little Theatre in the Adelphi was waiting for the play, but 'somehow it never got finished or produced'. The published extracts of correspondence between the two authors suggests that this was due to their being equally 'lazy or remiss'.[68]

Even if her own play remains very much of its time and place, it is still more than mere amusement for a good cause. Moreover, this experimentation with a new genre shows that Ella Hepworth Dixon kept abreast of literary and social movements until the First World War when, like many of her contemporaries, whether militant, constitutional or anti-suffrage, she channelled her energies elsewhere into more practical domains. Thereafter, as discussed in previous chapters, the only substantial piece of work she produced was her autobiography, which even she describes as 'sketches'. Nevertheless, she remained almost permanently in work and continued to write occasional articles for various journals until just before her death in 1932.

---

[67] *Ibid.* pp. 204-205.
[68] *Ibid.* p. 207.

Afterword

In many ways, Ella Hepworth Dixon personifies the conflicting interests and contradictions at the heart both of the New Woman phenomenon and the world of journalism in which she spent the whole of her life. Whilst remaining single and childless, she was neither a 'self-assertive, heartless, sexless thing' nor a febrile bag of nerves, much less a source of pity or ridicule. Like the journalist heroine of *The Story of a Modern Woman*, she may have begun earning her living in journalism thanks to her family connections and more precisely in the shadow of a famous father. Unlike her heroine, however, she was better able to defy the constraints imposed upon women both inside and outside her profession. For, while it cannot be denied that family circumstances certainly facilitated her entry into the world of journalism, it seems highly unlikely that such contacts would have kept her almost permanently in work for practically half a century.

I hope to have shown that rather than being merely a New Woman, Ella Hepworth Dixon was very much a Modern Woman. She may not have burned for her faith, and for this reason may attract the scorn of more engaged feminists. On the other hand, she does appear to have maintained the course she set herself and was admirably able to fulfil the ambitions expressed by the heroine of her novel 'to make her way in the world and compete with men'.[1] By her very example, writing for periodicals of various kinds throughout her life as well as editing a woman's magazine, and even becoming a selling-point for journals, she made important contributions to the development of the profession of journalism for women. At the same time she maintained a somewhat detached, gently ironic gaze on life, which, I would argue, remains as fresh and delightful to present-day readers as to her contemporaries.

[1] *The Story of a Modern Woman*, p. 88.

Appendix 1

Ella Hepworth Dixon's Birth and Death Certificates

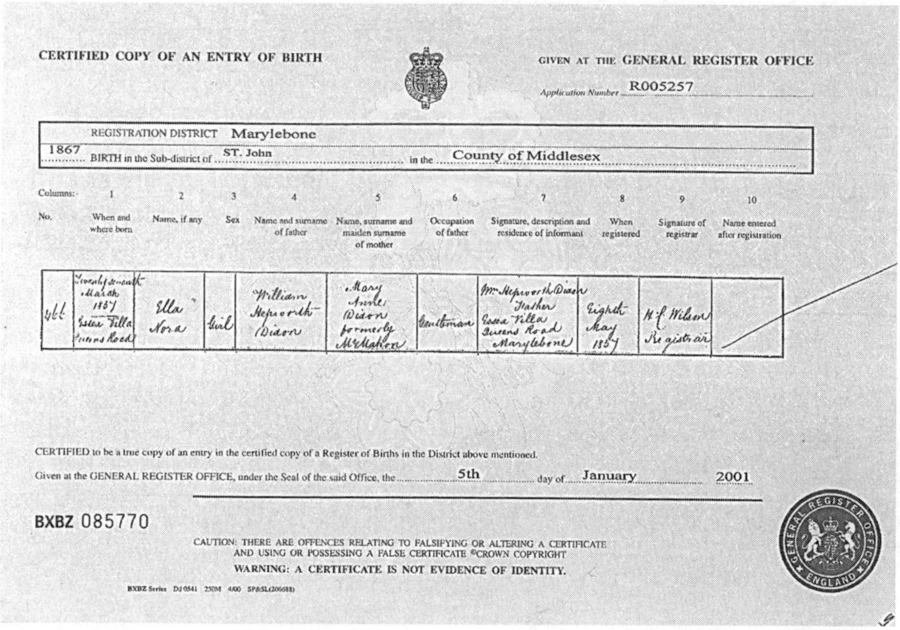

CERTIFIED COPY OF AN ENTRY OF BIRTH

GIVEN AT THE GENERAL REGISTER OFFICE

Application Number R005257

REGISTRATION DISTRICT Marylebone

1867 BIRTH in the Sub-district of ST. John in the County of Middlesex

Columns:-	1	2	3	4	5	6	7	8	9	10
No.	When and where born	Name, if any	Sex	Name and surname of father	Name, surname and maiden surname of mother	Occupation of father	Signature, description and residence of informant	When registered	Signature of registrar	Name entered after registration
466	Twenty seventh March 1857 Essex Villa Queens Road	Ella Nora	Girl	William Hepworth Dixon	Mary Anne Dixon formerly McMahon	Gentleman	Wm Hepworth Dixon Father Essex Villa Queens Road Marylebone	Eighth May 1857	H. C. Wilson Registrar	

CERTIFIED to be a true copy of an entry in the certified copy of a Register of Births in the District above mentioned.

Given at the GENERAL REGISTER OFFICE, under the Seal of the said Office, the 5th day of January 2001

BXBZ 085770

CAUTION: THERE ARE OFFENCES RELATING TO FALSIFYING OR ALTERING A CERTIFICATE AND USING OR POSSESSING A FALSE CERTIFICATE ©CROWN COPYRIGHT

WARNING: A CERTIFICATE IS NOT EVIDENCE OF IDENTITY.

BXBZ Series DJ 0541 250M 4/00 SP&SL(206088)

GENERAL REGISTER OFFICE ENGLAND

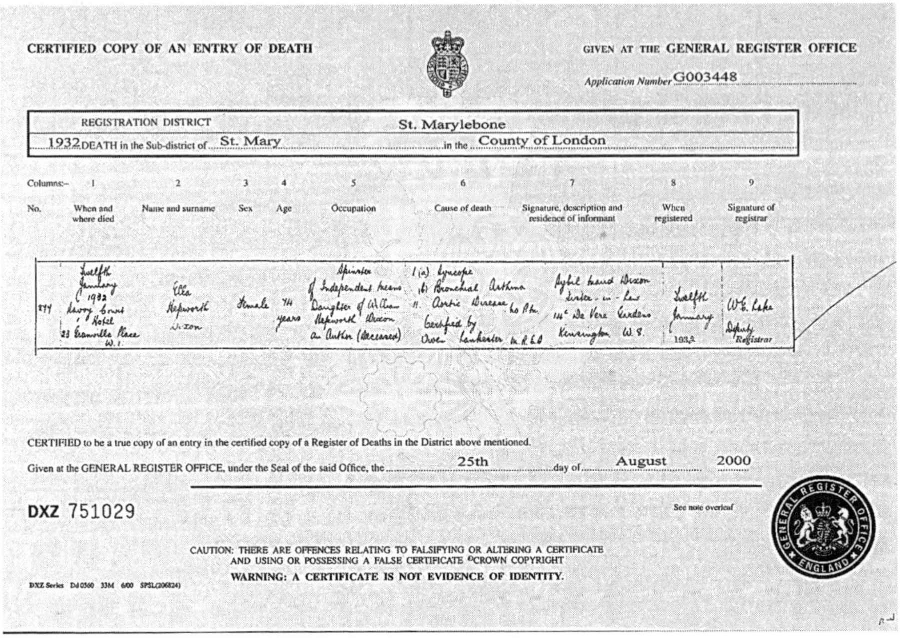

CERTIFIED COPY OF AN ENTRY OF DEATH — GIVEN AT THE GENERAL REGISTER OFFICE

Application Number G003448

REGISTRATION DISTRICT St. Marylebone

1932 DEATH in the Sub-district of St. Mary in the County of London

Columns:–	1	2	3	4	5	6	7	8	9
No.	When and where died	Name and surname	Sex	Age	Occupation	Cause of death	Signature, description and residence of informant	When registered	Signature of registrar
274	Twelfth January 1932 Savoy Court Hotel 23 Granville Place W.1.	Ella Hepworth Dixon	Female	74 years	Spinster of Independent means Daughter of William Hepworth Dixon an Author (Deceased)	1 (a) Syncope (b) Bronchial Asthma II. Aortic Disease no P.M. Certified by Owen Lankester M.R.C.S.	Sybil Maud Dixon Sister-in-Law 14c De Vere Gardens Kensington W.8.	Twelfth January 1932	W.G. Lake Deputy Registrar

CERTIFIED to be a true copy of an entry in the certified copy of a Register of Deaths in the District above mentioned.

Given at the GENERAL REGISTER OFFICE, under the Seal of the said Office, the 25th day of August 2000

DXZ 751029

See note overleaf

CAUTION: THERE ARE OFFENCES RELATING TO FALSIFYING OR ALTERING A CERTIFICATE AND USING OR POSSESSING A FALSE CERTIFICATE ©CROWN COPYRIGHT

WARNING: A CERTIFICATE IS NOT EVIDENCE OF IDENTITY.

DXZ Series Dd 0560 33M 6/00 SPSL(206824)

Appendix 2

Chronology of Ella Hepworth Dixon's Literary Career[1]

1880s

The World: 'Town and Country Tales', Christmas stories, occasional articles on travel, and article on Leeds Music Festival instead of Shaw when Arthur Sullivan was conducting. Mostly anonymous, occasionally signed 'E.H.D.'
Sunday Times, January-April, 1888: short story and 'Chats with Celebrities'. First evidence of signature in full.
London Society Holiday Number, June, 1888: short story.
The Woman's World, 1888-1890: short stories and articles.
The Lady's Pictorial Christmas Number, 1889: short story.

1890s
The World: as above, last story 1899.
The Woman's World: last story 1890.
Lady's Pictorial: Christmas stories and from 1895-1921 weekly column, originally entitled 'Pensées de Femme'.
My Flirtations, 1892, serialized in *Lady's Pictorial*, then published in book form by Chatto and Windus under pseudonym 'Margaret Wynman'.
Woman, 1890-1893: short stories, including Holiday and Christmas stories.
The Story of a Modern Woman, 1894, serialized in *Lady's Pictorial*, then published in book form by Heinemann.
The Englishwoman, March–August, 1895: editor.
Pall Mall Magazine, 1895: short story.

[1] As mentioned in chapter two, when Ella Hepworth Dixon began her long career many articles and short stories were simply unsigned, as was the custom, so, whilst every effort has been made to trace and identify her contributions to the numerous periodicals for which she wrote, this has not always proved possible. Likewise, during the First World War many propaganda articles were understandably anonymous. Where in doubt I have preferred to abstain from ascribing work erroneously to her pen. Moreover, on some occasions, as with the *Woman Christmas Number* of 1894, material is simply missing from the otherwise rich resources at Colindale; at other times, as with *The World* July–December 1892, the material is unfit for use.

The Humanitarian: July, 1895, 'The Place of Realism in Fiction' (Ella Hepworth Dixon's opinion expressed along with Gissing, Daudet et al.) and July, 1899, 'Why Women are Ceasing to Marry'.
The Yellow Book, April, 1896: 'The Sweet o' the Year'.
Interviewed by *Lady's Realm* on 'The Ideal Lover' December, 1896 and 'The Desirability of Long Engagements' August, 1899.
The Ladies' Field, March, 1898–March, 1903: weekly column, and Christmas stories from 1899.

1900s
Lady's Pictorial: weekly column and occasional story, last story 1905.
The Ladies' Field, March-May, 1900: 'The Way of the War' and Christmas stories, last story 1903.
New York Independent, 26 July, 1900: 'London in Khaki', pp. 1794-1796.
Interviewed by *Lady's Realm* on 'The Happiest Period in a Woman's Life' 1901.
Daily Mirror, November-December, 1903: short articles.
One Doubtful Hour and Other Sidelights on the Feminine Temperament 1904, collection of short stories published by Grant Richards.
Pall Mall Magazine, 1906-1907: short stories.
The Sketch, 1907-1917: weekly column.
The Toyshop of the Heart unpublished play, performed 1908.

1910s
Lady's Pictorial: weekly column.
The Sketch: weekly column.
Illustrated London News, 1914: monthly articles from January 17-July 18.
Unsigned propaganda during WW1 in *Daily Mail* and *Manchester Guardian.*

1920s
Manchester Daily Dispatch, March, 1921-February, 1923: occasional articles.
Westminster Gazette, November, 1921-January, 1928 (when it amalgamated with the *Daily News)*: weekly articles - Social Causeries, R.A. shows, 'The real Max Beerbohm' June 9, 1923; inspired articles in *Punch*: 'Is Music in Danger?' (October 28, 1926, p. 486) and 'Local Atmosphere' (September 7, 1927, p. 259).
The Empire Review, 1929: 'Ladies' Clubs'.

1930s
As I Knew Them, 1930, published by Hutchinson and Company.
The Empire Review, 1931: 'The New Egypt' - last article.

Appendix 3

Chronology of Ella Hepworth Dixon's Short Fiction

1886
'Full-stop or Period' (unsigned), 'Town And Country Tales', *The World* (October 6), pp. 17-18.

1888
'Dr. Patmore's Patient', *Sunday Times* (January 29), p. 8.
'An Unconventional Girl', *London Society Holiday Number* (June), pp. 90-100.
'Murder - or Mercy?', *The Woman's World* (October), pp. 466-469.
'A Winter Idyl', *The Lady's Pictorial Christmas Number*, pp. 25-27.

1889
'A Dear Little Girl', *The Lady's Pictorial Christmas Number*, pp. 21-24.

1890
'A Garden in the South', *The Woman's World* (March), pp. 247-250.
'An Idyl of the Engineers', *Woman* (July 10), pp. 13-14.
'A Literary Lover', *The Woman's World* (October), pp. 638-641.
'A Suburban Tragedy', *Lady's Pictorial* (December 27), pp. 1104-1105.

1891
'Two Carnivals', *Woman* (January 1), pp. 10-12.
'Condemned', *Woman* (April 9), pp. 15-16.
'Number Twenty-nine' (unsigned), 'Town And Country Tales', *The World* (April 15), pp. 29-32.
'What Women Worship', *Woman* (June 3), pp. 14-16.
'Wyllie's Wife', *The Lady's Pictorial Christmas Number*, pp. 17-23.

1892
'My Flirtations' (unsigned), *Lady's Pictorial* (January 23–April 30).

1893
'Like to Like' (signed 'Margaret Wynman'), *Woman Holiday Number*, pp. 3-10.

1894
'The White Death', *Christmas Number of The World* (November 22), pp. 22-26.
'A Man of Pleasure', *The Lady's Pictorial Christmas Number*, pp. 17-19.

1895
*'A Scribbler's Comedy', *Pall Mall Magazine* Volume V, pp. 286-294.
*'The World's Slow Stain', *Christmas Number of The World* (November 21), pp. 59-61.
*'The Disenchantment of Diana', *The Lady's Pictorial Christmas Number*, pp. 9-12.

1896
*'The Sweet o' the Year', *The Yellow Book* Volume IX (April), pp. 158-163.
*'Its Own Reward', *Christmas Number of The World* (November 26), pp. 50-53.
'The Goddess from the Machine', *The Lady's Pictorial Christmas Number*, pp. 1-5.

1897
'A London Episode', *Christmas Number of The World* (November 25), pp. 50-53.
*'One Doubtful Hour', *The Lady's Pictorial Christmas Number*, pp. 16-21.

1898
'His Sweet Disaster', *Lady's Pictorial* (November 26), pp. 4-9.

1899
'The Head Upon the Charger', *Christmas Number of The World* (November 16), pp. 26-29.
'The Absent-mindedness of Puggy Armstrong', *The Ladies' Field* (November 25), pp. 509-510.
*'The Kidnapping of Phil Kynaston', *Lady's Pictorial* (November 25), pp. 805-807.

1900
*'When Purfleet Came Back from the War', *The Ladies' Field* (December 1), pp. 484-486.

1901
'The Plain Miss Pendlestone', *Lady's Pictorial* (November 23), pp. 937-940.
'The Resolution of Rupert Strangeways', *The Ladies' Field* (November 30), pp. 488-490.

1902
*'The Fortune of Flora', *Lady's Pictorial* (November 22), pp. 850-853.
*'Mademoiselle Mankovich', *The Ladies' Field* (November 29), pp. 457-459.

1903
'The Romance of an Unsuccessful Man', *The Ladies' Field* (November 21), pp. 449-450.

1905
'The Wooing of Lord Warminster', *Lady's Pictorial* (November 25), pp. 860-861.

1906
'The Ambition of Pravny', *Pall Mall Magazine* (September), pp. 346-354.

1907
'The Capture of Miss Cohen', *Pall Mall Magazine* (February), pp. 229-234.

*republished in 1904 collection *One Doubtful Hour and Other Sidelights on the Feminine Temperament.*

Appendix 4

Brief Chronology of Marion Hepworth Dixon's Literary Career

1890s

'Marie Bashkirtseff: A Personal Reminiscence', *Fortnightly Review*, 47 (February, 1890), pp. 276-282.

'Charles Chaplin', *Magazine of Art*, 14 (1891), pp. 408-415.

'Stanhope A. Forbes, A.R.A.', *Magazine of Art*, 15 (1892), pp. 181-188.

'Onslow Ford, A.R.A.', *Magazine of Art*, 15 (1892), pp. 325-330.

'Thomas Faed, R.A.', *Magazine of Art*, 16 (1893), pp. 268-275.

'A Reminiscence of Henrietta Montalba', *The Art Journal* (July 7, 1894), pp. 215-217.

'Fair Children', *Magazine of Art*, 18 (1895), pp. 330-332.

'A Thief in the Night', *The Yellow Book* Volume IV (January, 1895), pp. 239-246.

'Let the Best Man Win', *English Illustrated Magazine* (February, 1895), pp. 47-52.

'Under the Lamp' – book reviews, *The Englishwoman* (March-August? 1895).

'A Desperate Remedy: A Dialogue', *The Englishwoman* (May, 1895), pp. 198-202.

'The Runaway', *The Yellow Book* Volume XIII (April, 1897), pp. 110-120.

'A Supper for Two: A Dialogue', *Christmas Number of The World* (November 17, 1898), pp. 57-59.

'Mr John S. Sargent as a Portrait-Painter', *Magazine of Art*, 23 (1899), pp. 112-119.

'Our Rising Artists: Miss Lucy E. Kemp-Welch, *Magazine of Art*, 23 (1899), pp. 481-487.

'Onlow Ford, R.A.', *Lady's Realm* (September, 1899), pp. 557-562.

'The Disenchantment of Dever Deming', *The Christmas Number of The World* (November 16, 1899), pp. 52-54.

1900s

'The Art of Mortimer Menpes', *Lady's Realm Christmas Number* (December 1900), pp. 205-214.

'Mr Walter Hunt: Animal Painter', *Magazine of Art*, 25 (1901), pp. 433-438.

'Our Rising Artists: Talbot Hughes', *Magazine of Art*, 26 (1902), pp. 1-6.

'Our Rising Artists: John H. Bacon', *Magazine of Art*, 26 (1902), pp. 193-198.

'Our Rising Artists: Eleanor Fortescue-Brickdale', *Magazine of Art*, 26 (1902), pp. 256-262.
'George Boughton, R.A.', *Lady's Realm* (February, 1902), pp. 445-452.
'Joseph Farquharson, A.R.A.', *Lady's Realm* (August, 1902), pp. 435-442.
'Arthur Hacker, A.R.A.', *Lady's Realm* (September, 1902), pp. 613-619.
'Jean Baptiste Greuze', *Lady's Realm* (January, 1903), pp. 335-341.
'Miss Lucy Kemp-Welch', *Lady's Realm* (March, 1903), pp. 575-582.
'The Miniatures of Vicountess Maitland', *Lady's Realm* (July, 1903), pp. 317-332.
'Solomon J. Solomon, A.R.A.', *Lady's Realm* (October, 1903), pp. 657-666.
'John H. Bacon, A.R.A.', *Lady's Realm* (November, 1903), pp. 25-32.
'Herbert Schmalz and his work', *Lady's Realm* (February, 1904), pp. 431-438.
'Mrs Louise Jopling', *Lady's Realm* (April, 1904), pp. 702-709.
'The Art of Mrs Stanhope Forbes', *Lady's Realm* (March, 1905), pp. 468-476.
'A Painter of Modern Life' (Frank Dicksee), *Lady's Realm* (March, 1905), pp. 565-572.
'The Art of David Murray, R.A.', *Lady's Realm* (July, 1905), pp. 273-280.
'The Art of John Da Costa', *Lady's Realm* (August, 1905), pp. 437-444.
'A Painter of the Summer. Mr H.S. Tuke, A.R.A.', *Lady's Realm*, (September, 1905), pp. 584-594.
'The Art of Henry Woods, R.A.', *Lady's Realm* (January, 1906), pp. 351-361.
'The Landscape Paintings of Mr H. Hughes Stanton', *Studio*, 42 (January 15, 1908), pp. 269-278 and *International Studio*, 34 (February, 1908), pp. 269-278.
'Visiting Cards a Hundred Years Ago' *Connoisseur*, 23 (January-April, 1909), pp. 192-200.

1910s

'Lady Alma-Tadema's Pictures', *Studio*, 50 (June 15, 1910), pp. 54-58 and *International Studio*, 41 (July, 1910), pp. 54-58.
'James Paterson R.S.A., R.W.S., *Studio*, 51 (December 15, 1910), pp. 190-202 and *International Studio*, 42 (January, 1911), pp. 190-202.
'Edward Stott: An Appreciation', *Studio*, 55 (February 15, 1912), pp. 3-9 and *International Studio*, 46 (March, 1912), pp. 3-9.
'The Paintings of Philip Connard', *Studio*, 57 (January 15, 1913), pp. 269-280 and *International Studio*, 48 (February, 1913), pp. 269-280.
'The Drawings of Kay Nielsen', *Studio*, 60 (November 15, 1913), pp. 116-125 and *International Studio*, 51 (December, 1913), pp. 116-125.

(From 1897 *Studio* was republished as *International Studio* in New York with volume one corresponding to volume ten of the original.)

Bibliography

Primary Sources

Fiction

Allen, Grant (1895), *The Woman Who Did*. Repr. Oxford: Oxford University Press, 1995.

Austen, Jane (1813), *Pride and Prejudice*. Repr. London: Dent, 1963.

Austen, Jane (1816), *Emma*. Repr. Harmondsworth: Penguin, 1964.

Balzac, Honoré de (1835), *Le Père Goriot, Old Goriot* (translated by M.A. Crawford). Harmondsworth: Penguin Classics, 1951.

Barr, Robert (1899), *Jennie Baxter, Journalist*. London: Methuen and Company.

Barrie, J.M. (1888), *When a Man is Single*. Repr. London: Hodder and Stoughton, 1923.

Beerbohm, Max (1912), *A Christmas Garland Woven by Max Beerbohm*. London: Heinemann.

Braddon, Mary (1862), *Lady Audley's Secret*. Repr. Oxford: Oxford University Press, 1987.

Brontë, Charlotte (1847), *Jane Eyre*. Repr. Harmondsworth: Penguin, 1966.

Broughton, Rhoda (1867), *Cometh up as a Flower*. Repr. London: Macmillan and Company, 1910.

Broughton, Rhoda (1870), *Red as a Rose is She*. Leipzig: Tauchnitz.

Caird, Mona (1894), *The Daughters of Danaus*. Repr. New York: Feminist Press, 1989.

Cholmondeley, Mary (1899), *Red Pottage*. Repr. London: Blond, 1968.

Collins, Wilkie (1862), *No Name*. Repr. Oxford: Oxford University Press, 1989.

D'Arcy, Ella (1895), *Monochromes*. London: John Lane.

Defoe, Daniel (1721), *Moll Flanders*. Repr. Harmondsworth: Penguin, 1978.

Dix, Gertrude (1895), *The Girl from the Farm*. London: John Lane.

Dixon, Ella Hepworth (1892), *My Flirtations*. London: Chatto and Windus.

Dixon, Ella Hepworth (1894), *The Story of a Modern Woman*. London: Merlin, 1990.

Dixon, Ella Hepworth (1894), *The Story of a Modern Woman*. Peterborough: Broadview, 2004.

Dixon, Ella Hepworth (1904), *One Doubtful Hour and Other Sidelights on the Feminine Temperament*. London: Grant Richards.

Dowie, Menie Muriel (1891), *A Girl in the Karpathians*. Repr. London: Philip and Son, 1892.

Dowie, Menie Muriel (1895), *Gallia*. Repr. London: Dent, 1995.

Egerton, George (Mary Chavelita Dunne Bright) (1893), *Keynotes* and (1894) *Discords*. Repr. London: Virago, 1983.

Egerton, George (1905), *Flies in Amber*. London: Hutchinson and Company.

Eliot, George (1859), *Adam Bede*. Repr. London: Dent, 1969.

Eliot, George (1871), *Middlemarch*. Repr. Oxford: Oxford University Press, 1956.

Gibbs, Philip (1909), *The Street of Adventure*. London: Heinemann.

Gilman, Charlotte Perkins (1899), *The Yellow Wallpaper*. Repr. London: Virago, 1981.

Gissing, George (1893), *The Odd Women*. Repr. London: Virago, 1980.

Grand, Sarah (1893), *The Heavenly Twins*. Repr. London: Heinemann, 1901.

Grand, Sarah (1898), *The Beth Book*. London: Heinemann.
Hardy, Thomas (1891), *Tess of the d'Urbervilles*. Repr. London: Penguin, 1978.
Hardy, Thomas (1895), *Jude the Obscure*. Repr. London: Macmillan and Company, 1971.
Hamilton, Cicely (1909), *Marriage as a Trade*. London: Chapman and Hall.
Hamilton, Cicely (1911), *Just to Get Married*. London: Chapman and Hall.
Iota (1894), *Children of Circumstance*, Leipzig: Tauchnitz.
Johnston, Sir Henry Hamilton (1920), *Mrs. Warren's Daughter: A Story of the Woman's Movement*. London: Chatto and Windus.
Johnstone, Edith (1894), *A Sunless Heart*. London: Ward, Lock and Bowden.
Keary, C.F. (1898), *The Journalist*. London: Methuen and Company.
Linton, Eliza Lynn (1888), *Sowing the Wind*. London: Chatto and Windus.
Macaulay, Rose (1922), *Mystery at Geneva*. London: Collins.
Macaulay, Rose (1923), *Told by an Idiot*. London: Collins.
Martineau, Harriet (1839), *Deerbrook*. Repr. London: Virago, 1983.
Paston, George (Emily Morse Symonds) (1899), *A Writer of Books*. Repr. Chicago: Academy Chicago Publishers, 1999.
Phillpotts, Eden (1905), *The Secret Woman*. London: Methuen and Company.
Schreiner, Olive (1883), *The Story of an African Farm*. London: Collins, 1924.
Syrett, Netta (1896), *Nobody's Fault*. London: John Lane.
Turgenev, Ivan (1859), *Home of the Gentry* (a.k.a. *Liza* and *A Nest of Nobles*). Repr. Harmondsworth: Penguin, 1970.
Ward, Mrs Humphrey (1894), *Marcella*. London: Macmillan and Company.
Winter, John Strange (Mrs Arthur Stannard) (1897), 'Jewels To Wear' in *'Princess Sarah' and Other Stories*. London: Ward and Lock.
Wood, Mrs Henry (1861), *East Lynne*. Repr. Peterborough: Broadview, 2000.
Woolf, Virginia (1927), *To the Lighthouse*. London: Dent, 1963.
Yonge, Charlotte (1856), *The Daisy Chain; Or, Aspirations*. Leipzig: Tauchnitz.

Drama

Barrie, J.M. (1995) *The Admirable Crichton, Peter Pan, When Wendy Grew Up, What Every Woman Knows, Mary Rose*. Oxford: Oxford University Press.
Chothia, Jean (ed.) (1998), *The New Woman and Other Emancipated Woman Plays*. (*The New Woman, The Notorious Mrs Ebbsmith, Votes for Women!,The Last of the De Mullins*.) Oxford: Oxford World Classics.
Dixon, Ella Hepworth (1908), *The Toyshop of the Heart*. (L.C.P. 1908/25.)
Fitzimmons, Linda and Viv Gardener (eds) (1992), *New Woman Plays*. (*Diana of Dobsons, Alan's Wife, Chains, Rutherford and Son*.) London: Methuen Drama.
Granville-Barker, Harley (1987), *Plays*. Cambridge: Cambridge University Press.
Hamilton, Cicely (1914), *Just to Get Married*. London: Samuel French.
Hamilton, Cosmo (1908), *Soldiers' Daughters*. (L.C.P. 1908/12.)
Heinemann, William (1895), *The First Step: A Dramatic Moment*. London: John Lane.
Ibsen, Henrik (1998), *Four Major Plays* (*A Doll's House, Ghosts, Hedda Gabler, The Master Builder*) (translated by James McFarlane and Jens Arup). Oxford: Oxford University Press.
Ibsen, Henrik (1896), *John Gabriel Borkman* (translated by William Archer). London: Heinemann, 1897.
Jones, Henry Arthur (1901),*The Liars*. London: Macmillan and Company.
Mayer, Gaston (1907), *French as He is Spoke*. (L.C.P. 1907/18) adapted from the French of Tristan Bernard.

Morgan, Fidelis (ed.) (1994), *The Years Between: Plays by Women on the London Stage 1900-1950*. London: Virago.

Pinero, Arthur Wing (1895), *The Notorious Mrs Ebbsmith*. London: Heinemann, 1916.

Pinero, Arthur Wing (1986), *Plays: The Schoolmistress, The Second Mrs Tanqueray, Trelawney of the 'Wells', The Thunderbolt*. Cambridge: Cambridge University Press.

Shaw, George Bernard (1898), *Plays Unpleasant*. Repr. London: Constable and Company, 1947.

Spender, Dale and Carole Hayman (eds) (1985), *How the Vote was Won and other Suffragette Plays*. London: Methuen.

Taylor, Tom (1850), *Still Waters Run Deep*. London: Thomas Hailes Lacy.

Non-Fiction

Arncliffe Sennett, Maud (1906-1936), Collected, annotated papers, including articles, press cuttings, letters, relating primarily to the Women's Suffrage Movement (British Library C.121.gp).

Arnold, Matthew (1887), 'Up to Easter', *The Nineteenth Century*, May, pp. 190-209.

Asquith, Margot (1937), *The Autobiography*. Harmondsworth: Penguin.

Atherton, Gertrude Franklin (1932), *Adventures of a Novelist (Autobiographical Reminiscences)*. London: Jonathon Cape.

Banks, Elizabeth (1902), *The Autobiography of a 'Newspaper Girl'*. London: Methuen and Company.

Banks, Elizabeth (1905), *The Long Day: The True Story of a New York Working Girl as Told by Myself*. New York: The Century Company.

Banks, Elizabeth (1928), *The Remaking of an American Girl*. London: Heinemann.

Bashkirtseff, Marie (1999), *Journal*. Volume 4. Edited by Lucile Le Roy. Lausanne: L'Age d'Homme.

Bennett, E.A. (1898), *Journalism for Women: A Practical Guide*. London: John Lane.

Bennett, E.A. (1903), 'The Truth about an Author'. Repr. in *Sketches for Autobiography*. Edited by James Hepburn. London: Allen and Unwin. 1979.

Bennett, E.A. (1913), 'The Author's Craft'. Repr. in *'The Author's Craft' and Other Critical Writings of Arnold Bennett*. Edited by Samuel Hynes. Nebraska: University of Nebraska Press. 1968.

Black, Helen C. (1893), *Notable Women Authors of the Day*. Glasgow: D.Bryce and Son.

Black, Helen C. (1896), *Pen, Pencil, Baton and Mask*. London: Spottiswoode and Company.

Breakell, Mary L. (1907), 'Marie Bashkirtseff: The Reminiscence of a Fellow Student', *Nineteenth Century and After*, 62, pp. 110-125.

Bulley, A. Amy and Margaret Whitley (1894), *Women's Work*. London: Methuen and Company.

Caird, Mona (1888), 'Marriage', *The Westminster Review*, 130, August, pp. 186-201.

Caird, Mona (1892), 'A Defence of the So-Called Wild Women', *The Nineteenth Century*, May, pp. 811-829.

Caird, Mona (1910), 'The Lot of Women', *The Westminster Review*, 174, July, pp. 52-79.

Cholmondeley, Mary (1918), *Under One Roof: A Family Record*. London: John Murray.

Cobbe, Frances Power (1894), *Life of Frances Power Cobbe: By Herself*. London: R. Bentley and Son.

Collet, Clara E. (1892), 'Prospects of Marriage for Women', *The Nineteenth Century*, April, pp. 537-552.

Cook, Lady, née Tennessee Claflin (1894), 'A Short History of Marriage', *The Westminster Review*, 141, pp. 380-395.

Crackanthorpe, B.A. (1894), 'The Revolt of the Daughters', *The Nineteenth Century*, March, pp. 23-31.

Crackanthorpe, B.A. (1895), 'Sex in Modern Literature', *The Nineteenth Century*, April, pp. 607-616.

Craik, Dinah Maria (1859), *A Woman's Thoughts about Women*. London: Hurst and Blackett.

Craik, Dinah Maria (1886), 'A Paris Atelier' in *Good Words for 1886*. Edited by Donald Macleod, London: Ibister and Company.

Dixon, Ella Hepworth (1899), 'Why Women are Ceasing to Marry', *The Humanitarian*, 14, pp. 391-396.

Dixon, Ella Hepworth (1930), *As I Knew Them*. London: Hutchinson and Company.

Dixon, Marion Hepworth (1890), 'Marie Bashkirtseff: A Personal Reminiscence', *Fortnightly Review*, February, pp. 276-282.

Dixon, William Hepworth (1880), *Royal Windsor*. Volume III. London: Hurst and Blackett.

Egerton, George (1958), *A Leaf from the Yellow Book*. Edited by T. de Vere White. London: Richards Press.

Eliot, George (1853), 'Margaret Fuller and Mary Wollstonecraft', *The Leader*, VI, pp. 988-999.

Eliot, George (1856), 'Silly Novels by Lady Novelists', *The Westminster Review*, October, pp. 442-461.

Eliot, George (1856), 'The Natural History of German Life', *The Westminster Review*, July, pp. 51-79.

Eliot, George, *Letters* (in 7 volumes). Edited by Gordon S. Haight, New Haven: Yale University Press, 1955.

Friswell, Laura Hain (1905), *In the Sixties and Seventies: Impressions of Literary People and Others*. London: Hutchinson and Company.

Gaskell, Mrs Elizabeth (1857), *The Life of Charlotte Brontë*. Repr. Harmondsworth: Penguin, 1977.

Gordon, Alice M. (1895), 'The After-Careers of University-Educated Women', *The Nineteenth Century*, June, pp. 959-960.

Gosse, Edmund (1895), 'The Decay of Literary Taste', *The North American Review*, p.161.

Grand, Sarah (1894), 'The New Aspect of the Woman Question', *The North American Review*, 158, pp. 270-276.

Graves, Algernon (ed.) (1901), *Graves Dictionary of Artists who have Exhibited in the Principal London Exhibitions from 1760-1893*, London: Henry Graves and Company Limited.

Hamilton, Cicely (1935), *Life Errant*. London: J.M. Dent and Sons Limited.

Hemery, Gertrude (1894), 'The Revolt of the Daughters. An Answer - by One of Them', *The Westminster Review,* 141, pp. 679-681.

Husband, Thomas F. (1894), *The Westminster Review*, 141, pp. 631-642.

James, Henry (1884), 'The Art of Fiction' in *Selected Literary Criticism*. Edited by Morris Shapira, Harmondsworth: Penguin, 1968.

James, William (1890), *The Principles of Pyschology*. New York: Henry Bolt and Company, 1998.

Jeune, May (1894), 'The Revolt of the Daughters', *The Fortnightly Review*, pp. 267-276.

Jopling, Louise (1928), *Twenty Years of My Life 1867-1887*. London: John Lane.

Keats, John (1958), *Letters*. Edited by Hyder Edward Rollins. Cambridge: Cambridge University Press.

Le Doeuff, Michèle (1996), "'And Every Man in His Cave ...'", Oxford Amnesty International Lecture.

Le Gallienne, Richard (1926), *The Romantic '90s*. London: Robin Clark, 1993.

Lee, A.L. (1894), 'The Impasse of Women', *The Westminster Review*, 141, pp. 566-568.

Lee, Vernon (1937), *Vernon Lee's Letters*. London: privately printed.

Lewes, G.H. (1850), 'A Gentle Hint to Writing Women', *The Leader*, May 18, p. 189.

Linton, E. Lynn (1862), 'Out Walking', *Temple Bar*, V, July, pp. 132-139.

Linton, E. Lynn (1868), 'The Girl of the Period', *Saturday Review*, March 14, pp. 339-340.

Linton, E. Lynn (1884), *Ourselves*. London: Chatto and Windus.

Linton, E. Lynn (1899), *My Literary Life*. London: Hodder and Stoughton.

Low, Frances (1904), *Press Work for Women: A Text Book for the Young Woman Journalist*. London: L. Upcott Gill.

Martineau, Harriet (1877), *Autobiography*. Repr. London: Virago, 1983.

Maugham, William Somerset (1958), *Points of View*. London: Heinemann.

Mackenzie, Tessa (ed.) (1895), *The Art Schools of London*. London: Chapman and Hall.

Mill, John Stuart, Harriet Taylor Mill and Helen Taylor. *Sexual Equality*. Edited by Ann P. Robson and John M. Robson. Toronto: University of Toronto Press, 1994.

Meredith, George (1970), *Letters*. Edited by C.L. Cline. Oxford: Clarendon Press.

Moore, George (1886), *Confessions of a Young Man*. Harmondsworth: Penguin, 1939.

Oliphant, Mrs (unsigned) (1877), 'Harriet Martineau', *Blackwood's Magazine*, April, pp. 472-496.

(M.O.W.O.) Mrs Oliphant (1896), 'The Anti-Marriage League', *Blackwood's Magazine*. January, pp. 135-149.

Oliphant, Mrs M.O.W. (1899), *The Autobiography and Letters of Mrs M.O.W. Oliphant*. Arranged and Edited by Mrs Harry Coghill. Edinburgh and London: William Blackwood and Sons.

Ouida (1894), 'The New Woman', *The North American Review*, 158, pp. 610-619.

Nieriker, May Alcott (1879), *Studying Art Abroad, and How to Do it Cheaply*. Boston: Roberts Brothers.

Peel, Mrs C.S. (1933), *Life's Enchanted Cup: An Autobiography, 1872-1933*. London: The Bodley Head.

Phillips, Ernest (1895), *How to Become a Journalist: A Practical Guide to Newspaper Work*. London: Sampson, Low, Marston and Company.

Robins, Elizabeth (1913), *Way Stations*. London: Hodder and Stoughton.

Sharp, Evelyn (1933), *Unfinished Journey*. London: Bodley Head.

Smyth, Ethel (1920), *Impressions That Remained*. London: Longman's, Green and Company.

Smyth, Ethel (1921), *Streaks of Life*. London: Longman's, Green and Company.

Stead, W.T. (1886), 'Government by Journalism', *The Contemporary Review*, 49, pp. 653-74.

Stead, W.T. (1886), 'The Future of Journalism', *The Contemporary Review*, 50, pp. 663-679.

Stead, W.T. (1892), *A Journalist on Journalism*. Edited by E.H. Stout, London: J.Haddon and Company.

Stead, W.T. (1893), 'The Pall Mall Gazette', *The Review of Reviews*, VII, pp. 139-154.

Stead, W.T. (1894), 'The Novel of the Modern Woman', *The Review of Reviews*, X, pp. 64-74.

Stead, W.T. (1897), 'After Seven Years', *The Review of Reviews*, XV, pp. 1-16.

Stutfield, Hugh E.M. (1895), 'Tommyrotics', *Blackwood's Magazine*, June, pp. 833-845.

Sykes, A.G.P. (1894), 'The Evolution of the Sex', *The Westminster Review*, 143, pp. 396-400.
Syrett, Netta (1939), *The Sheltering Tree*. London: Geoffrey Bles.
Toye, Francis (1950), *For What We Have Received: An Autobiography*. London: Heinemann.
Woolf, Virginia (1925), 'Modern Fiction', *The Common Reader:* First Series. London: Hogarth Press, 1984, pp. 146-154.
Woolf, Virginia (1928), *A Room of One's Own*. Harmondsworth: Penguin, 1963.
Woolf, Virginia (1929), 'Women and Fiction' in *Granite and Rainbow*. London: Hogarth Press, 1958, pp. 76-84.
Woolf, Virginia (1939), 'A Sketch of the Past' in *Moments of Being*. New York: Harvest Brace Jovanovich, 1976.
Wollstonecraft, Mary (1792), *A Vindication of the Rights of Women*. Harmondsworth: Penguin, 1975.
Zillhardt, Madeleine (1932), *Louise-Catherine Breslau et Ses Amis*. Paris: des Portiques.

Secondary Sources

Allen, Walter (1954), *The English Novel*. Repr. Harmondsworth: Penguin, 1958.
Allen, Walter (1981), *The Short Story in English*. Oxford: Oxford University Press.
Ardis, Ann L. (1990), *New Women, New Novels: Feminism and Early Modernism*. New Brunswick: Rutgers University Press.
Armstrong, Nancy (1987), *Desire and Domestic Fiction*. New York: Oxford University Press.
Auerbach, Nina (1978), *Communities of Women*. Cambridge, Mass.: Harvard University Press.
Ayres, Brenda (ed.) (2003), *Silent Voices: Forgotten Novels by Victorian Women Writers*. Westport, Conn. and London: Praeger.
Baile de Laperrière, Charles (ed.) (1996), *The Society of Women Artists Exhibitors 1855-1996: A Dictionary of Artists and Their Works in the Annual Exhibitions of The Society of Women Artists*. Calne: Hilmarton Manor Press.
Barstow, Susan Torrey (2003), '"Hedda is All of Us": Late-Victorian Women at the Matinee', *Victorian Studies*, Volume 43, Number 3, pp. 387-412.
Beaumann, Nicola (1983), *A Very Great Profession: The Woman's Novel 1914-39*. London: Virago, 1995.
Beetham, Margaret (1996), *A Magazine of Her Own? Domesticity and Desire in the Woman's Magazine 1800-1914*. London: Routledge.
Benjamin, Walter, *Charles Baudelaire: a Lyric Poet in the Era of High Capitalism* (translated by Harry Zohn). London: New Left Books, 1973.
Benstock, Shari (ed.) (1988), *The Private Self: Theory and Practice of Women's Autobiographical Writings*. London: Routledge.
Best, Geoffrey (1979), *Mid-Victorian Britain 1851-70*. Glasgow: Collins.
Bjorhovde, G. (1987), *Rebellious Structures: Women Writers and the Crisis of the Novel, 1880-1900*. Oslo: Oslo University Press.
Blain, Virginia, Patricia Clements and Isobel Grundy (eds) (1990), *The Feminist Companion to Literature in English. Women Writers from the Middle Ages to the Present*. London: B.T. Batsford Limited.
Booth, Michael and Joel H. Kaplan (eds) (1996), *The Edwardian Theatre: Essays on Performance and the Stage*, Cambridge: Cambridge University Press.

Booth, Wayne C. (1962), *The Rhetoric of Fiction*. Chicago: University of Chicago Press.

Boumelha, Penny (1982), *Thomas Hardy: Sexual Ideology and Narrative Form*. Sussex: Harvester.

Brake, Laurel (1994), *Subjugated Knowledges: Journalism, Gender and Literature in the Nineteenth Century*. Basingstoke: Macmillan.

Brandon, Ruth (1990), *The New Women and the Old Men: Love, Sex and the Woman Question*. London: Secker and Warburg.

Briggs, Asa and Daniel Snowman (eds) (1996), *Fins de Siècle: How Centuries End, 1400-2000*. New Haven: Yale University Press.

Brodski, Bella and Celeste Schenck (eds) (1988), *Life/Lines: Theorizing Women's Autobiography*. Ithaca: Cornell University Press.

Broughton, Trev Lynn (1999), *Men of Letters, Writing Lives: Masculinity and Literary Auto/Biography in the Late Victorian Period*. London: Routledge.

Casteras, Susan P. (1987), 'The End of the Century and Conflicting Fantasies of Femininity' in *Writing about Art*. Edited by Carole Gold Calo, Englewood Cliffs, New Jersey: Prentice-Hall, 1994.

Chadwick, Whitney (1994), *Women, Art and Society*. London: Thames and Hudson.

Cherry, Deborah (1993), *Painting Women: Victorian Women Artists*. London and New York: Routledge.

Cherry, Deborah (2000), *Beyond the Frame: Feminism and Visual Culture, Britain 1850-1900,* London and New York: Routledge.

Christensen Nelson, Carolyn (1995), *British Women Fiction Writers of the 1890s*. New York: Twayne Publishers.

Clark, Ian (1989), *Edwardian Drama: A Critical Study*. London: Faber.

Coward, Rosalind (1984), *Female Desire: Women's Sexuality Today*. London: Paladin.

Cunningham, Gail (1978), *The New Woman and the Victorian Novel*. London: Macmillan.

Daiches, David (1968), *A Critical History of English Literature*. London: Secker and Warburg.

Davidoff, L. and C. Hall (1987), *Family Fortunes: Men and Women of the English Middle Classes,1780-1850*. London: Hutchinson.

Dellamora, Richard (ed.) (1999), *Victorian Sexual Dissidence*. Chicago: The University of Chicago Press.

Demoor, Marysa (2000), *Their Fair Share: Women, Power and Criticism in the 'Athenaeum', from Millicent Garrett Fawcett to Katherine Mansfield, 1870-1920*. Aldershot: Ashgate.

Dijkstra, Bram (1986), *Idols of Perversity: Fantasies of Feminine Evil in Fin de Siècle Culture*. Oxford: Oxford University Press.

Dowling, Linda (1986), *Language and Decadence in the Victorian Fin de Siècle*. Princeton: Princeton University Press.

DuPlessis, Rachel Blau (1985), *Writing Beyond the Ending: Narrative Strategies of Twentieth Century Women Writers*. Bloomington: Indiana University Press.

Dyos, H. J. and Michael Wolff (eds) (1973), *The Victorian City: Images and Realities*. London and Boston: Routledge and Kegan Paul.

Fehrer, Catherine (1989), 'The Julian Academy: Paris 1868–1939' in Exhibition Catalogue, Shepherd Gallery, New York.

Felman, Shoshana (1991), *What Does a Woman Want?* Baltimore: The Johns Hopkins Press.

Feltes, N.N. (1986), *Modes of Production of Victorian Novels*. Chicago: University of Chicago Press.

Fernando, Lloyd (1977), *'New Women' in the Late Victorian Novel*. University Park: Pennsylvania State University Press.

Fetterley, Judith (1978), *The Resisting Reader*. Bloomington: Indiana University Press.

Flint, Kate (1993), *The Woman Reader 1837-1914*. Oxford: Clarendon Press.

Forster, E.M. (1927), *Aspects of the Novel*. Repr. Harmondsworth: Penguin, 1968.

Fryer, Jonathon (2000), *Robbie Ross: Oscar Wilde's True Love*. London: Constable.

Gardner, Viv and Susan Rutherford (eds) (1992), *The New Woman and Her Sisters: Feminism and Theatre, 1850-1914*. New York: Harvester Wheatsheaf.

Gilbert, Sandra and Susan Gubar (1979), *The Madwoman in the Attic: The Woman Writer and the Nineteenth-Century Literary Imagination*. New Haven: Yale University Press.

Gillooly, Eileen (1999), *Smile of Discontent: Humor, Gender, and Nineteenth-Century British Fiction*. Chicago: The University of Chicago Press.

Hanson, Clare (1985), *Short Stories and Short Fictions, 1880-1980*. Basingstoke: Macmillan.

Hanson, Clare (ed.) (1989), *Re-reading the Short Story*. Basingstoke: Macmillan.

Harris Elree I. and Shirley R. Scott (1997), *A Gallery of Her Own: An Annotated Bibiliography of Women in Victorian Painting*. New York and London: Garland.

Harrison, Craig (ed.) (1999), *The Essence of Art: Victorian Advice on the Practice of Painting*. Aldershot: Ashgate.

Heilbrun, Carolyn G. (1988), *Writing a Woman's Life*. New York: Ballantine.

Heilmann, Ann (ed.) (1998), *The Late-Victorian Marriage Question: A Collection of Key New Woman Texts*. London: Routledge/Thoemmes Press.

Heilmann, Ann (2001), *New Woman Fiction: Women Writing First-Wave Feminism*, Basingstoke: Macmillan.

Helsinger, Elizabeth K., Robin Lauterbach Sheets, and William Veeder (1983), *The Woman Question: Society and Literature in Britain and America 1837-1883*. 3 Vols., Chicago: University of Chicago Press.

Hobsbawm, Eric (1987), *The Age of Empire, 1875-1914*. New York: Pantheon.

Holquist, Michael and Walter Reed (1980), 'Six Theses on the Novel - and some Metaphors' in *New Literary History*. Austin: University of Texas Press.

Homans, Margaret (1986), *Bearing the Word: Language and Female Experience in Nineteenth-Century Women's Writing*. Chicago: University of Chicago Press.

Hunter, Fred (1992), 'Women in British Journalism' in *The Encyclopedia of The British Press 1422-1992*. Basingstoke: Macmillan.

Hurley, Kelly (1996), *The Gothic Body: Sexuality, Materialism and Degeneration at the Fin de Siècle*. Cambridge: Cambridge University Press.

Huyssen, Andreas (1986), *After the Great Divide: Modernism, Mass Culture, Postmodernism*. Indianapolis: Indianapolis University Press.

Jelinek, Estelle (1986), *The Tradition of Women's Autobiography: From Antiquity to the Present*. Boston: G.K. Hall/Twayne Publishers.

Johnston, Judith (1997), *Anna Jameson: Victorian, Feminist, Woman of Letters*. Aldershot: Scolar Press; Vermont: Ashgate.

Kanner, Barbara Penny (ed.) (1997), *Women in Context: Two Hundred Years of British Women Autobiographers. A Reference Guide and Reader*. New York: Prentice Hall.

Kaplan Joel H. and Sheila Stowell (1994), *Theatre and Fashion: Oscar Wilde to the Suffragettes*. Cambridge: Cambridge University Press.

Keating, Peter (1989), *The Haunted Study: A Social History of the English Novel 1875-1914*. London: Secker and Warburg.

Kemp, Sandra, Charlotte Mitchell and David Trotter (eds) (1997), *Edwardian Fiction: An Oxford Companion*. Oxford: Oxford University Press.

Kooistra, Lorraine Janzen (1995), *The Artist as Critic: Bitextuality in Fin de Siècle Illustrated Books*. Aldershot: Scolar Press.

Kranidis, Rita S. (1995), *Subversive Discourse: the Cultural Production of Late Victorian Feminist Novels*. New York: St. Martin's Press.

Lecarme, Jacques & Eliane Lecarme-Tabore (1997), *L'Autobiographie*. Paris: Armand Colin.

Ledger, Sally and Scott McCracken (eds) (1995), *Cultural Politics at the Fin de Siècle*. Cambridge: Cambridge University Press.

Ledger, Sally (1997), *The New Woman: Fiction and Feminism at the Fin de Siècle*. Manchester: Manchester University Press.

Levine, Philippa (1987), *Victorian Feminism 1850-1900*. London: Hutchinson.

Lewis, Linda M. (2003), *Germaine de Staël, George Sand, and the Victorian Woman Artist*. Columbia and London: University of Missouri Press

Liddington, Jill and Jill Norris (1978), *One Hand Tied Behind Us: The Rise of the Women's Suffrage Movement*. London: Virago.

Lionnet, Françoise (1989), *Autobiographical Voices: Race, Gender, Self-Portraiture*. Ithaca: Cornell University Press.

London, Bette (1999), *Writing Double: Women's Literary Partnerships*. Ithaca: Cornell University Press.

Marcus, Laura (1994), *Auto/biographical Discourses: Theory, Criticism, Practice*. Manchester: Manchester University Press.

Marks, Patricia (1990), *Bicycles, Bangs, and Bloomers: the New Woman in the Popular Press*. Lexington: Kentucky University Press.

Marsh, Jan and Pamela Gerrish Nunn (1997), *Pre-Raphaelite Women Artists*. London: Thames and Hudson.

Miller, Nancy K. (1981), 'Emphasis Added: Plots and Plausibilities in Women's Fiction', *PMLA*. Vol. 96. pp. 36-48.

Mitchell, Juliet and Ann Oakley (eds) (1976), *The Rights and Wrongs of Women*. Harmondsworth: Penguin.

Mitchell, Sally (1981), *The Fallen Angel: Chastity, Class and Women's Reading 1835-1880*. Ohio: Bowling Green University Popular Press.

Mitchell, Sally (1995), *The New Girl: Girls' Culture in England 1880-1915*. New York: Columbia University Press.

Moers, Ellen (1963), *Literary Women*. New York: Doubleday and Company.

Mulvey, Laura (1993), *Visual and Other Pleasures*. Basingstoke and London: Macmillan.

Newey, Vincent and Philip Shaw (eds) (1996), *Mortal Pages, Literary Lives: Studies in Nineteenth-Century Autobiographies*. Aldershot: Scolar Press.

Noël, Denise (1988), *'L' Académie Julian : Les Ateliers Pour Dames 1868–1907'*. unpublished *Mémoire de Maîtrise*.

Nunn, Pamela Gerrish (1987), *Victorian Women Painters*. London: The Women's Press Limited.

Nunn, Pamela Gerrish. (1996), *Problem Pictures: Women & Men in Victorian Painting*. Aldershot: Scolar Press.

Nunn, Pamela Gerrish (ed.) (1986) *Canvassing: Recollections by Six Victorian Women Artists*. London: Camden Press.

Nussbaum, Felicity (1989), *The Autobiographical Subject: Gender and Ideology in Eighteenth-Century England*. Baltimore: The Johns Hopkins University Press.

O'Connor, Frank (1962), *The Lonely Voice: A Study of the Short Story*. Cleveland: The World Publishing Company.

Onslow, Barbara (2000), *Women of the Press in Nineteenth-Century Britain*. Basingstoke: Macmillan.

Orr, Clarrisa Campbell (ed.) (1995), *Women in the Victorian Art World*. Manchester: Manchester University Press.

Parker, Rozsika and Griselda Pollock (1981), *Old Mistresses: Women, Art and Ideology*. London: Pandora.

Parsons, Deborah L. (2000), *Streetwalking the Metropolis: Women, the City, and Modernity*. Oxford: Oxford University Press.

Peterson, Linda H. (1999), *Traditions of Victorian Women's Autobiography: The Poetics and Politics of Life Writing*. Charlottesville: University of Virginia Press.

Poovey, Mary (1984), *The Proper Lady and The Woman Writer*. Chicago: University of Chicago Press.

Poovey, Mary (1989), *Uneven Developments: The Ideological Work of Gender in Mid-Victorian England*. Chicago: University of Chicago Press.

Powell, Kerry (1997), *Women and Victorian Theatre*. Cambridge: Cambridge University Press.

Pykett, Lyn (1992), *The 'Improper' Feminine*. London: Routledge.

Pykett, Lyn (1995), *Engendering Fictions: The English Novel in the Early Twentieth Century,* London: Edward Arnold.

Pykett, Lyn (ed.) (1996), *Reading Fin de Siècle Fictions*. London: Longman.

Reynolds, Kimberley (1990), *Girls Only? Gender and Popular Children's Fiction in Britain, 1880-1910*. Hemel Hempstead: Harvester Wheatsheaf.

Riley, Denise (1988), *Am I that Name? Feminism and the Category of 'Women' in History*. Basingstoke: Macmillan.

Rose, Phyllis (1984), *Parallel Lives*. London: Chatto and Windus.

Rowbotham, Sheila (1973), *Hidden from History*. Repr. London: Pluto Press. 1992.

Sanders, Valerie (1989), *The Private Lives of Victorian Women: Autobiography in Nineteenth-Century England*. New York: Harvester Wheatsheaf.

Shattock, Joanne and Michael Wolff (eds) (1982), *The Victorian Periodical Press: Samplings and Soundings*. Leicester: Leicester University Press.

Shattock, Joanne (1994), *The Oxford Guide to British Women Writers*. Oxford: Oxford University Press.

Showalter, Elaine (1978), *A Literature of their Own*. London: Virago.

Showalter, Elaine (1985), *The Female Malady: Women, Madness, and English Culture 1830-1980*. New York: Pantheon Books.

Showalter, Elaine (1990), *Sexual Anarchy*. New York: Viking.

Sinnema, Peter W. (1998), *Dynamics of the Pictured Page: Representing the Nation in the 'Illustrated London News'*. Aldershot: Ashgate.

Smith, Sidonie (1987), *A Poetics of Women's Autobiography: Marginality and the Fictions of Self-Representation*. Bloomington and Indianapolis: Indiana University Press.

Smith, Sidonie and Julia Watson (eds) (1998), *Women, Autobiography, Theory; A Reader*. Wisconsin: University of Wisconsin Press.

Spens, Michael (ed.) (1993), *Studio International Special Centenary Number*, Volume 201, Number 1022/1023 1993. *High Art and Low Life*: *The Studio* and the *fin de siècle*. (Incorporating the Catalogue to the Exhibition *High Art and Low Life:* 'The Studio' *and the Arts of the 1890s*. Victoria and Albert Museum, 23 June - 31 October, 1993.)

Sontag, Susan (1978), *On Photography*. New York: Straus and Giroux.

Stanley, Liz (1992), *The Auto/biographical I: The Theory and Practice of Feminist Auto/biography*. Manchester: Manchester University Press.

Stetz, Margaret and Mark Samuels Lasner (1990), *England in the 1890s: Literary Publishing at the Bodley Head*. Washington: Georgetown University Press.

Stetz, Margaret (1994), 'New Grub Street and the Woman Writer of the 1890s' from *New Approaches to British Fiction of the 1890s*. ed. by Nikki Lee Manos and Meri Jane Rochilson. London: Macmillan.

Stetz, Margaret (2001), *British Women's Comic Fiction, 1890-1990: Not Drowning, but Laughing*. Aldershot: Ashgate.

Stetz, Margaret (2004), *Gender and the London Theatre 1880-1920*. High Wycombe: Rivendale Press.

Stewart, Garrett (1996), *Dear Reader: The Conscripted Audience in Nineteenth Century British Fiction*. Baltimore: The Johns Hopkins University Press.

Stokes, John (1989), *In the Nineties*. Hemel Hempstead: Harvester Wheatsheaf.

Stokes, John (ed.) (1992), *Fin de Siècle/ Fin du Globe*. Basingstoke: Macmillan.

Stowell, Sheila (1992), *A Stage of Their Own: Feminist Playwrights of the Suffrage Era*. Ann Arbor: The University of Michigan Press.

Stubbs, Patricia (1979), *Women and Fiction: Feminism and the Novel, 1880-1920*. Sussex: Harvester.

Sutherland, John (1988), *The Longman Companion to Victorian Fiction*. Harlow: Longman.

Taylor, Barbara (1983), *Eve and the New Jerusalem: Socialism and Feminism in the Nineteenth Century*. London: Virago.

Thirlwell, Angela (2003), *William and Lucy: The Other Rossettis*. London and New Haven: Yale University Press.

Thompson, Nicola Diane (1996), *Reviewing Sex: Gender and the Reception of Victorian Novels*. Basingstoke: Macmillan.

Tickner, Lisa (1987), *The Spectacle of Women: Imagery of the Suffrage Campaign, 1907-1914*. London: Chatto and Windus.

Trewin, J.C. (1976), *The Edwardian Theatre*. Oxford: Blackwell.

Tuchman, Gaye (1989), *Edging Women Out: Victorian Novelists, Publishers, and Social Change*. London: Routledge.

Varty, Anne (ed.) (2000), *Eve's Century: A Sourcebook of Writings on Women and Journalism, 1895-1918*. London: Routledge.

Vicinus, Martha (ed.) (1980), *Suffer and Be Still: Women in the Victorian Age*. London: Methuen.

Vicinus, Martha (1985), *Independent Women: Work and Community for Single Women, 1850-1920*. Chicago: University of Chicago Press.

Watson, Martha (1999), *Lives of Their Own: Rhetorical Dimensions in Autobiographies of Women Activists*. Columbia: University of South Carolina Press.

Weisberg, Gabriel P. and Jane R. Becker (eds) (1999), *Overcoming All Obstacles: the Women of the Académie Julian*. New York: The Dahesh Museum.

Wilson, Elizabeth (1992), 'The Invisible *Flâneur*', *The New Left Review*, Volume 191, pp. 90-110.

Whyte, Frederic (1928), *William Heinemann: A Memoir*. London: Jonathon Cape.

Wolff, Janet (1985), 'The Invisible Flaneuse' in *Theory, Culture and Society* special issue 'The Fate of Modernity', Volume 2, Number 3.

Yeldham, Charlotte (1984), *Women Artists in Nineteenth-century France and England: their Art Education, Exhibition Opportunities and Membership of Exhibiting Societies and Academies*. London: Garland.

Young, G.M. (1952), *Portrait of an Age*. Oxford: Oxford University Press.

Index

For ease of reference 'Ella Hepworth Dixon' has been abbreviated to 'EHD'. References marked with one asterisk (*) indicate fictional works by EHD, and those marked with two asterisks (**) indicate her non-fictional works.